DISCARD

CONTAINMENT AND REVOLUTION

Containment and Revolution is the first volume in the series entitled *Studies in Imperialism and the Cold War* edited by David Horowitz for the Bertrand Russell Centre for Social Research, London

Containment
and
Revolution

Edited by David Horowitz

BEACON PRESS · *Boston*

Contents

Preface by Bertrand Russell   5

Introduction   9
David Horowitz

Myths of the Cold War   13
Isaac Deutscher

American Intervention in Russia: 1917–20   26
William Appleman Williams

The World War and the Cold War   76
John Bagguley

A Conservative Critique of Containment: Senator Taft   125
on the Early Cold War Program
Henry W. Berger

Counter-Insurgency: Myth and Reality in Greece   140
Todd Gitlin

The Origins of China's Foreign Policy   182
John Gittings

Revolution and Intervention in Vietnam   218
Richard Morrock

Notes on Contributors   251

Preface

by Bertrand Russell

THE launching of this series of volumes on the cold war and imperialism comes at a time of important changes. Never before in the West have so many people been prepared to look afresh at the last quarter of a century. For many years I have endeavoured to oppose the destructiveness of the cold war and the menace which it represents to all mankind. I am convinced that such opposition must be strengthened by a thorough examination of the origins and development of the cold war. To us in the West, some of the facts were at first obscured by propaganda, others by the tyranny of Stalin. Similarly, in the Third World, many were misled by the semblance of independence or the hope of economic aid. Out of this confusion has emerged the certainty of the United States of America as the wealthiest and most powerful nation in history. Its relationship to the rest of the world deserves the closest attention. There is an essential unity in the cold war, economic and foreign policies of the United States. This is created by the constant search for raw materials and markets, the imposition of poverty upon a large proportion of the world's population and the use of US military power in dozens of countries to protect the interests of American capitalism and destroy those who dare to resist. Aggression is more than a facet of imperialism: the determination to conquer, dominate and exploit is the very essence of imperialism. Such aggression is not only unjust: in the nuclear age it must be impermissible. In the face of the massive governmental propaganda to which we are all subjected, there is a need for a critical and independent analysis of these years, which is both radical and substantial, using the abundant documentation of scholarship for the purposes of clarifying issues and preparing the ground for more effective opposition to those who would exploit or destroy us all. It is for these purposes that this series exists.

CONTAINMENT AND REVOLUTION

Introduction

THE conflict which we call the cold war has already entered its third decade and, despite lulls at various times and places, shows little sign of any real overall abatement, any indication that a final global settlement is in sight. Indeed, as the power vacuums of the initial postwar period, particularly in Europe, have been filled, and as new centres of national power have emerged over the world's surface, the very feasibility of such a settlement has been increasingly put in doubt. More and more it is apparent that instead of moving closer to that peaceful world order envisioned at the end of World War II, the various protagonist powers may be moving further and further away from the possibility of any general resolution of the cold war.

In fact, this peculiar development and duration of the conflict suggests that the very term 'cold war' may be a misleading description. For unlike its prototype, this 'war' increasingly has no locality in terms of geo-political space, no specifiable and therefore resolvable issue. Moreover, except for divided Germany, its contested areas are themselves shifting and non-delimitable—expressions rather than causes of the general conflict.

In the early years of the cold war, however, it was possible for intelligent and perceptive analysts to see the conflict as indeed concrete and specific in content, with definable issues hanging in the balance. These issues were held to be the terms of a European peace settlement, which, in turn, would mean a withdrawal of the three allied armies, which had met in the centre of the European continent along the armistice line from Stettin to Trieste. Had these terms been negotiated then, and the allied armies withdrawn—so it was believed—'the material cause and reason of the conflict' would have been dealt with, and the conflict itself resolved.*

Such views are now no longer seriously maintained. No intelligent observer today would be so rash as to suggest that the achievement of a European settlement and withdrawal, even if it were now possible, would signify an end to the cold war as such, or lead, for example, to a general United States withdrawal from its thousand and more military bases overseas. Moreover, this has been the case (though it may not always have been so obvious) at least since the

* Walter Lippmann, *The Cold War*, New York, 1947.

triumph of the Chinese Revolution in 1949, when the cold war conflict firmly established itself well beyond its European Frontiers.

The now obsolete view that the cold war conflict was basically about a set of more or less clearly defined issues and contested areas was first urgently raised in 1947 at the time when the Truman Doctrine was proclaimed. The Doctrine had sought to present the developing conflict between the Soviet Union and the United States as a struggle between 'two ways of life', and—so it was argued—had thereby threatened to extend the contested issues to a metaphysical realm in which no resolution short of the unattainable victory of one side was possible. Instead of limiting the conflict, by concentrating on the concrete issues of the peace treaties for Germany and Austria and the withdrawal of the allied armies from the armistice line, the Truman Doctrine escalated its terms to an apocalyptic level which afforded no room for negotiation or compromise.

With the hindsight provided by two decades of cold war history, we may well ask whether such views were valid, even at the time at which they were put forward. That is to say, we may ask not whether certain problems that were created could have been avoided by more sober and realistic policies—since there is every reason to believe they could have—but: Was the postwar conflict itself really containable in its early stages, as was contended, and is its present global extension and apparent limitlessness really the product of a clash between metaphysical creeds (communism and anti-communism), the ideologically conditioned unreason of national politics in the atomic era?

The evidence would seem to suggest that such a conception of the cold war, prevalent as it may still be among some historians of the period,* is not in fact soundly based, that the global nature of the cold war reflects the clash of real global forces, and not merely the aberrant and uncontainable crusading instincts of leading politicians and statesmen on both sides. Thus, the Truman Doctrine of 1947 was already promulgated to deal with an issue that had deeper and more globally situated roots than the terms of the postwar peace settlement in Europe, or the power conflict between the United States and the Soviet Union. For the Truman Doctrine was promulgated to deal with a *social revolution* in Greece, and Washington's open-ended commitment to suppress revolutions, which was expressed in the Doctrine, was obviously made also with an eye to the billions of dollars that the United States was then pouring into China in an unsuccessful effort to halt the advance of communist revolution there. Even on the evidence of the early cold war period, therefore, it is clear that the global scale of the conflict was the result of a real global

* E.g. Louis J. Halle, *The Cold War As History*, London, 1967.

phenomenon: the spread of revolution in the contemporary era of world social development, and the decision of the United States to assume its role, as the newly dominant capitalist world power, of guardian of the global *status quo*.

Of course, in the early cold war period, the rhetoric in Washington referred primarily to the threat of Soviet expansion and military aggression. Both the Chinese and the Greek revolutions were portrayed by western statesmen and political writers as *Russian* attempts to take over these countries, examples of the Kremlin's remorseless determination—if not resolutely opposed—to conquer the postwar world. Those in a position to know and assess the real facts at the time, however, had no such illusions either about Russian intentions, or about the nature of the postwar conflicts and the forces at work in their development.

George F. Kennan was, until 1946, stationed in the US embassy in Moscow. He was then brought to Washington to become Director of the Policy Planning Staff of the State Department, and to formulate the theory, if not the actual programme, of containment. In May 1965, at a lecture delivered at the Graduate Institute of International Studies at Geneva, Kennan offered revealing insight into his own conception of 'the problems that confronted American policy-makers in 1947.'* In Kennan's own words: 'It was perfectly clear to anyone with even a rudimentary knowledge of the Russia of that day, that the Soviet leaders had no intention of attempting to advance their cause by launching military attacks with their own armed forces across frontiers.' Such a procedure, he pointed out, 'fitted neither with the requirements of the Marxist doctrine, nor with Russia's own urgent need for recovery from the devastations of a long and exhausting war, nor with what was known about the temperament of the Soviet dictator himself.' The real 'threat', according to Kennan, was the threat of *revolution*, particularly in Europe, 'the conspiratorial action of Communist-trained and inspired minorities,' who hoped to seize and retain 'dictatorial power *within* their respective national orbits.'

At the time, therefore, Kennan supported the Marshall Plan, which was designed to strengthen the economies and social structures of the countries of western Europe. He likewise criticised (privately) the formation of NATO as a 'military defense against an attack no one was planning.' NATO could only have been conceived, thought Kennan, by 'people capable of envisaging a favorable future for Europe only along the lines of a total military defeat of the Soviet Union or of some spectacular, inexplicable and wholly improbable collapse of the political will of its leaders.'

* Mimeographed lecture, delivered May 11, 1965.

Not only was NATO addressed to the 'wrong' problem, according to Kennan (although if the political collapse of the Soviet regime were an envisaged objective of the alliance, as the evidence suggests, then it would certainly have had relevance to the problem with which Kennan was concerned), but NATO had severe negative consequences for a European settlement as well. For by drawing a line 'arbitrarily' across Europe, and establishing on one side a series of obligations not shared by the peoples on the other, NATO had 'added depth and recalcitrance to the division of the continent and virtually forced individual countries to choose sides.' Indeed, from the moment that NATO was formed, 'the peaceful solution of Europe's greatest problems on any basis other than that of the permanent division of Germany and the continent, with the implied consignment of the Eastern European peoples to inclusion for an indefinite period in the Soviet sphere of power, became theoretically almost inconceivable. . . .' In other words, with the creation of NATO 'the problem of German unification, the removal of the division of the continent generally, the reintegration of the peoples of Central and Eastern Europe into the European community . . . all these great objectives, vital to any hopeful vision of Europe's future as also to the prospects for world peace, were sacrificed at a stroke. . . .'

Kennan's lucid if belatedly revealed perspective on the origins of the cold war and the division of Europe in the postwar period for the first time (in terms of orthodox analysis) begins to place a proper emphasis on the preponderant role and responsibility of the United States, which enjoyed such overwhelming advantages in economic and military power during this period, in shaping the cold war conflict. Moreover, by showing the fear of revolution to be close to the centre of Washington's cold war policy, Kennan also provides justification, from an unusually authoritative source, for the appraisal of the cold war which lies behind the conception of the present volume and the series of volumes which it initiates. For to treat the cold war as the particular expression of a more basic social phenomenon, the postwar phase of a long-term historical development, as this series does, is still a highly unorthodox procedure. It is our belief, however, that as the 'cold war' progresses, the rightness of this conception will become more and more evident, until it is generally regarded by serious historians as the only proper way to understand the nature and course of the contemporary world conflict.

DAVID HOROWITZ
Director, Bertrand Russell
Centre for Social
Research

Myths of the Cold War*

ISAAC DEUTSCHER

Many of the contributors to this volume belong to the same political generation as those who have organised the 'teach-ins' and similar protests in America, while among the others, Isaac Deutscher and William Appleman Williams have been this generation's teachers. In printing Deutscher's speech to the Berkeley Teach-In (see note below), we wish not only to preserve this brilliant critique of the orthodox version of the cold war, but to emphasise the profound connection between the criticism of ideas and the criticism of practice.

IMMEDIATELY after World War II when the western powers embarked upon the reversal of alliances, upon the great conflict with their former Soviet ally, people usually spoke about the two colossi, the American and the Russian, that faced each other in hostility across a power vacuum. It was assumed that one of the colossi, the Russian, threatened the American, the western. What people did not realise then, what the governments did not tell them, was that of these two colossi, one—the American—emerged from World War II in full-blooded vigour and strength, immensely wealthy, with hardly any losses suffered in the war compared with the other allies, with barely a scratch on its skin; whereas the other colossus, the Russian, lay almost prostrate, bleeding profusely from all its wounds. And it was that almost prostrate, bled white colossus who was assumed to create a major military threat to Europe—to threaten an invasion of Europe. That colossus, Russia, lost in the last war over 20 million people in dead alone. When, after the war, the first population census was carried out in the Soviet Union, it turned out that in the age groups that were older than 18 years at the end of the war, that is, in the whole adult population of the Soviet Union, there were only *31 million men compared with 53 million women*. For many, many years only old men, cripples, children and women tilled the fields in

* This is the text of the speech given by Isaac Deutscher at the Berkeley Teach-In on Vietnam, May 21–22, 1965. It has been specially revised by Mr Deutscher for inclusion in this volume.

13

the Russian countryside. Old women had to clear, with bare hands, the immense masses of rubble from their destroyed cities and towns. And this nation which had lost 20 million men in dead alone—and only think how many of the 31 million men that were left alive were the cripples and invalids and the wounded of the world war and how many were the old-aged—this nation with so tremendous, so huge a deficit in its population, this nation, of which a whole generation was lost, this nation was supposed to threaten Europe with an invasion! And until quite recently the threat of that invasion was still assumed to be real. NATO was formed in order to counter that threat! Yet any specialist in population statistics could have counted the number of years that it would take Russia to fill these gaps in her manpower.

Moreover, from the end of the war until the proclamation of the Truman Doctrine in 1947, the Russians had demobilised their armies so rapidly that they reduced them from eleven and a half million men at the end of the war to less than three million. Only *after* the formation of NATO did they start remobilising, but they had such difficulties with their manpower that in the course of another three or four years they called to arms not more than another two million men. Of course Russia could not—even if we were to argue on the most cynical grounds, even if we assumed that she had the most wicked rulers—Russia could not threaten anyone in that situation. And it is not only I who say so. The former American ambassador to Moscow, Mr George F. Kennan, whom we knew in those years as the advocate of the containment policy, who was the chief policy planner of the State Department, declared recently in a lecture at Geneva University in Switzerland (I am quoting from the London *Times* of May 12, 1965), that 'after the Second World War, American policy makers could see Communism only in terms of a military threat. In creating NATO . . . they had drawn a line arbitrarily across Europe against an attack no one was planning.' Mr Kennan, who in those years preached a containment policy, declares now (better late than never!) that the containment policy had nothing to contain. He says that the NATO powers had drawn a line arbitrarily across Europe 'against an attack no one was planning.' Then he goes on to put it even more emphatically: 'After the war the Soviet Union did not want or need to overrun other countries.' And the *Times* correspondent adds: 'In his first lecture here in Geneva a week ago, Mr Kennan said that erroneous Western concepts had given rise to many of the postwar difficulties and permitted Communist domination to extend farther west than might otherwise have been the case.' That is, he says, Russia was provoked into self-defensive expansion by the policies of the NATO powers. That is not what *I* say, but the former American

ambassador in Moscow. 'The Atlantic Pact,' he says, 'was unfortunate because it was quite unnecessary.' Yet this Atlantic Pact,
according to a man whom we considered as one of its architects, this
'unnecessary' Atlantic Pact, continues to dominate and determine
western policy till this day.

Now this assumption of a military threat from a major communist
power reappears in absolutely every crisis, up to and including the
crisis in Vietnam. We have seen how, after fifteen years, the myth of
that threat is exploded by one of the myth-makers; need it take
another fifteen years before one of the present myth-makers, before
one of those who *now* speak of the threat from a major communist
power, will explode the myth? Need it take another fifteen
years?

There was yet another set of illusions and myths characteristic of
the psychology and mentality of our ruling classes: the myth of
American nuclear superiority, the myth of an absolute unchallengeable American superiority. If, on the one hand, Russia's actual,
immediate ability to strike at the west was, to put it very euphemistic-
ally, greatly over-stated, Russia's potential strength, her capacity for
industrial development, was greatly and ridiculously under-rated.
Those who are old enough will remember what the experts told us
in those years: Russia, they said, will never have an atomic bomb
because she doesn't have the uranium ore. Then it was that Russia
didn't have the engineering resources to produce nuclear energy. Then
Russia didn't have the know-how. And then, when Russia *did* explode
the bomb, we were told that she couldn't produce nuclear weapons
in sufficient numbers to change the military situation. Then we were
told that the Russians would never have the means of delivering those
warheads. And then we were told that Russia couldn't produce the
H-bomb. Illusion after illusion. A chain of illusions, one exploded
after another. And yet, until the Russian Sputnik soared into outer
space, the assumption of America's unchallengeable technological
superiority in every field, in every military field, was taken for granted
—in America, and also in Britain and in the whole of western
Europe.

What accounts for this curious arrogance and wishful thinking?
I believe that our rulers sincerely—*sincerely*—thought that the
Russians would never challenge the west in the field of nuclear energy.
Brought up in the capitalist system, they were convinced that a social
order in which so-called private initiative, the 'private initiative' of
the big trusts and cartels, the 'private initiative' of the financial
oligarchies doesn't operate, they assumed that such a system couldn't
really work and couldn't produce nuclear energy. This was the
arrogance of an old ruling class, convinced that its 'way of life' and

its way of operating a national economy was the only rational and reasonable one, and that a new social order was an aberration. Since the beginning of history, declining social classes and ruling groups have assumed that any new social system opposed to theirs couldn't possibly work. This is the secret of the illusions and the myths in which our ruling classes believe. And when some of these illusions were exploded, when the illusion about America's unchallengeable superiority was exploded, the reaction to it was equally irrational: Panic! Waves of panic spread over the whole west. And now, when it turns out that even backward China, the China that the west had kicked around and trampled upon for a century, that even backward China is developing its nuclear industry, we hear those panicky and insane voices that tell us that perhaps if a few bombs are dropped on China's nuclear installations, the growth of that giant will be properly interrupted at the right time. Quite apart from the wickedness, the profound inhumanity and immorality of such talk—which one would still like to hope does not·affect or reflect official American policy, but I am not sure that it doesn't—quite apart from that, what a non-sensical illusion it is, that by dropping a few bombs you can really stop the growth, the industrial growth and modernisation, of the greatest nation in the world. Once again, arrogance—incredible, fathomless arrogance—and wishful thinking combine to produce something that future historians will cite as examples of the degeneration of the human mind.

The next set of cold war assumptions consists in the identification of communism and subversion. One wonders if the Atlantic alliance and the expenditure of hundreds of billions of dollars all over the west are really necessary to stop subversion. And can it stop subversion? But we may be told, did not Russia at one time, and does not China now, really aim at subverting western civilisation? It is one of the most unintelligent assumptions made in the west that Stalin or his successors were or are committed to the idea of international revolution. Those who have given themselves some trouble to study Soviet history know that what Stalin and even his successors represented was a profound conservatism, the conservatism of a new privileged post-revolutionary bureaucracy which was, and to a large extent still is, interested primarily in preserving the *status quo* both within the Soviet Union and without. At Yalta and Teheran during the last war Stalin divided the world with Churchill and Roosevelt into zones of influence. In October 1944 that grotesque gentlemen's agreement was concluded between Stalin and Churchill in which these noble men divided Europe in such a way that western Europe should go to capitalism, to the western powers, and in eastern Europe, as Churchill himself put it, Russia should exercise a ninety per cent predominance. In Greece, Britain was to exercise a ninety per cent predominance; and in Yugoslavia the influence should be divided on a precise basis of 50–50.

This ungentlemanly gentlemen's agreement provides the key to the history of the cold war. What has really happened is this: our ruling classes were, during the last war, in a paradoxical and self-contradictory situation; in their own interest they had to ally themselves with communism (or with Stalinism, which to them was communism); they had to ally themselves with Stalin against Nazism. The necessities of this alliance, and its strategic pressures, induced them to yield eastern Europe to victorious Stalin as his zone of influence. To speak from a Marxist viewpoint there was something very paradoxical in the attitude of the British and the American possessing classes. They yielded eastern Europe, a large and important part of the continent, to their class enemy. After the war, they had second thoughts; after the war, they wanted to get it back. That was the idea of containment. They wanted to contain Stalin on the old frontiers of the Soviet Union. And they dreamt of the great 'roll-back'. It was, so to speak, the guilty bourgeois conscience of our ruling classes that dictated to them the attempt to *regain* from the Russians the zone of influence they had yielded to them. Hence NATO; hence the reversal of alliances. However, Stalin insisted on the letter of the bargain—of the Yalta and Teheran bargain. Stalin said, 'You yielded eastern Europe to me; I am not going to give it back to you.' Stalin, who in his dealings with his own people was absolutely unscrupulous and ruthless, who was most ruthless and most cruel in dealing with communists, the same Stalin was in a bizarre Byzantine way scrupulous, legalistically scrupulous, in his bargains with his bourgeois allies. He claimed the advantage they had yielded to him: he gripped eastern Europe. He stuck to the letter of his wartime agreements with Churchill and Roosevelt; but he also respected his obligations. He yielded western Europe to them; he had 'resigned' from western Europe. He had committed himself to respect the predominance of the bourgeois order in postwar western Europe and he carried out his obligations. Long before the Truman Doctrine was proclaimed, Stalin had very effectively saved western Europe for capitalism; he had saved western Europe from communism.

This is no paradox. If you study the postwar history of Europe, you will see that in the postwar conservative, clericalist governments of France and Italy, the communists sat as junior partners. They disarmed their own communist resistance. They urged the workers to behave moderately, not to demand high wages, to help capitalism in its reconstruction. There would have been no restoration of

17

capitalism in western Europe without Stalin. And we were told that communism, that Russia, was planning subversion. If the Russian government, if Stalin's government, was plotting anything, it was plotting the restoration of capitalism in western Europe. In Greece, where according to the gentlemen's agreement Britain was given a 90 per cent predominance, when the Greek communists struggled and were being crushed by British tanks, Stalin did not utter even a murmur of protest. The Soviet press didn't write a word about it for weeks at the time of the civil war in Greece. And this we were then told was communist aggression. And Yugoslavia! In Yugoslavia, we now know that the communists carried out a revolution under Tito's leadership, despite Stalin's obstruction. Stalin did all that he could to prevent them. We know that in China too Mao Tse-tung ordered the last military offensives that were to end in the triumph of Chinese communism against Stalin's advice, against Stalin's obstruction. To the end, Stalin urged Mao Tse-tung to yield to Chiang Kai-shek and to allow his partisans (who had fought for over 20 years in the hills and from the caves) to be incorporated in Chiang Kai-shek's armies. Happily, Mao Tse-tung was no Togliatti and no Thorez and went on fighting for the triumph of the Chinese Revolution. I'm saying this not as an adherent or admirer of Mao's various other policies.

Now it is true that Stalin carried out the Stalinisation of all the countries of eastern Europe. But up to the moment of the formation of NATO he was still very cautious. He didn't want to antagonise bourgeois opinion in the west; and anti-communist parties still sat in the coalition governments of eastern Europe, just as the communists sat in the governments of France and Italy. Only after the proclamation of the Truman Doctrine, when the communists were ejected from the governments of France and Italy—and it was common knowledge in Paris and Rome what role the pressure of the American embassies there played in that ejection—it was only when the communists were ejected from the western European governments that the anti-communists were ejected from the eastern European governments, and that the single-party system was established with the help of the totalitarian terror of Stalin's police all over eastern Europe. It was allegedly in the name of freedom, for the sake of the freedom of eastern Europe that NATO was formed, and the Truman Doctrine was proclaimed. Yet the effect of NATO and of the Truman Doctrine was precisely to hasten the process of the Stalinisation of eastern Europe.

But was all the talk about Moscow-inspired subversion so hollow? Behind all that talk there was one real emotion which was and is gripping our ruling classes and our governments to this day: whether subversion threatened or not, our ruling classes were and are really frightened of revolution. They are especially frightened of any revolution behind which there is no Russian and no Chinese hand. The more a revolution is spontaneous, the more a revolution develops by its own momentum, the more are our ruling classes frightened of it. They have assumed the roles of the gendarmes of counter-revolution, and this is the root of all the trouble. They are the belated 20th century Metternichs. Metternich sought, after the defeat of Napoleon, to preserve feudalism in Europe and suppressed all revolution, until he was overthrown in 1848. Our present-day Metternichs say, of course, that they are struggling against subversion by offering economic aid to poverty-stricken peoples—they talk of the generosity of Marshall Aid, and so on. We have recently heard how the Vietnamese have been offered economic aid, but if they don't behave well, if they don't respond immediately to our offer, then of course the bombing of North Vietnam must be resumed. Either you take my economic aid or I bomb you. This is as in the famous German lines: 'Und willst du nicht mein Bruder sein, da schlag ich dir den Schädel ein.' Which in a free amateurish English translation means: 'and if you don't want to be my brother and pal, then I am going to smash your wicked skull.'

Of course, in order to preserve peace in the world you have to be tough: you mustn't appease the Russians, you mustn't appease communism. There is much talk in America just now about the 'hawks' and the 'doves', and our policy-makers assume, of course, that the hawks and doves are bred only here in the west. The Russians, apparently, don't have those breeds of birds. Certainly, if we in the west send out our ferocious hawks in sufficiently great numbers the Russians will, of course, send out their doves to meet them. And the Chinese will presumably do the same.

This illusion, too, has been repeatedly defeated and exploded. In truth, throughout the cold war the west hasn't been able to record any significant and lasting success anywhere. Wherever it has managed to stem revolution it has done so only with Russian cooperation. Where they lacked that cooperation, our 'hawks' haven't brought anything of which they could boast, which they could show as their gain. I shall not here go back deeper into the history of the cold war. I shall only say that in the major crises of recent years—in Berlin, in Cuba, and even earlier in the Korean War—all that the west's so-called tough policy has ever achieved in all these cases were stalemates, humiliating stalemates—stalemates for which there was no need in the first instance. There was no need to provoke struggles and fights which had to end in stalemates.

Let me now turn to yet another set of cold war assumptions: our policy-makers once assumed that the entire so-called Soviet bloc was a single monolith. They assumed, of course, what most Sovietologists told them. Their Sovietologists told them that Russia was making no industrial progress, that all allegations of progress were Red propaganda. Their Sovietologists told them that Russia was just one huge depressed area, a single concentration camp. There was, indeed, no lack of concentration camps in the Soviet Union under Stalin; but the actual reality was far more contradictory and complex, for progress and oppression, progress and retrogression went hand in hand. However, the Sovietologists were talking all the time of the one terrible monolith. When, in 1953, a few—very, very few—of us forecast the breaking up of Stalinism and the dissolution of that 'monolithicism', our policy-makers would not believe it and dismissed it as wishful thinking. I'm speaking here from my own experience, for in 1953 I myself made this forecast in a book, *Russia After Stalin*, and I got many such official reactions.

There was one man, however, among western statesmen who saw the de-Stalinisation coming, who saw a change in the climate of Soviet opinion, and advocated a new approach to Russia. And that was Churchill, the prompter of the cold war, the man who had, in his 1946 Fulton speech, called upon the west to rally against Russia. But in 1953 it was he who spoke about the change in the situation and appealed to his NATO colleagues for a new, more conciliatory approach to Russia. He was disavowed by the White House and ridiculed by his own Foreign Office, although he was then the British Prime Minister. It couldn't be that Russia should change; in Russia nothing was changing. Then, again, when the monolith was breaking up to such an extent that the Russo-Chinese conflict was developing, and when some of us were writing about that conflict before it came into the open, our great experts and policy-makers dismissed this, too, as wishful thinking.

I myself wrote in 1958 and 1959 articles on this subject in a well-known American periodical and a spokesman for the State Department declared that what Deutscher wrote about a conflict between Russia and China was just a Soviet canard, a canard put out by Soviet propaganda in order to disarm western vigilance. In truth, Soviet propaganda was saying nothing about the conflict; it was, on the contrary, making a profound secret of it and denying it flatly. But the State Department knew that what I was writing about the Soviet-Chinese controversy was meant to soften up the west vis-à-vis Khrushchev and to advertise Khrushchev as the conciliatory communist with whom the west could talk. And that was, of course, Soviet propaganda.

When the whole reality of the Russo-Chinese conflict became apparent, how did our policy-makers react to it? Again they swung to the other extreme and began to place great hopes on Russia. We were then told that Russia, becoming more and more bourgeois, was developing in 'our direction'; China became the villain of the piece. And the whole wisdom of western policy consisted now in driving a wedge between Russia and China. The war in Vietnam was the wedge to be driven between Russia and China. But how recklessly that wedge is being driven, how crudely, and in how unintelligent a manner. The driving of the wedge between Russia and China, which was to separate Russia and China, seems rather to be bringing them closer together; temporarily at least the Vietnamese war has effected a certain limited rapprochement between Moscow and Peking. The ideological differences are there, but many Russians and Chinese feel that they ought to present a common front over Vietnam. American policy-makers apparently didn't give any thought to the fact that only a few weeks after the 1964 American attacks in the Bay of Tonkin, Khrushchev fell. He fell, among other things, precisely because he advocated with excessive zeal a rapprochement with America and advertised hopefully, to the entire communist world, the latent 'sanity' of the official American policy. And, of course, the American attack on Vietnam was a refutation of Khrushchev's conciliatory policies.

We have seen how the impotence of the anti-communist containment policy has been revealed again and again. That policy has proved impotent because no weapons, no armed intervention and no napalm bombing can stop a revolution which develops by its own momentum, a revolution rooted in the faith, the sufferings, and the experience of an entire people or of its working masses. General de Gaulle, who is certainly not the hero of my novel, has learned the lesson in Algeria. He was confronted there with the revolution of a small, primitive, unarmed or badly-armed nation. And half a million (*half a million!*) French soldiers were fighting against the Algerian insurgents for years; and they had behind them the French section of the Algerian population. Yet they were impotent! Impotent against the revolution of a small and weak nation determined to fight for its existence.

'Ah!' say the defenders of armed intervention, 'But how do you know that such a native revolution is developing in Vietnam by its own force and momentum? Is it not all directed from the North?' There is, I suggest, one infallible test of whether an armed struggle is really the outcome of a genuine, broadly based revolution or not. To get at this test, I suggest that you note the contrast between the wars in Vietnam and Korea. In Southern Korea there was really no genuine revolution when the Northerners invaded it. And so the American troops and the others who participated in the hostilities under the banner of the United Nations had an easy job. They took the whole of Southern Korea in a matter of days almost. Why is it that in Southern Vietnam the troops of intervention are isolated on little bases, surrounded on all sides by the Viet Cong? Those familiar with the characteristics of civil wars in peasant countries know that in such a country no army can hold the ground and win unless it has the support of the peasantry on the spot. Those who are confined to small bases are so confined because the whole surrounding territory is for them 'enemy' territory, because the population of the surrounding areas is against them. Such was the pattern of the Russian civil war and of the Chinese. The Whites, the counter-revolutionary forces, were defeated because every village was for them enemy territory and in every village the ground was burning under their feet. This is what is happening also in South Vietnam, what is happening there to the Americans and the · highly unreliable forces of the South Vietnamese government. They are surrounded, hermetically surrounded, by a hostile element; and the hostile element is the peasantry that cooperates with the Viet Cong. Very few newspapers in the west have publicised the fact that the National Liberation Front of South Vietnam has carried out a land reform there and has distributed the estates of the landlords among the peasants. In other words, the peasants have a *vested interest* in the victory of the Viet Cong. They know that if behind American tanks and official South Vietnamese troops the landlords come back, the land will be taken away from the peasants who would also become victims of class revenge.

All these latest developments in the cold war are having their effect; and western Europe is weary of the illusions and misconceptions of the cold war. It is also very weary of the recklessness of American policy. Too grave risks are involved. It isn't a matter of chance that General de Gaulle pursues the 'anti-American' policy, that he plays the anti-American card. He woos the French people, and knows that his anti-American gestures have their appeal and evoke popular support. This gives you a measure of what is the reaction in the world to the present crisis. There is really a bitter irony in this fact, because two decades ago, after World War II, and even later, western Europe —bourgeois Europe—prayed for the American presence in Europe; people like de Gaulle were afraid of nothing more than of America's relapse into isolationism: American isolationism was considered the evil thing, and it was American internationalism that aroused great hopes. But what the world got, what western Europe got, was not American internationalism, but a malignant parody of it. We have seen American policy-makers carrying out one half of Theodore Roosevelt's advice: 'Carry a big stick'; but not the other, the more clever half: 'and speak softly.' They carry around their big stick, and talk very loudly. Are we to admire this as the image of American internationalism?

The effect of this American policy on eastern Europe is very grave indeed. I have no illusions about the feelings of the eastern European peoples towards the Russians. I'm myself Polish by origin and I know how deeply Russia has wounded the national feelings and sentiments of the eastern Europeans, and how this revenges itself on the relations between the peoples of eastern Europe and Russia. But eastern Europe sees also West Germany where the dominant social groups are still (or rather, are again) the Krupps and the other big magnates of the Ruhr industry, who once backed Hitler; they are now the main support, the mainstay of NATO in Europe. Can you visualise with what horror Poles, Czechs and Russians—those peoples who lost in the war 20 million and six or seven million more dead, those peoples who *knew* the inferno of Nazism as no one else in the world has known it—can you imagine with what feelings they watch America basing its whole policy, the policy that is supposed to defend our freedom, on that most cruel, most reactionary, and potentially always mad German imperialist class?

I would like to sum up very briefly the conclusion of my argument. In Vietnam it is not only American policy but the whole western cold war strategy that has reached an impasse. For nearly two decades western policy has moved in a maze of misconceptions and miscalculations, and amid the wreckage of its own illusions, in order to run now into a blind wall. It is time to draw a balance of this long and terrible venture, to count the political and moral costs of the cold war, and to assess soberly the risks. Unfortunately, I cannot say that I am setting my hopes very high for the immediate future. I do not see the approach of the great cease-fire that would end the cold war. To some extent this cold war may have been unavoidable. The antagonisms and the tensions between the powers cannot be conjured out of existence. The conflict between capitalism and socialism—all too often misrepresented as a conflict between democracy and communism—is not nearing a solution. The hostility between colonialism or neo-colonialism and the peoples of Asia and Africa and Latin America will not soon blow over. But if the stark realities of these multiple conflicts must remain with us, it may yet be possible for all the forces involved to behave more rationally, to shake off the hysteria and insanity of the cold war, to dispel the fog of myths and false scares, and to reduce the suicidal intensity of the conflict.

I still believe that class struggle is the motive force of history, but in this last period, class struggle has all too often sunk into a bloody morass of power politics. On both sides of the great divide, a few ruthless and half-witted oligarchies—capitalist oligarchies here, bureaucratic oligarchies there—hold all the power and make all the decisions, obfuscate the minds and throttle the wills of nations. They even reserve for themselves the roles of our spiritual protagonists and expound for us the great conflicting ideas of our time. The social struggles of our time have degenerated into the unscrupulous contests of the oligarchies. Official Washington speaks for the world's freedom, while official Moscow speaks for the world's socialism. All too long the peoples have failed to contradict these false friends, either of freedom or of socialism. On both sides of the great divide the peoples have been silent too long and have thus willy-nilly identified themselves with the policies of their governments. The world has thus come very close, dangerously close, to a division between revolutionary and counter-revolutionary nations. This to my mind has been the most alarming result of the cold war. Fortunately, things have begun to change. The Russian people have been shaking off the old conformism and have been regaining a critical attitude towards their rulers. Things are also changing in the United States. They are changing because the world, after all, is something like a system of interconnected vessels where the level of freedom and critical thinking tends to even out. I am sure that without the Russian de-Stalinisation there would not have been the amount of freedom and critical thinking that there is in America today. And I am also sure that continued exercise of freedom and continued voicing of criticism and continued critical political action in America will encourage the further progress of freedom in the communist part of the world. Freedom in the Soviet Union was suppressed and stifled mostly during the rise of Nazism. That was the time of the great purges. It was stifled again and trampled over again throughout the cold war or most of the cold war. The more Americans exercise their freedom in opposing their own rulers, the more will the Russians too feel encouraged to speak up critically against the mistakes and blunders of their government.

We are nevertheless not able to get away from the severe conflicts of our age; and we need not get away from them. But we may perhaps for the time being lift those conflicts above the bloody morass into which they have been forced. The division may perhaps once again run *within* nations rather than *between* nations. And once the divisions begin to run within nations, progress begins anew, progress towards the *only* solution of our problems (not of all our problems, but of the critical political and social ones), progress towards a socialist world, towards *one socialist world*. We can and we must give back to class struggle its old dignity. We may and we must restore meaning to the great ideas, the conflicting or partly conflicting ideas, by which mankind is still living; the ideas of liberalism, democracy, and communism—yes, the idea of communism.

American Intervention in Russia: 1917-20*

WILLIAM APPLEMAN WILLIAMS

THE increasingly antagonistic policy of the United States towards the Soviet Union during the last months of World War II, and on into the years of the cold war, was not the result of a fundamental change in the outlook of American policy-makers. American leaders had never, either in the mid-1930s or between 1941 and 1944, abandoned or reversed the basic opposition displayed by the United States from the outset of the Bolshevik Revolution. Various individuals and groups had questioned or criticised that policy, but they had never been able to effect any significant modification of its essentially negative character.

Washington had always been willing to deal with the Soviets when and as the Soviets accepted American premises, terms and proposals. This attitude was even predominant among the liberals and leftists who were so pro-Soviet during a brief period in the 1930s. They did not accept the Soviet Union for what it was and then try to evolve a relationship designed to benefit both parties. They saw Russia as the realisation of *their* hopes and desires; and when this proved false as well as self-centred they reacted largely in the manner of all narcissists.

The men who made policy were more integrated and realistic in at least one important respect. They did not try to realise their own visions by projecting them eastward and interpreting the mirage as reality. A few of them did consider the possibility of inducing the Russians, either by persuasion or by economic aid, to accept significant parts of the American programme, and even tried to convince their fellow policy-makers that such an approach was worth a serious effort. But even those men were concerned with tactical compromise—not with a broad, positive strategic accommodation. And the majority of policy-makers thought principally, if not exclusively, in terms of strategic confrontation and containment.

The painful and dangerous results of that antagonism and

* This is a revised version of an essay that originally appeared in the American journal *Studies on the Left*. A new introduction and conclusion have been added.

26

opposition prompted many of its central proponents, such as George Frost Kennan, to defend their action on the grounds that there was no other choice. These arguments maintained that the Soviets, from the beginning in 1917, were either evil *per se,* or else, as in Kennan's view, so psychically disturbed as to be understandable only in terms of metaphors comparing them to wind-up toys that could be stopped only by immovable walls. Permanent frustration, according to his somewhat novel psychology, would produce a healthy acceptance of confinement and perhaps a slow return to sanity.

A psychological analysis of Kennan's argument might offer significant insights into the dynamics of American policy in general, but even that undertaking would have to be predicated upon an accurate reconstruction of American policy and action. In its own right, furthermore, such a review provides the basis for explaining and understanding both the origins and the nature of American antagonism towards the Soviet Union. Among other important results, such an inquiry makes it clear that American policy-makers were fully conscious of what they were doing and why they were doing it; and that the Soviet leaders displayed a readiness to compromise and accommodate that American leaders, both then and later, were neither willing to admit nor prepared to act upon. It also offers a major insight into why the basic policy was never changed, and why its unhappy consequences were compounded through the ensuing years down to and including the war in Vietnam.

I
ATTITUDES AND POLICIES ON THE EVE OF REVOLUTION

On the eve of the Russian Revolution, as the United States was preparing to enter World War I, President Woodrow Wilson and Secretary of State Robert Lansing were seriously engaged in formulating the basic features of the peace settlement that the United States wanted to secure at the end of the conflict. Both men were deeply committed to overseas economic expansion, and to the Open Door Policy of 1899–1900 that guided American policy-makers in their efforts to secure and maintain free access for American economic power around the globe. Wilson's short outline of February 7, 1917 for the peace settlement accordingly laid particular emphasis on freedom of the seas, territorial guarantees, and security for trade expansion—'equal opportunities of trade with the rest of the world.'[1]

In reply to the President's request for comments,[2] Lansing, who sought in all his diplomacy to 'reaffirm explicitly the principle of the "Open Door",' offered two astute recommendations. Instead of a vague treaty involving the principle of the open door, he proposed a very specific 'mutual agreement not to form any international combination or conspiracy to interfere with the commercial enterprises or to limit the equal trade opportunities of any nation.' Lansing wanted to leave the way open for expansion 'as a result of increased population or an accumulation of capital desiring investment in territory under national control.' Wilson saw the point. He changed his formulation so that it opened the door for 'natural expansion peaceably accomplished.'[3]

As this episode indicates, Wilson's moralism did not exclude an early, persistent, and hard-headed concern for America's overseas economic expansion. This emphasis was not surprising in view of his assumptions that 'society is an organism,' and that 'we have not a large enough market or the means of disposing of the surplus produce'—'Our domestic markets no longer suffice. We need foreign markets.'[4] Amplifying and projecting his axiom that society was 'an organism,' Wilson argued that business 'is the foundation of every other relationship, particularly of the political relationship.' Since 'the organic cooperation of the parts is the only basis for just Government,' it followed that 'the question of statesmanship is a question of taking all the economic interests of every part of the country into the reckoning. Just so soon as the business of this country has general, free, welcome access to the councils of Congress,' he concluded, 'all the friction between business and politics will disappear.'[5]

'If America is not to have free enterprise,' Wilson stated flatly, 'then she can have freedom of no sort whatever.'[6] The integration of economic and political freedom in an organic whole was the ideal to be realised, and Wilson viewed the office of the President as the agency of such integration, and the overseas economic expansion of the American system as a crucial means of achieving that goal. He was deeply impressed by Frederick Jackson Turner's frontier thesis as an explanation of America's past prosperity and democracy, and took it over as a guide for policy to maintain those desirable conditions. Having entered upon the course of commercial empire after the closing of the frontier, Wilson saw the United States inexorably involved in a struggle to 'command the economic fortunes of the world.' The prize was control of the overseas market to soak up the surpluses—'the market to which diplomacy, and if need be power, must have an open way.'[7] In December 1919 President Wilson made it clear that the government 'must open these gates of trade, and open them wide; open them before it is altogether profitable to open them, or altogether reasonable to ask private capital to open them at a venture.'[8]

*　　　*　　　*

As though in microscopic illustration of his macroscopic theory about society as an organism, Wilson's economic ideas were integrated with his political ideology, and with his moral views and moralistic temperament. Expansion which produced well-being and constitutional government for its practitioners was by definition moral. The more so, indeed, because it carried the same benefits to others. Americans were thus the 'custodians of the spirit of righteousness, of the spirit of equal-handed justice.'[9] Wilson was candidly prejudiced in favour of 'those who act in the interest of peace and honor, who protect private rights, and respect the restraints of constitutional provisions.'[10] This inclined him strongly against helping those who 'show that they do not understand constitutional process.'[11] Yet his Christianity, and the demands of American foreign policy as he defined them, made it extremely difficult for Wilson actually to dismiss any society from any and all consideration. But the competing demands of Christian ethics and national expansion created tremendous moral tension, and Wilson's commitment to the principle of self-determination served only to intensify the dilemma.

His basic approach to resolving the conflict is of central importance to any understanding of his ultimate decision to intervene in Russia. 'When properly directed,' he noted, 'there is no people not fitted for self-government.'[12] Such being the case, the role of the United States was to discipline, educate, and guide the laggards and the mistaken. Wilson thus set about to 'teach the South American republics to elect good men,' and to use the power of the United States to establish a government in Mexico 'under which all contracts and business and concessions will be safer than they have been.'[13]

This integrated moral and economic expansionism provides the root explanation of Wilson's extensive political, economic, and military intervention in various Caribbean countries (Haiti, Nicaragua and the Dominican Republic), and in the Mexican Revolution. Paradoxically, it also was the basis of his decision in 1913 to forego open and vigorous support for the American bankers involved in the reorganisation loan to China. Wilson wanted to return to a pure version of the Open Door Policy under which Americans would act independently for their own and Chinese benefit.

Simultaneously with his refusal to back the bankers, therefore, the President acted to push American penetration of China. The government and the private entrepreneurs, he explained to American officials who might have misunderstood his earlier action, 'certainly wish to participate, and participate very generously, in the opening to the Chinese and to the use of the world the almost untouched and perhaps unrivalled resources of China.' He went on to 'urge and support' such activity, and promised government assistance in providing 'the banking and other financial facilities which they now lack and without which they are at a serious disadvantage.'[14]

This determination to participate in 'the economic development of China' prompted the Wilson administration to move firmly (if in the beginning somewhat deliberately) against Japan's threat in 1915 to establish extensive control over China. Wilson not only expressed 'grave concern' over the specific challenge, but candidly and forcefully spoke of his commitment in the basic issue of 'the maintenance of the policy of an Open Door to the world.'[15] This explicit and unqualified statement of his foreign policy strategy goes far beyond explaining Wilson's response to Japan's Twenty-One Demands. It provides the central definition of his diplomacy, and reveals the underlying nature of his conception of the League of Nations. That institution was in his mind, and from the very beginning, conceived and designed to establish and guarantee the principle of the Open Door Policy as the basis of international relations.

Given the nature of his integration of morality, politics, and economics around the Open Door Policy, Wilson's opposition to revolutions becomes quite comprehensible. Such social upheavals were immoral disruptions of America's programme. The President's thought, concludes Professor Harley Notter, 'disclosed itself as antipathetic to unsettled political conduct and to revolution as a method of government.' Nor was there any question concerning Wilson's position on socialism. He analysed it as 'either utterly vague or entirely impracticable.' His conclusion was unequivocal. 'I do not believe in the programme of socialism.' The danger it posed, however, could 'be overcome only by wiser and better programmes, and this is our duty as patriotic citizens.'[16]

Anti-socialism was thus defined as an essential component of American patriotism. But such an approach did not really resolve the contradiction and dilemma in Wilson's integrated liberal outlook. It only served to infuse one casuist solution with the emotions of nationalism. For, by the logic of the *principles* he avowed, Wilson was bound to accept and tolerate socialism as a legitimate expression of self-determination and as a respectable Christian heresy. By those principles, therefore, his commitment to American free-enterprise expansion as the engine of general peace and prosperity, and of political and moral salvation for mankind, had to be restrained in the face of socialist efforts to accomplish the same objectives. By defining anti-socialism as a manifestation of patriotism, however, Wilson distorted the Christian and liberal doctrine of the right of self-defence into a justification of—if not a rallying cry for—militant and righteous opposition to socialism. As will be seen, Wilson's personal understanding of this conflict defines the tragic core of the whole story of American intervention in Russia.

A review of the outlooks of the key officials who, together with Wilson, were involved in making American policy towards the Bolshevik Revolution suggests several further generalisations. First, none of them was naïve or innocent. They very seldom blundered into either success or failure. Many more times than not they won because they shrewdly picked their spots and deployed their power effectively; and when they lost it was because they were bested in tough competition in the course of which they gave almost as good as they took. All of them, furthermore, had extended experience in business and politics, and many of them had participated in the demanding labour of thinking inclusively and incisively about those matters. They were also men who had to come to terms with—and practised—the kind of routine casuistry that often seems to be inherent in the conduct of big business, big law, domestic politics, and diplomacy. They were not dishonest in the usual meaning of that term, and they were not hypocrites. They were simply powerful and influential men of this world who had concluded, from hard experience and close observation, that all of the truth all of the time was almost always dangerous. Hence they did not use all of the truth all of the time.

Secondly, these American decision-makers viewed economics as of extremely great, if not of literally primary, importance in the dynamic operation of the American system. This does not mean that they were motivated by personal pocketbook considerations. It means that they thought about economics in a *national* sense; as an absolutely crucial variable in the functioning of the system *per se,* and as the foundation for constitutional government and a moral society. And all of them viewed overseas economic expansion as essential to the continued successful operation of the American free-enterprise system.

Finally, these men shared a central conviction that the good society —and the good world—were defined by the forms and the substance of Western Civilisation as they had manifested themselves in the United States at the hour of the Bolshevik Revolution. Some were conservatives concerned to preserve aspects of the status quo that they considered particularly valuable. Others were reformers more interested in improving the existing order. But all of them shared a fundamental belief in, and a commitment to, the established system. This is by no means surprising, but an explicit awareness of it is essential to understanding their policy towards the Bolshevik Revolution.

*   *   *

II
The Crucial Decision of Principle

The Bolshevik Revolution challenged Wilson and his American leaders, both as individuals and as a group, in many central areas of their beliefs, ideas and objectives. And they knew it—every one. Inherently and explicitly opposed to the Revolution, they found themselves in a veritable thicket of dilemmas as they approached the broad policy problem. These difficulties can be summarised as follows:

How was it possible to oppose the Bolsheviks effectively and yet—
1. not compromise their own moral values and ideological precepts?
2. not risk the successful conduct of the war against Germany?
3. not allow Japan to establish itself in a position from which it could bolt and bar the open door in China?
4. and not unite other Russians behind the Bolsheviks?

Such was the problem. It was an extremely difficult one, and there should be no surprise that Secretary of State Lansing was occasionally depressed, or that Wilson repeatedly complained about 'sweating blood' over the Russian question.

American leaders were not totally unprepared for the Bolshevik coup on November 7, 1917. Ambassador to Russia David Roland Francis and others had described the Bolsheviks as radicals, and had kept Washington relatively well-informed of their activities throughout the summer and early autumn. And everyone was aware that the general Russian situation had become increasingly unstable.

Lansing gave considerable thought to the dangers of the situation on August 8, 1917. He knew of 'the strong opposition developing against' the Kerensky government, and was hence 'very skeptical' of the Premier's chances to survive as the leader of the general Russian Revolution. The revolution, Lansing concluded, was a fundamental one, and would therefore go through what he considered to be the usual historical cycle of such upheavals: 'First, Moderation. Second, Terrorism. Third, Revolt against the New Tyranny and restoration of order by arbitrary military power.' For the moment, at any rate, the situation was 'demoralized.' That meant, at least to the Secretary, that the United States 'should therefore prepare for the time when Russia will no longer be a military factor in the war,' and await the opportunity to act during the third stage of the revolution.[17]

This conclusion was reinforced by a memorandum on war strategy that Lansing received in October. The Army War College discounted any possibility of 'action through Russia.' Routine logistics difficulties and the classic admonition against dividing one's forces explained part of the decision. More important was the judgment that 'the invasion of Russia is, in itself, not a definite objective on the part of Germany.' The issue 'will be settled on the Western Front.' In addition, 'certain political considerations render advisable the presence of English troops in Mesopotamia and in Egypt, and of French and Italian troops in Greece.' Hence it would be difficult to muster an effective force for action in Russia. And finally, and perhaps as important as any reason in the minds of those who made the decision, 'the English and the French, rather than the Russians, are our natural allies.'[18]

On November 7, the day the Bolsheviks took power, Lansing was giving serious attention to a dispatch from the American Consul General in Russia Maddin Summers. Having apparently given up on Kerensky even before he was finally toppled, Summers was casting about for acceptable and reliable replacements. He was concerned for 'all classes of Russians standing for law and order.' Lansing was alerted by the warning, and sent it on to Secretary of War Newton D. Baker with a covering letter that reinforced the consul's report.[19] This episode indicates the early date at which Americans were concerned with strengthening conservative elements in Russia, but some of the most revealing evidence about the immediate reaction of American leaders to the triumph of the Bosheviks was provided by reporters of the *New York Times*.

It was 'thought certain,' one of them learned after a cabinet meeting of November 9, that the United States and its allies would recognise and extend aid to the anti-Bolshevik forces. One official said the Bolsheviks would be treated as 'international outcasts.' And another noted, in an amazing preview of what ultimately happened, that Vladivostok would probably be used as the main base for operations against the Bolsheviks.[20] On the next day, moreover, the reporter was told that it was 'a logical deduction' that aid shipments to Russia would be stopped until the Bolsheviks were overthrown.[21] In this case, in any event, the logic pointed the way towards policy and the assistance was terminated.

President Wilson's speech to the annual convention of the American Federation of Labour on November 12 provided the next public clue to adminstration thinking and policy. His broad theme was the need to strengthen and accelerate the war effort, and he specifically wanted labour to buckle-down and produce mountains of arms and other supplies. Radicals who fomented labour unrest were troublesome enough, but radicals who wanted to end the war before Germany was overwhelmed were particularly dangerous. The President explicitly mentioned the Bolsheviks in this connection and called them 'ill-informed.' Then he smeared American pacifists (and other critics of the war) by the demagogic device of describing them as being 'as fatuous as the dreamers of Russia.'[22] There would seem little reason to speculate about Wilson's early attitude towards the Bolsheviks. He was antagonistic.

Intervention as a consciously anti-Bolshevik operation was decided upon by American leaders within five weeks of the day Lenin and Trotsky took power. On November 19, for example, Ambassador Francis appealed publicly to the Russian people to 'remove the difficulties that beset your path.'[23] A week later Summers warned Lansing that, true to their radical socialism, the Bolsheviks were 'inciting the Proletariat against law-abiding citizens.' Action was imperative: 'strongly advise ... protest against present regime.'[24] And on December 1, 1917, the Inter-Allied Conference in Paris began a three-day discussion of intervention in Siberia as a means of keeping the supply lines open to anti-Bolshevik forces organising in southern Russia.

At this juncture, when overt anti-Bolshevism was clearly on the rise, the British made a suggestion which became the basis of the grand strategy of talking about action against the Bolsheviks in terms of something else. London warned on November 22 that 'any overt step taken against the Bolsheviks might only strengthen their determination to make peace, and might be used to influence anti-Allied feeling in Russia, and so defeat the very object we were aiming at.'[25] Colonel Edward House, one of the most influential advisers in Wilson's personal entourage, agreed with this strategy. He was specifically upset and worried about the consequences of various straightforward anti-Bolshevik remarks in the United States, and other attacks on the revolutionaries as enemies. He therefore advised Wilson and Lansing on November 28 to change the form of expressing such sentiments. 'It is exceedingly important,' he explained, 'that such criticisms should be suppressed. It will throw Russia into the lap of Germany if the Allies and ourselves express such views at this time.'[26]

These developments serve to raise the general question of the inter-relationship between the fighting of the war and the evolution of intervention against the Bolsheviks. More precisely defined, the issue concerns the way the commitment to defeating Germany affected American policy towards the Bolsheviks. It is true, of course, that the war against Germany limited the number of troops that the United States (and the other Allies involved in combat in Europe) could deploy for direct intervention. And America's top military commanders consistently opposed intervention because it would weaken the Western Front.

But the crucial point is that President Wilson overruled this purely military argument once he decided to intervene. He did so, moreover, in the late spring and early summer of 1918, at a time when American forces were being committed against the big German push as a preliminary to a major counter-offensive. It can hardly be over-emphasised, indeed, that Wilson made the decision to intervene in Russia with American troops *before* the Germans were stopped in the Second Battle of the Marne (July 18—August 6, 1918).

It is also undeniable that the Allies and the United States wanted to sustain military pressure on the Germans from the east. To this end they had exerted heavy influence on the Kerensky government right up to the hour of its collapse. But the leaders of the United States persistently refused to seek that objective through even short-run collaboration with the Bolsheviks. In this sense, and it is an important one, a strategic objective of the war took second priority behind strategic opposition to the Bolsheviks.

It should be clear that neither the British nor Colonel House were attacking, or suggesting a change in, the policy of opposition to the Bolsheviks. The advice was to suppress—to knowingly hide—the fact that the policy was anti-Bolshevik because general awareness of that fact could cause grave consequences. Furthermore, the Bolsheviks were treated as revolutionaries. There was no assumption, implication, or assertion that they were agents of the imperial German government. Colonel House and the others were simply afraid that open opposition might *drive* the Bolsheviks into some kind of a bargain with the Germans.

Lansing saw the point of this argument and momentarily agreed with the advice. But nobody giving the advice offered any concrete suggestion as to a different mode of referring to the Bolsheviks in public. Lansing solved the problem in a very natural way. He began to talk about the Bolsheviks in terms of 'German intrigue.'[27] As his diary reveals, however, Lansing did not actually think that the Bolsheviks were literally German agents. In one sense, he was merely using the possible danger as a weapon to forestall its realisation. In another, the psychological, he was projecting the fear about what the Bolsheviks might do in response to American action as a description of what the Bolsheviks were in fact doing—a description that provided a legitimate basis for American action. This was perhaps the first instance of such behaviour in American-Soviet relations, but it certainly was not the last.

This approach led American officials into the confusing practice of using two sets of terminology with reference to the Bolsheviks—they were 'German agents' in public discourse and 'dangerous social revolutionaries' in private discussions. American leaders also tended to see the Bolsheviks as men who indirectly furthered German purposes, at least when considered within the framework of the war, and sometimes talked of them in those terms. But they never abandoned their basic definition of the Bolsheviks as radical revolutionaries.

For that matter, Lansing very quickly began to question the wisdom of the advice from House and the British. He really preferred to attack the Bolsheviks publicly for the real reasons they were being opposed, and thereby bring the basic issue out into the open. Sometime between December 2 and 4 (and probably on the 3rd), he prepared a long memorandum stating the basis of American anti-Bolshevism. It contained no nonsense about Lenin and Trotsky as agents of German intrigue. They were defined and discussed as radical socialist revolutionaries bent upon a general revolution in keeping with their beliefs. As far as Lansing was concerned, therefore, they could be understood and dealt with only in terms of 'a determination, frankly avowed, to overthrow all existing governments and establish on the ruins a despotism of the proletariat in every country.' Including Germany.

Hence it was 'unwise to give recognition to Lenin, Trotsky and their crew of radicals.' The United States was dedicated to 'the principle of democracy and to a special order based on liberty.' The Bolsheviks openly challenged that unique system and should be dealt with accordingly. The first step, Lansing argued, was to prepare and issue a ringing public declaration of opposition and follow through with an announcement that the Bolshevik government would not be recognised.[28]

Lansing carried his argument to Wilson on December 4. According to the Secretary, Wilson 'did not think it was opportune to make a public declaration of this sort at the time it was suggested. He nevertheless approved in principle the position I had taken and directed that our dealings with Russia and our treatment of the Russian situation be conducted along those lines.' Ray Stannard Baker, one of Wilson's intimate associates and his official biographer, supports Lansing's account.[29] So do subsequent developments. On December 6, for example, Lansing advised Francis (and other American officials abroad) that 'the President desires American representatives withhold all direct communication with Bolshevik Government.'[30]

Some commentators, most notably George Frost Kennan, have explained Wilson's refusal to act on Lansing's request by referring to the President's speech of that day (December 4) asking the Congress to declare war on Austria-Hungary. Kennan's argument is that

Wilson did not want to blunt the impact of that performance. There is some point to this comment, but the President could have made such a statement on Russia in a few days. The reason he did not do so is very probably bound up in the way that Wilson had followed House's advice in referring to Russia in the war message. He called the Bolsheviks 'masters of German intrigue' who 'lead the people of Russia astray.'[31]

It seems very likely that Wilson had reacted favourably to the suggestion from House because it offered him a way to ease the very pressing contradiction and dilemma in his ideology. Fundamentally opposed to socialism, he avowedly 'stood resolutely and absolutely for the right of every people to determine its own destiny and its own affairs.'[32] By referring to the Bolsheviks as German agents, however, the President could define the issue of self-determination in a way that excluded the programme of the Bolsheviks. He thereby categorised the Bolsheviks as instruments of external influence rather than as agents of internal revolution. Wilson could thus oppose the Bolsheviks on the grounds of their having violated the right of self-determination instead of having to acquiesce in—or even assist—their efforts to determine Russia's 'own destiny and its own affairs.'

But such public rhetoric did not serve to change the facts—or to resolve the real dilemma. There is persuasive evidence to indicate, moreover, that Wilson knew this as well as, if not better than, anyone else. As he admitted to Lincoln Colcord on December 6, for example, the great bulk of the information reaching him defined the Bolsheviks as radical social revolutionaries rather than as German agents.[33] And his next action was predicated upon that knowledge, and upon his estimate that such radicalism threatened vital American interests in the Far East.

This decision was a response to Bolshevik agitation in Harbin, Manchuria, which served as the headquarters for the joint Russo-Chinese management of the Chinese Eastern Railway. The United States had been involved, ever since 1905, in a struggle with Japan for predominant influence over that railroad and the associated opportunities for trade and investment in Manchuria and China. And it seemed, at the time of the Bolshevik Revolution, that America would succeed in reasserting the kind of influence it had enjoyed in that area prior to the Russo-Japanese War.

This opportunity to consolidate the traditional strategy of the Open Door Policy was threatened when the Bolsheviks challenged the authority of the existing Russian manager of the Chinese Eastern, General Dmitri L. Horvat, who was a man amenable to American influence. The first warning went from the American consul in

Harbin to the Minister to China Paul S. Reinsch.[34] And three weeks later the developments had verified the storm signal. 'Situation Harbin serious,' Reinsch cabled Lansing. 'General Horvat ready to conduct joint administration with Bolsheviks.' Reinsch then advised support for a plan to send Chinese troops to counter the Bolshevik pressure. That would block the radicals and also prevent Japan from moving in with troops and thereby threatening the American position.[35]

Actually, of course, the Bolsheviks had a legitimate claim to control or replace Horvat. He was the Russian representative on the railroad board under the terms of a Russo-Chinese treaty. A new government in Russia (or China) had a legal right to exercise its authority under the terms of that agreement. With some reason, however, Reinsch and his superiors feared that Bolshevik participation in the management of the railroad might conflict with the realisation of American objectives under the Open Door Policy.

Wilson and Lansing approved the basic idea of denying treaty rights to the Bolsheviks. Their only concern was that China might fail in the specific operation, or initiate general military operations, and thereby give the Japanese an excuse to march in as the saviours of the Chinese Eastern. Hence they offered a strong warning against allowing the Chinese to open any military action they could not handle. All went well. By the end of the month, Reinsch (who had referred to the Bolsheviks as 'revolutionaries' throughout the crisis) reported that the Chinese had deployed over 3,000 men and that the operation was a success. The Bolsheviks were checked, and Harbin became a centre of anti-Bolshevik intrigue.[36]

By that time, Lansing and Wilson had worked out the basic strategy of American intervention against the Bolsheviks. On December 7, as he considered the crisis in Harbin, Lansing again reviewed the general Russian situation.[37] The Bolsheviks represented 'a despotism of the proletariat.' Thus 'the correct policy for a government which believes in political institutions as they now exist and based on nationality and private property is to leave these dangerous idealists alone and have no direct dealings with them.' The Bolsheviks, he judged, 'are wanting in international virtue.' They sought 'to make the ignorant and incapable mass of humanity dominant in the earth.' For such reasons, he discounted the rumours that they were German agents: 'I cannot make that belief harmonise with some things they have done.'

Lansing then evaluated the existing situation in the light of his general theory that revolutions progressed through three phases: 'First, Moderation. Second, Terrorism. Third, Revolt against the New Tyranny and restoration of order by arbitrary military power.' The Bolsheviks represented the second, 'black period of terrorism' of the general Russian Revolution which had started in March 1917, while Generals Alexeev and Kaledin were the chief candidates 'for a strong, commanding personality to arise ... gather a disciplined military force ... restore order and maintain a government' which could carry Russia on into the post-Revolutionary era.

Lansing's urge to act in line with this analysis was shortly reinforced by advice from two men whose views he respected. On December 9, he received a report from Summers reviewing a long discussion of the anti-Bolshevik problem that the Consul had held with a close associate of Generals Alexeev and Kaledin. Summers was convinced that they had strength 'sufficient to reestablish order' if they received official encouragement and material support from the United States and its allies. He strongly recommended such assistance.[38] On the same day Lansing had a long discussion of the situation with Major Stanley Washburn. The major reinforced the consul. Their combined effect was to convince Lansing that there was a chance to accelerate affairs in Russia into phase three of the Revolution.

On December 10, therefore, Lansing proposed such action to Wilson. The Secretary's operational plan involved breaking 'Bolshevik domination' by supporting 'a military dictatorship backed by loyal disciplined troops.' Following the advice of Summers (which he sent along to Wilson), Lansing reported that the 'only apparent nucleus for an organised movement sufficiently strong to supplant the Bolsheviki and establish a government would seem to be the group of general officers with General Kaledin.' He would 'in all probability obtain the support of the Cadets and of all the *bourgeoisie* and the land-owning class.' 'Nothing is to be gained by inaction,' Lansing concluded, 'that is simply playing into the Bolsheviki's hands ... I do not see how we could be any worse off if we took this course because we have absolutely nothing to hope from continued Bolshevik domination.'[39]

Wilson responded favourably. He spent an hour and twenty minutes discussing the proposal with Lansing on the night of December 11. The Secretary's diary tells the story: 'went over the Russian situation particularly strength of Kaledin movement.'[40] They decided to aid the anti-Bolshevik forces, and the next day Lansing asked for clearance on the financial side from Secretary of the Treasury William G. McAdoo. The money was available: 'This is O.K. so far as I am concerned.'[41] The President, who wanted action 'immediately,' quickly authorised the operation: 'This has my entire approval.'[42]

As should be apparent from the language of American policy-makers, this decision to intervene was based on their opposition to the radical nature of the Bolshevik Revolution. The *strategy*, that is to say, was anti-revolutionary. Any opposition movement, Lansing explained in his action dispatch, 'should be encouraged even though its success is only a possibility.'[43] The decision to intervene, as even Kennan has acknowledged, was 'a major decision of principle.'[44]

Lansing was not able, however, to persuade Wilson to oppose the Bolsheviks openly on the fundamental issue of their radicalism. As a result, the *rhetorical tactics* of intervention followed the suggestions offered at the end of November by House and the British. The operation was to be kept secret, and was cast in the idiom of strengthening the Eastern Front against Germany.[45]

But this tactic of intervention should not lead to confusion about the strategic grounds on which decision was based. To ask whether the intervention was not *really* anti-German or anti-Japanese is to misconceive the nature of the problem. Action through Russia aimed at Germany or designed to check the Japanese in the far east—or both—could have been formulated and implemented through co-operation or collaboration with the Bolsheviks. American leaders were aware of that option and upon occasion skittishly considered it as a basis for policy. But they always rejected it on the grounds that opposition to the Bolsheviks claimed first priority. Anti-Bolshevism was the central causative and determining element in American intervention in Russia, an intervention which was in principle decided upon between December 10 and 12, 1917.

III
VALIDATING THE DECISION TO INTERVENE

Various Americans raised fundamental questions about the policy of opposing the Bolsheviks. Two of the most significant and influential of these critics based their opposition on their experiences in Russia. One was Colonel William V. Judson, the American military attaché. The other was Raymond Robins, a devoted midwestern follower of Theodore Roosevelt who had gone to Russia as the Rough Rider's personal selection on the Red Cross mission to supply non-military aid—and political advice and support—to the Kerensky government. Robins later became head of the mission and quickly established himself as a quasi-official liaison man between the United States and the Bolsheviks.

Robins and Judson were convinced that America's central objectives —the defeat of Germany and a long-range strategic relationship with Russia—depended upon recognising and supporting the Bolsheviks. Neither man was a radical or what in later years came to be called a fellow-traveller. But they did understand the scope of the revolution, they did correctly estimate the odds in favour of the Bolsheviks retaining power, and they did realise that the Bolsheviks were inclined, as their difficulties became increasingly serious, to turn to the United States for aid. Robins and Judson wanted to exploit the opportunity thus offered to achieve immediate and future benefits.*

Both men knew of the plan to aid Kaledin and opposed it vigorously. Judson warned on December 17 that it 'would be absolutely futile and ill-advised.' The Bolsheviks were not German agents, and they realised that their revolution was mortally threatened by German ambitions in Russia. Hence the proper and effective strategy was to support the Bolsheviks against the Germans.[46] Combined with similar arguments advanced by Robins, Judson's efforts led Francis to offer to modify his own anti-Bolshevik position.

While it is probably impossible to establish with full certainty the precise meaning of this offer by Francis, we know that he advised Lansing on December 24 that 'Bolshevik power is undoubtedly greatest in Russia.' For this reason, and because of the growing Bolshevik fear and antagonism towards the Germans, and the indications that Lenin was interested in American aid, Francis said he was 'willing therefore to swallow pride, sacrifice dignity, and with discretion ... [establish] relations with Soviet Government .. [to] influence terms of peace.'[47]

This dispatch serves to date the beginning of a period of some ambivalence and drift in American policy that lasted until mid-February 1918, when Wilson and Lansing firmly reiterated the principle and the policy of intervention against the Bolsheviks. This hiatus was caused by the convergence of three principal difficulties: the practical problem of translating the principle of intervention into action without creating serious dangers to other aspects of American policy; the power and persistence of the argument that American objectives could best be attained through some kind of cooperation with the Bolsheviks; and Wilson's exhausting bout with the inescapable realisation that intervention contradicted the principles of both his personal ethic and his liberal ideology.

In the face of these difficulties, Lansing's first response when he received the cable from Francis offering to open talks with the

* Judson had personal discussions with Francis concerning policy matters; and, through various official channels and the influence of his friend Postmaster General Albert Burleson, his ideas also came directly to the attention of Lansing and Wilson. Robins talked policy with Francis almost every day, and his views and suggestions entered the State Department and the White House through that channel as well as through the efforts of his many personal and political friends in New York and Washington.

Bolsheviks was to carry on in the spirit of the decision to intervene. He promptly conferred with 'Polk on Bolshevik menace to the world,' warned his agent in South Russia to be particularly discreet in negotiations to support Kaledin, and then turned to the problem of checking Japan's desire to use the anti-Bolshevik policy as a springboard for further expansion in Asia.[48]

The Secretary confronted the Japanese ambassador on December 27, and his argument speaks for itself. 'I told him that the view of this Government was that it would be unwise for either the United States or Japan to send troops to Vladivostok as it would undoubtedly result in the unifying of the Russians under the Bolsheviks against foreign intervention.'[49] Whatever one's judgment of the strategy of anti-Bolshevism, it cannot be denied that Lansing used considerable finesse in acting on the chosen tactical approach. He used the threat of Bolshevik victory to block Japanese manoeuvres with the intention and expectation that the refusal to intervene directly would keep the Bolsheviks from consolidating their power.

This tactic for implementing the strategy of anti-Bolshevism had much to recommend it, especially its objective of blocking a Bolshevik appeal to Russian nationalism. But there were many difficulties involved in putting it into operation effectively. For one thing, Washington policy-makers were being bombarded by requests for more overt action against the Bolsheviks.[50] And Francis did not ease the tension and uneasiness when he sent along a Bolshevik appeal for world revolution.[51] Neither did Miles offer much concrete assistance. The Departmental expert started off the new year with a long memorandum, but it was nothing more than a verbose recommendation to stick with the decision of principle that had been made in December. His particular formulation—'continue ... support of elements of law and order in the south, but ... not exploiting Russia to carry on a civil war'—may very well have served mainly to dramatise the dilemmas of the policy agreed upon.[52]

Wilson could say, as he did, that the memo outlined 'a sensible program,' but that did not solve the problems.[53] And the pressures to act were increasing each day. In response to the entreaties to give active support to the anti-Bolsheviks, therefore, Wilson shortly approved sending the cruiser *Brooklyn* to Vladivostok as a show of force against the radicals (and as a cautionary hint to the Japanese). That was no more done, however, than Lansing was back with another plea to bring the anti-Bolshevik policy into the open.

Prompted by the Bolshevik appeal to the world that Francis had transmitted, Lansing attacked 'the fundamental errors' of the radicals and asked for prompt and effective countermeasures. The Bolsheviks, the Secretary warned, are appealing 'to a class and not to all classes of society, a class which does not have property but hopes to obtain a share by process of government rather than by individual enterprise. This is of course a direct threat at existing social order in all countries.' The danger was that it 'may well appeal to the average man, who will not perceive the fundamental errors.' Furthermore, the Bolsheviks threatened to subvert the principle of nationalism by advancing 'doctrines which make class superior to the general conception of nationality ... Such a theory seems to me utterly destructive of the political fabric of society and would result in constant turmoil and change. It simply cannot be done if social order and governmental stability are to be maintained.'

Nor were the Bolsheviks merely talking about the 'abolition of the institution of private property.' They had 'confiscated private property' in Russia. That could lead only to 'the worst form of despotism.' 'Here seems to me,' Lansing concluded, 'to lie a very real danger in view of the present social unrest throughout the world.' 'In view of the threat against existing institutions,' the Secretary asked Wilson to consider a blunt counterattack. He was 'convinced' that it was impossible to cooperate in any way with the Bolsheviks.[54]

Lansing had written a powerful letter. Had it reached the President under different circumstances, it is possible that Wilson would have accepted it outright as a guide for policy. And it may have exerted a less dramatic but vital kind of influence, quietly working away in Wilson's mind during the next two months. But it had immediately to compete with a resurgence of the argument to oppose the Germans by aiding the Bolsheviks, a logic that served additionally to remind the President of his moral and ideological dilemma.[55] Hence Wilson again deferred making a bold move.

Lansing promptly launched a counterattack against this competing advice. He first conferred with the Secretary of War 'on Russian situation.' Lansing was anxious, among other things, to expedite Judson's recall from Russia. The military attaché was an effective critic of official policy, and the Secretary wanted him removed from a position which gave his views some standing and influence inside the government. Then Lansing and Baker joined Secretary of the Navy Josephus Daniels for another discussion of the Russian question with President Wilson. It lasted 40 minutes and was the first of several which took place during the next 10 days.[56]

The ultimate result of these and associated conferences was a validation of existing policy (and Judson's recall), which, however, did not occur until Wilson had endured another of his periodic crises over the moral and ideological issues of anti-Bolshevism. This developed as the Bolshevik international appeal intruded itself upon

Wilson's long-term project of announcing his peace programme to the world. When the President would have delivered his now famous Fourteen Points Speech (of January 8, 1918) in the absence of Bolshevik competition for leadership of the peace movement is a moot point; but there is no doubt that, in its given form, the address was intimately bound up with policy towards the revolution in Russia.

As Wilson admitted in a striking and oft-quoted phrase, policy towards Russia was 'the acid test' of American and allied ideas and intentions. He laid bare the central elements of his dilemma. The United States should give Russia 'an unhampered and unembarrassed opportunity for the independent determination of her own political development and national policy,' and provide 'assistance also of every kind that she may need and may herself desire.' Only in that way could America and its allies demonstrate 'their comprehension of her needs as distinguished from their own interests, and of their intelligent and unselfish sympathy.'

Considered in isolation from other documents bearing on its nature and meaning, Wilson's speech can be interpreted as a manifestation of his ambivalence and anguished inability to come to a hard decision to implement the anti-Bolshevik decision of December 12, 1917. In context, however, the speech is a document in evidence of Wilson's willingness to modify his principles when they threatened to limit American power and expansion. For as Colonel House noted at the time, the President 'resented' the Bolsheviks and was trying to use them in order to appeal through and over their authority to the Russian populace. House's analysis was shortly verified in the course of a public argument over the meaning of the speech for policy towards the Bolsheviks.

The fight developed when William Boyce Thompson, an industrialist and financier who was a powerful and influential friend of Robins, asserted in a newspaper article that the speech meant that Wilson would seek some accommodation with the Bolsheviks. This claim was promptly and vigorously denied by William English Walling, who had access to Wilson's views on the Russian issue. 'It is utterly impossible,' he asserted in explaining the President's remarks, that the Bolshevik government 'should be recognised by America.' And a bit later, when Walling advised Wilson that aid to the Bolsheviks would be 'playing with fire,' the President remarked to Lansing that the warning contained 'an unusual amount of truth' and furnished 'a very proper basis for the utmost caution' in making policy decisions.[57]

The reason American intervention against the Bolsheviks took such a deceptively passive form for many months was not that Wilson drew back from the policy, but that it was deemed necessary to keep the way clear for anti-Bolshevik forces within Russia to defeat the radicals. As Lansing told the Allies on January 16, American leaders still feared that direct, military intervention might 'offend those Russians who are now in sympathy with the aims and desires which the United States and its cobelligerents have at heart in making war and might result in uniting all factions in Siberia against them [and in support of the Bolsheviks].'[58]

Wilson continued to be bothered when anyone raised the alternative of maintaining pressure on the Germans, and checking the Japanese, by collaboration with the Bolsheviks, but his basic attitude was revealed by his very positive response to a militantly anti-Bolshevik policy recommendation submitted by Samuel Gompers, President of the American Federation of Labor, and Walling.[59]

The Gompers-Walling memorandum, dated February 9, 1918, arrived at a time when Wilson was particularly weary of the constant strain connected with the war effort and the Russian problem. 'I do not know that I have ever had a more tiresome struggle with quicksand,' he had just written Senator John Sharp Williams, 'than I am having in trying to do the right thing in respect of our dealings with Russia.'[60] Hence it may have been particularly encouraging to have Gompers come forward in vigorous and determined opposition to recognition of the Bolsheviks and to any kind of dealings with them.[61] Here was the same advice Lansing had been offering, and it was coming from the other side of the class line. And the Secretary was unquestionably pleased by the President's reaction: the memorandum 'deserves a very careful reading' as 'a very proper basis of the utmost caution in the conduct of the many troublesome affairs' connected with Russian policy.

'It is really a remarkable analysis,' Lansing replied, 'of the dangerous elements which are coming to the surface and which are in many ways more to be dreaded than autocracy; the latter is a despotism but an intelligent despotism, while the former is a despotism of ignorance. . . . It is a condition which cannot but arouse the deepest concern.' 'I am more than ever convinced,' the Secretary concluded, 'that our policy has been the right one and should be continued.'[62]

Lansing promptly acted to sustain that policy in the face of evidence that his critics were gaining ground. Francis had upset the Department considerably with his dispatch of February 7, advising his superiors that he was 'endeavoring to establish gradually working relations' with the Bolsheviks. Whatever the ambassador had in mind, Miles interpreted the news as the sign of a dangerous development. 'This indicates,' he warned, 'that Ambassador is getting in touch with Bolshevik government. Does he need instruction?' As one who had always seen Robins as an outsider who ought to be put back in his proper place, Miles had no doubts about the source of the trouble. 'I gather Ambassador is being strongly influenced by Robins and he may splash over if we don't look out.'[63]

Lansing moved quickly to prevent such an eventuality, and to sustain the right policy. He bluntly told Francis that the United States was 'by no means prepared to recognise Bolshevik government officially.'[64] Then he again explained to the British that military action in Siberia would be 'particularly unfortunate' because it would 'tend to estrange from our common interests [a] considerable portion of the people in Russia.'[65] But in reiterating that argument, the Secretary entered the qualifying comment that such action would be unwise '*now*.'[66] As the caveat indicated, the form of intervention was a tactical matter. Tactics are altered with changing circumstances, and American leaders were shortly to change their tactics and begin the search for an effective way to undertake more active, overt intervention against the Bolsheviks.

IV
THE MORAL AND PRACTICAL DILEMMAS OF ACTION

The vigorous reassertion in February 1918 of the fundamentally anti-Bolshevik attitudes of American leaders placed President Wilson under increasing pressure from the logic of his own outlook to intervene directly in Russia. His problem henceforward was to find a way to act against the Bolsheviks that would enable him to resolve or rationalise his moral dilemma, that would be effective against the revolutionary forces and that would offer a way of preventing Japan from exploiting intervention to weaken or even subvert the Open Door Policy in Asia.

It is not surprising, therefore, that Wilson and Lansing slapped aside a serious and dramatic French proposal to try collaboration with the Bolsheviks, or that they did so in an instantaneous and ruthless refusal. This striking reversal of earlier French policy, which favoured military intervention, evolved in response to the clear indications that the Bolsheviks needed and wanted allied assistance against the Germans. Renewed German operations in northern Russia prompted Trotsky to advise the coalition of revolutionaries in Murmansk on March 1 and 2, 1918, that it was 'obliged to accept any help from the Allied Missions.' Lenin supported that decision and later issued general orders to resist the Germans.[67]

American and French representatives in Moscow knew of these

decisions, and interpreted them as verification of their own estimates of Bolshevik policies. The American military advisers, who had been seeing Trotsky almost as often as Robins, filed strong recommendations in favour of supporting the Bolshevik effort against the Germans. Coupled with his continuing evaluation of the nature and meaning of the Revolution *per se,* this convergence of events led the French military attaché, Jacques Sadoul, to extend even further his own talents and energy in an effort to convince his superiors in Russia and Paris that cooperation was both the most rational and the most promising policy for France to follow.

Combining strong emotion and powerful logic with persuasive language, Sadoul's argument momentarily carried the day. The French government reconsidered its heretofore militant anti-Bolshevism, supported Sadoul's negotiations with the Bolsheviks, and formally asked the United States if it would join in general collaboration with Lenin and Trotsky.[68] American leaders considered the French proposal on February 19, conducting their talks in the context of a militantly anti-Bolshevik memorandum prepared by Miles.

The United States, Miles argued, defined democracy in terms of 'the political freedom of its people.' On the other hand, the Bolsheviks held that democracy was based on 'equal economic freedom.' His conclusion was unequivocal. 'Fundamentally, these two conceptions are as different as black from white. It is idle to attempt to reconcile them as so many do. They are wholly different and cannot be reconciled.' The Bolshevik view was 'revolutionary in the deepest sense,' and its advocates 'have hitherto lived in the shadow.'[69] It is apparent, and should be made explicit, that American leaders were every bit as inflexible and deterministic as they accused the Bolsheviks of being; and, further, that it was the Bolsheviks who proved to be the more willing to diverge from the dictates of their theoretical and general opposition to collaboration with capitalist nations.

The decision on the French proposal was wholly in keeping with the logic and tone of the memorandum by Miles. He had not, of course, changed anybody's mind. But his analysis did reinforce the existing anti-Bolshevik consensus. Lansing personally took the French request to President Wilson. His brief pencilled notation documents their attitude: 'This is out of the question. Submitted to Pres't who says the same thing.'[70] American leaders were of course interested in re-establishing resistance to the Germans on the eastern front, but they were not sufficiently anti-German to overcome their anti-Bolshevism.

Robins had no direct knowledge of this mid-February decision, and his efforts to arrange such cooperation with the Bolsheviks came to a climax between February 22, when the Bolshevik Central Committee voted to accept aid from the allies (with Lenin casting the crucial vote), and March 5, when Trotsky and Lenin gave Robins a written and specific inquiry designed to initiate a serious discussion concerning aid from the United States.[71]

There is some evidence that a full copy of this document failed to reach Washington until after the Bolsheviks ratified the Brest-Litovsk treaty of peace with Germany. Even if this is true, and the evidence is not wholly convincing, the delay is far less significant than such writers as George Frost Kennan have made it appear. *Top American leaders already had explicit knowledge of the Bolshevik interest in obtaining assistance from the United States.* Furthermore, and as Washington was advised by several American military representatives in Russia, ratification of the treaty with Germany did not prevent the Germans from reopening their offensive—or the Bolsheviks from opposing that new attack as best they could. As late as March 26, for example, Francis told Lansing that the Red Army 'is the only hope for saving European Russia from Germany.'[72] American policy-makers *could* have responded favourably to the overture from Lenin and Trotsky whenever it actually did arrive. For that matter, they could have offered such negotiations on their own initiative. They did neither.

Wilson's message to the Congress of Soviets of March 10 made it clear beyond any question that he had no intention even of exploring the possibilities of such cooperation.[73] He bluntly told the Russian people that the United States, despite its great sympathy for their travail, was not going to help them through the Bolshevik government. His words further carried the strong implication that the Bolsheviks were in league with the Germans. This document was prepared, moreover, in the course of continuing discussions designed to evolve a plan of intervention which would resolve the moral and practical dilemmas confronting Wilson and other American leaders. By February 26, for example, Lansing was referring in his conversations with Wilson to 'our proposed policy.'[74] The resulting decision seems to have been produced by several convergent pressures, and was based upon a rather subtle strategy for controlling the variables involved in intervention.

After their proposal to collaborate with the Bolsheviks had been dismissed out of hand, the French returned to nagging Wilson for some kind of intervention in Siberia. The British supported this campaign to break down the President's resistance. And the Japanese, of course, continued their own push for permission to move on to the mainland of Asia. These pressures on the United States were powerful in and of themselves, and gained additional strength from the political and psychological circumstances. Wilson was opposing other allied suggestions, for example, and he seems to have felt that he might gain some political ground by agreeing to some form of intervention. The psychological factor involved the fatigue which was apparent in Wilson and Lansing. They were tired men, and were no doubt particularly weary of the Russian issue. The inclination to go on in and be done with it may have become quite strong once they had turned their backs on the idea of working with or through the Bolsheviks.

Even so, there was more than political higgling and *ennui* involved in Wilson's decision in February to approve Japanese intervention. For one thing, Lansing and Wilson seem to have concluded that Japan might do something regardless of American or allied approval. 'My own belief,' Lansing fretted in a letter to the President on February 27, 'is that Japan intends to go into Siberia anyway.'[75] This raised the very difficult question of how to limit and control the Japanese. Lansing first encouraged the Chinese to hold the line in Manchuria. He told them that the United States wanted 'the Chinese Government to take over and guard that part of the Trans-Siberian Railroad system [i.e., the Chinese Eastern Railway] which passes through Manchuria.'[76] And, since the Chinese already had troops near Harbin, and could send more, this was not an empty gesture.

A second move was based on the old adage of publicly committing a suspect to a self-denying pledge as a way of preventing the crime. Wilson and Lansing had a perfect opportunity to do this: a Japanese spokesman had voluntarily offered such assurances.[77] It is not so often realised, however, that France and the other allies were also concerned to check Japan. Perhaps the intensity of the French desire to act has obscured this point. While it is true that neither France nor England was as sensitive to Japanese operations in Manchuria, or in north China, as the United States was, it is *not* true that they were indifferent to the implications of an unrestrained Japanese move on to the mainland—particularly in view of Tokyo's seizure of Shantung Province, and its Twenty One Demands of 1915. And, because it was a late-comer to the scramble for concessions in Asia, and because it was rather self-conscious about its lack of success prior to the war, Italy manifested an even stronger resistance to unilateral, unchecked Japanese intervention.

Lansing had clear evidence of this concern before Wilson acted between February 27 and March 1. The French were 'very emphatic' and very explicit: 'A full understanding and agreement would have to be had with Japan by all the other leading Allied powers, providing for the retirement of Japanese troops from Russian soil after the war, in addition to certain other guarantees.' As if to make doubly sure that the meaning was understood, the French 'evinced a keen curiosity as to the reason for the United States Government's opposing exclusive Japanese intervention.'[78]

France ideally preferred to bind Japan with a treaty, but Lansing demurred: that approach would involve the Senate, and the ensuing debate would cause jarring complications.[79] A full, public discussion of policy towards Russia was not desirable from the point of view of the Wilson administration. That would open the way for Robins, Thompson and other critics to force modifications in—or perhaps even a major change of—existing policy. The European powers acquiesced, and expressed themselves as being 'quite satisfied with the way the matter is being handled by the President.'[80]

This support from England, Italy and France for the manoeuvre to control the Japanese encouraged Wilson and Lansing to feel, at least temporarily, and in conjunction with reports from Reinsch, Summers, and other American agents, that they could move in behind the Japanese and influence events in Russia along American lines through the use of economic power and diplomatic influence.[81] Wilson's memorandum of the night of February 27 was a device to commit the Japanese to their own professions of moderation by announcing them publicly as the basis for American acquiescence in intervention. The United States, Wilson explained, 'wishes to assure the Japanese Government that it has entire confidence that in putting an armed force into Siberia it is doing so as an ally of Russia, with no purpose but to save Siberia from the invasion of the armies and intrigues of Germany with entire willingness to leave the determination of all questions that may affect the permanent fortunes of Siberia to the Council of Peace.'[82]

This sly but all-inclusive caveat was intended to trap the Japanese. On the one hand, they dared not reject such a pleasant essay in praise of their integrity. On the other hand, it would do them no good to ignore it because in that contingency the United States could use it as an aide-memoire of an understanding based on earlier Japanese assurances. And, armed with the support of its European associates, America could feel confident of winning its point at the peace conference. In a real sense, Wilson was warning Japan to observe the conditions he specified or face united opposition.

Within 72 hours, however, Wilson withdrew even this support for Japanese intervention. The change, he told Polk, was 'absolutely necessary.'[83] Several reasons account for the abrupt shift. The President was repeatedly and vigorously warned that the United States could not count on controlling Japan through the stratagem of a self-denying pledge. These critics, such as Colonel House, argued that Wilson's approach risked creating an awful choice for the United States if the Japanese should decide to stay in Siberia, or turn their troops southward into China. If either of those conditions developed, the United States would have either to abandon the Open Door Policy or go to war against Japan. This analysis served to dramatise the second negative consideration, which was simply that Wilson was not ready to move immediately with a programme of economic aid that would buttress American influence and also strengthen Russian and Chinese opposition to Japan.

In addition, the President also seems to have reconsidered the broad situation and, as a result, to have fallen back on the original strategy of December 1917, which was based on the axiom that direct intervention would provoke the Russians to support the Bolsheviks. Some Americans felt this would be particularly apt to occur if the Japanese went in alone; their reasoning being that racial antagonisms would be intensified by the memory of the Russian defeat in the Russo-Japanese War. And, finally, Wilson's central moral dilemma about intervention had been sharpened by reminders from men like Colonel House. They emphasised the loss of American influence if the principle of self-determination was so blatantly ignored.

All in all, the reversal of policy may well have been Wilson's finest moral hour. Torn by the conflict between his opposition to the Bolsheviks, which involved his entire political, economic, and social philosophy, and his deep involvement with the essential right of self-determination, the President chose to honour the moral axiom. Wilson's moral courage was no doubt reinforced by the fear that, given the existing circumstances, the Japanese outlook would triumph instead of his own. But the consideration should not be allowed to obscure either the intensity of Wilson's moral turmoil over intervention, or the central relationship between the agony and the change in policy. A man so essentially moralistic as Wilson could hardly be expected to view the Bolsheviks as anything but heretics, and to such men the heretic is even more dangerous than the non-believer. In this sense, at any rate, the surprise lies not so much in Wilson's final intervention, but rather in the strength and persistence of his moral qualms about such action. The liberal conscience ultimately broke down, but its initial resistance was greater than sometimes seems to be the case long after the crisis.

While it did not cause Wilson's change of mind, the Italian opposition to unilateral Japanese action may well have encouraged the President as he reconsidered the issue. Clearly seeking to creep in under the umbrella of the Open Door Policy, Italy made 'three conditions' for its support of any Japanese move. Tokyo's action 'should be satisfactory' to the United States, the intervention 'should be *not* by Japan alone,' and 'guarantees should be given by Japan that they do not intend to hold territory.'[84]

Wilson's circular note of March 5 announcing that he now opposed unilateral Japanese intervention provides what is almost a diagram of his thinking on the general subject. He remarked first on the 'most careful and anxious consideration' that he had given 'to the extreme danger of anarchy' in Siberia. This social and political situation was the root cause of the crisis, and intervention might in the end be necessary to control matters before they got completely out of hand. But he was 'bound in frankness to say that wisdom of intervention seems . . . most questionable.' Then, in what was at once a veiled expression of his fears about Japan and his commitment to the right of self-determination, he warned that 'all the assurances in the world would not prevent what Germany is doing in the West.'

In conclusion, Wilson revealed that he had fallen back on the strategic estimate evolved early in December 1917. Military intervention would generate 'a hot resentment' in Russia, 'and that whole action might play into the hands of the enemies of Russia, and particularly the enemies of the Russian revolution, for which the Government of the United States entertains the greatest sympathy in spite of all the unhappiness and misfortune which has for the time being sprung out of it.'[85]

And to Wilson, as to American leaders in general, the Bolsheviks were both the cause and the substance of that unhappiness and misfortune. In their minds, at any rate, the Bolsheviks were not considered part of the Russian Revolution for which the United States entertained 'the greatest sympathy.' As Assistant Secretary of State Long put it in a personal letter to Reinsch, American policy was concerned with supporting 'the original revolution.'[86]

V
The Decision to Intervene

Wilson did not abandon the idea of intervention on March 5; he merely refused to support one of many tactics of intervening. The President continued his search for some way to go into Siberia as the dominant power in an allied force including Japan and then begin economic and political operations in support of the anti-Bolshevik movement. There is no evidence that the discussions to evolve an effective way to accomplish this objective had been significantly influenced by the occasional rumours about German military operations in Siberia. Lansing reviewed these stories in a memorandum to Wilson on March 19, and concluded that Admiral Knight's evaluation was valid.

Knight concluded that it was 'impossible' for any significant part of the military stores in Vladivostok to be destroyed; that there was 'absolutely no danger' they would reach the Germans; and that there was 'no evidence' of any serious German influence in Siberia. He added that Lenin and Trotsky, and their Bolshevik followers in the far east, were revolutionaries—not German agents. And he concluded with a strong recommendation that it was 'of first importance' that Japan 'should not be permitted to act alone.'[87]

Lansing did become somewhat concerned, between March 21 and 24, 1918, over a new flurry of reports that the Bolsheviks were converting some German and Austrian prisoners-of-war to their radical ideology, and then using them in military operations against the anti-Bolshevik forces in Siberia. If this turned out to be true, the Secretary anticipated that 'we will have a new situation in Siberia which may cause a revision of our policy.' His reference to a 'new situation,' makes it clear that neither the Bolshevik-as-German-agent theory, nor the fear of a German campaign in Siberia, was a causative factor in the discussions of intervention that took place between November 7, 1917, and March 20, 1918. Lansing's approach to the new reports, furthermore, was wholly conditional. He was merely doing what any responsible official would have done: 'we should consider the problem on the hypothesis that the reports are true and be prepared to act with promptness.'[88]

Wilson commended the Secretary for his foresight, but did not think the situation called for action. 'I do not find in them,' he replied, 'sufficient cause for altering our position.'[89] The stories reappeared from time to time, but decisions were not made on the assumption that they were true. In April, for example, both Reinsch and the Czech leader Thomas Masaryk advised Wilson and Lansing that the tales were not worth serious attention, and most certainly were not a reliable basis for policy decisions. Reinsch's estimate was based on extensive first-hand information. He put 'much work' into his efforts to find out what was going on in Siberia, and his chief agent in the field, Major Walter S. Drysdale (the American military attaché in Peking) was a man with 'a great deal of good sense.'[90]

An early report to Reinsch, prepared by a Colonel Speshneff on March 9, told of finding the prisoners employed 'as clerks, [and] some of them work as painters, carpenters, shoemakers, tailors, hairdressers, etc.' Speshneff wanted American intervention 'in the internal affairs directed against the Bolsheviki,' but he did not base his plea on the danger from the prisoners-of-war. He was simply against the Bolsheviks. Drysdale's review on March 19 of the evidence he had collected during a field trip was unequivocal: 'not a single armed prisoner was seen and there is little probability that any of the prisoners are armed.' Three weeks later, on April 10, he reaffirmed that estimate. 'Some very few of the prisoners' at Chita were being converted politically, and were 'fighting as workmen, for the workmen's cause, against the Bourgeoisie.'

As one Austrian explained to Drysdale, 'they were helping their brother labourers in Russia against Semenoff and the Bourgeoisie.'[91] This situation might with some accuracy have been described under the heading of Austrians-as-Bolsheviks, but it was positive disproof of the argument that the Bolsheviks were German agents. And, as the men on the scene reported, there were no other armed prisoners. These on-the-spot dispatches, and Reinsch's summary of them for Washington, put an end even to Lansing's conditional and hypothetical worry about the prisoners-of-war.

On the other hand, the idea of supporting the Bolsheviks against Germany continued to show life. Robins sustained his campaign for that policy to the point of antagonising Consul Summers beyond his endurance. But, when Summers asked for a transfer, Lansing promptly and effectively exerted pressure on the Red Cross directors to recall Robins from Russia. That did not put an end to the advice to collaborate with the Bolsheviks, however, for American military representatives continued to recommend the same policy after Robins was ordered to return to the United States.

These men, who had agreed with Judson's estimate of the situation in November and December 1917, had no illusions about a political honeymoon with the Bolsheviks. They understood that Lenin and Trotsky were fighting the Germans to save the revolution—not as a disinterested favour to the Allies. Some of them may also have sensed, as Robins did, that the Bolsheviks were becoming aware that they —or any Russian government, for that matter—needed allies against Japan and Germany. Even before World War I, Robins had concluded from a general analysis of the world political system that an American-Russian entente offered security for both countries.

The military representatives may not have gone that far in thinking, but they did argue that short-run collaboration was the most intelligent and practical course of action. Ambassador Francis allowed them to continue their discussions with Trotsky, and even to offer some technical assistance, even though he intended that any army organised by Trotsky would be 'taken from Bolshevik control' and used against the revolutionaries.[92] He thought any agreement with the Bolsheviks would help sustain them in power, and considered that 'cost will be too dear.'[93]

Sometime in the second or third week of April, at a stage when the German prisoner-of-war scare had been thoroughly discredited, President Wilson began an active search for some anti-Bolshevik group through which he could inject American power directly into the Russian situation. 'I would very much value a memorandum,' he advised Lansing on April 18, 'containing *all* that we know about these several *nuclei* of self-governing authority ... in Siberia. It would afford me a great deal of satisfaction to get behind the most nearly representative of them if it can indeed draw leadership and control to itself.' Like the decision of December 10, 1917, to aid Kaledin in southern Russia, this letter makes it clear that American policy-makers were thinking of intervention as an anti-Bolshevik operation. The problem in the spring of 1918 was to find a winner; not only, of course, in order to defeat the Bolsheviks, but also to block the Japanese.

Further conversations between the two men seem almost certainly to have taken place during the next few days, even though no written record survives. This is strongly suggested, for example, by a dispatch Lansing sent to the American ambassador in France on April 23. For, in briefing the ambassador so that he would be able to discuss intervention with the French authorities, the Secretary clearly implied that such talks had occurred. Belgium and Italy, Lansing explained, had requested the United States to move a total of 450 officers and men, along with some armoured cars, from Nagasaki and Vladivostok to the Western Front. *Acting on its own,* the American government had suggested in reply that it would be wise to leave the troops in the far east.

That reply, Lansing explained, 'was predicated upon the possibility of intervention in Siberia. It seemed inadvisable to bring away from there troops carrying flags of co-belligerents when it might be embarrassing to send back there other such troops.' This action did not commit Wilson and Lansing to intervention, but it certainly indicates that they were discussing it seriously enough to keep non-Japanese troops in readiness. This conclusion is reinforced by Lansing's final cautionary word to the American ambassador in France: 'it is felt to be highly desirable that the matter should not be discussed with other persons.'[94]

Lansing and Wilson kept a sharp watch on the progress of the anti-Bolshevik leader Grigori Semenov during the ensuing month. Semenov was a Cossack who had served first as a Tsarist officer; then after the March Revolution, he had gone to Siberia to raise a volunteer force of Mongols against the Germans. Caught in the east when the Bolsheviks took power, Semenov promptly began to fight them. He was vain, arrogant and undemocratic, but his nerve and ruthlessness made him effective in the field—at least for a long enough time to attract the attention of American policy-makers. And, since neither Wilson nor Lansing favoured negotiating any understanding with the Bolsheviks about intervention in Siberia, Semenov attracted their interest and concern.

The Secretary of State made it clear that he opposed any agreement with the Bolsheviks, even for the purpose of checking the Germans or the Japanese, because that 'would array us against Semenov and the elements antagonistic to the Soviets.' That should not be done. Wilson agreed, and on May 20 reiterated his instructions of April 18: 'follow very attentively what Semenov is accomplishing and whether or not there is any legitimate way in which we can assist.'[95]

The President's clear and persistent concern to evolve some way of aiding the anti-Bolsheviks was reinforced during these weeks by an increasing campaign involving various anti-Bolshevik groups in the United States. They wanted to move in with economic aid, and then stay for a share in the post-Bolshevik economic pie.[96] Wilson was interested in such plans, but his own thinking about intervention ran along the more narrow and specific line of aid to the anti-Bolshevik groups in their military operations. The door had to be opened, as it were, before the economic benefits—and influence—could flow through it. The President's approach of course involved economic assistance, but not in the precise form then being advocated by the various clusters of opinion in the United States. This difference between their outlooks became apparent in a second letter of May 20 from Wilson to Lansing.

A dispatch from Reinsch urging action prompted Wilson to ask the Secretary if the moment for intervention had arrived. 'Situation in Siberia seems more favorable than ever,' Reinsch judged on May 16, 'for effective joint action of Allies and American initiative . . . Should America remain inactive longer friendly feeling is likely to fail.' Lansing was definitely interested in Reinsch's argument, perhaps even partially persuaded, but not wholly convinced.

He was aware that Semenov's 'policy is to keep the Siberian Railway open and overthrow the Bolsheviki,' and that his successes offered 'the prospect of forcing an amalgamation of all the different elements seeking reconstruction in Siberia.' But the Secretary still worried about the danger of antagonising the rank and file anti-Bolshevik Russians, even though support for Semenov could be combined with assistance to the Czecho-Slovak troops that were in

Siberia. Lansing concluded, therefore, that the time was not yet 'opportune' for direct intervention.[97]

Wilson admitted the importance of not antagonising the non-Bolshevik Russians, and of checking the Japanese, but those tactical difficulties did not lead him to abandon the search for a way to implement the strategy of anti-Bolshevism. He was prepared, as he told the British, to 'go as far as intervention against the wishes of [the Russian] people knowing it was eventually for their good providing he thought the scheme had any practical chance of success.' Joint intervention offered good possibilities of rallying the people against the Bolsheviks, but unilateral Japanese action would probably antagonise all the Russians 'excepting for a small reactionary body who would join anybody to destroy the Bolsheviks.'

Asked if this meant that the allies should 'do nothing at all,' Wilson replied 'No.' 'We must watch the situation carefully and sympathetically and be ready to move whenever the right time arrives.' While waiting for an invitation to intervene from a successfully organised anti-Bolshevik group, Wilson wanted to prepare the way for effective operations by strengthening the economic situation in the non-Bolshevik areas of Siberia.[98] Even as the President was thus reiterating his commitment to the fundamental strategy of anti-Bolshevik intervention, Lansing was modifying his tactical caution.

The Secretary received on May 26 a long letter from George Kennan, an old friend who was generally considered to be one of America's leading experts on Russian affairs. Kennan's advice and recommendations were militantly anti-Bolshevik. Lansing was impressed. 'I have read the letter with especial interest because it comes from the highest authority in America on Russia.' The Secretary naturally found it 'gratifying that his own views were very similar' to those expressed by Kennan. The only significant disagreement concerned the 'wisdom of intervention in Siberia.'

Kennan was convinced that intervention was tactically workable as well as strategically desirable. Lansing wholly agreed on the strategy of anti-Bolshevism, but was 'not so sure' that the tactic of direct intervention would prove successful. He explained, however, that the issue was receiving 'very careful consideration' by the administration. And, because Kennan 'had so clearly analysed the state of affairs,' Lansing promised to 'lay it [the letter] before the President.'[99]

Lansing received more of the same kind of advice when he returned to the Department of State the next morning. A dispatch from Ambassador Page in London advised the Secretary that a League for the Regeneration of Russia in Union with Her Allies had been established in Rome, and was receiving support from Russians in

England. It was militantly anti-Bolshevik, appealed directly to the United States for aid and suggested a 'strong central government around which all sane elements would group themselves against Bolsheviks and Germans.'[100]

As he considered this development, the Secretary learned that the allied ambassadors in Paris had agreed on the necessity and wisdom of intervention. They argued that it 'must take place with or without the consent of the Bolshevik government,' which in itself 'has become far less important.'[101] Next, on May 30, Reinsch added his 'urgent appeal' to act on the 'extreme need for Allied action in Siberia.' Russia, he explained, 'is craving for order and will follow those who establish it. Only if established through Allied assistance will order be compatible with development of democracy.'[102]

All this was enough to prompt Lansing to warn Francis once again of the extreme care required in any *ad hoc* dealings with the Bolsheviks. 'I am confident,' the Secretary hopefully reminded the ambassador, 'you will appreciate the delicacy with which your actions ... must be conducted.' The Bolsheviks must not be allowed to receive or create any impression of American collaboration or assistance that would 'alienate the sympathy and confidence of those liberal elements of Russian opinion which do not support Bolsheviki.'[103] As these instructions suggest, policy-makers in Washington were moving ever more rapidly towards overt intervention in support of their established anti-Bolshevism, and they wanted to rally all possible Russian support for the action.

On the next day, June 2, Lansing learned that a unit of Czecho-Slovak troops in Siberia had engaged the Bolsheviks. These men had fought with the Russians after deserting from the Austrian Army, but the Treaty of Brest-Litovsk left them without a war, and arrangements had been made by the French and the embryonic Czech government-in-exile, in negotiations with Lenin and Trotsky, for them to proceed via Siberia to the Western Front. Given the tensions in Russia, it would have taken a combination of great patience, extraordinary discipline, excellent communications, and unusual luck for such a contingent to avoid some clashes with the Bolshevik regional authorities. The odds against a peaceful remove to Vladivostok were simply too great, and a series of bitter outbreaks occurred along the Trans-Siberian Railway.

Lansing's first response in this situation was to assure Ambassador Page of the administration's sympathy and concern with the anti-Bolshevik League for the Regeneration of Russia. 'Deeply interested in program for regeneration of Russia,' he replied, 'with which this Government, in the main, agrees.' Then he alerted Francis to the increasing possibility of intervention through the subtle device of telling the ambassador that the Department was 'considering carefully' his own proposal of May 2 for such action.[104] Assistant Secretary Long shortly thereafter reviewed for Lansing the advantages offered by intervention in liaison with the Czechs. They were 'antagonistic to the Bolsheviks,' and 'available to be used as a military expedition to overcome Bolshevik influence, and under Allied guidance to restore order.'[105] As indicated by these and other dispatches of the period, American policy-makers straightforwardly discussed intervention as an anti-Bolshevik operation.

As the momentum for intervention increased among government policy-makers, Lansing became somewhat worried by a growing public discussion of the issue. The Secretary was afraid that the agitation would force the government to move before it was ready. Referring to the criticism of the government for the breakdown and failure of the aircraft construction programme, Lansing warned against losing control of the intervention issue in a similar manner. 'I see signs,' he wrote to Wilson on June 13, 'in Congress and outside of a similar situation arising in connection with Russia.' The Secretary's idea was to have Herbert Hoover take charge of an economic commission that would in turn provide an excellent public image of intervention. 'Armed intervention to protect the humanitarian work done by the Commission,' Lansing noted, 'would be much preferable to armed intervention before this work had begun.'[106]

Wilson probably appreciated the political finesse inherent in Lansing's suggestion, but the President was strongly inclined to proceed first with armed intervention in support of the Czechs and other anti-Bolshevik forces. In that frame of mind, he responded favourably to Reinsch's analysis of June 13. Reinsch was very high on the Slavs: with 'only slight countenance and support they could control all of Siberia against the Germans.' The minister's reference to Germans did not mean that he had changed his mind about the nature of the Bolsheviks or about the danger of a German conquest of Siberia. He knew from Drysdale that the Czechs were anti-Bolshevik, and agreed with his subordinate that it was crucial to keep the Bolsheviks from mounting an effective counterattack.

The reference to Germany concerned his fear that an increasing number of prisoners-of-war might side with the Bolsheviks in view of the Czech attacks. He did not anticipate a German offensive in Siberia.[107] Neither Wilson nor Lansing misread Reinsch's dispatch to mean that the nature of the danger had become German instead of Bolshevik. The President saw the Czechs as a strong, effective force which he could support against the Bolsheviks, and one which was also anti-Japanese and anti-German. That was precisely the kind of a nucleus he had been looking for since at least as early as the middle of April.

Wilson's central line of thought, and its anti-Bolshevik nature, was clearly revealed in his reaction to a favourable review and estimate of the All-Russian Union of Co-operative Societies. The leader of that organisation, after expressing his opposition to the Bolsheviks, asked the United States to take the lead in intervention.[108] The President's comment of June 19 on the report indicates not only his anti-Bolshevik objectives, but suggests very strongly that he had made his personal decision to intervene. The co-ops, he remarked, should be considered 'instruments for what we are now planning to do in Siberia.'[109]

This interpretation is reinforced by another move Wilson made on the same day. He asked Secretary of War Baker to prepare a campaign plan for Siberia, using as a starting point a memorandum which proposed to undertake intervention by gathering and organising support from the bourgeoisie in Siberia and the rest of Russia.[110] The army's reply was drafted by Chief of Staff General Peyton C. March. The war, he argued, would 'be won or lost on the western front.' Siberian intervention, 'considered purely as a military proposition,' was 'neither practical nor practicable—a serious military mistake.'[111]

Wilson overruled this argument during a White House conference on July 6, 1918. He did so in full knowledge of the German assault on the Western Front. He also knew that the Czechs had overthrown the Bolsheviks in Vladivostok, and that they offered a general base of operations against the Bolsheviks throughout Siberia. Lansing had the same information. He noted on June 23 that the Czechs were 'fighting the Red Guards along the Siberian line,' and added on July 2 that they were fighting 'to eject the local Soviets.' As he commented in a private memo in July, the Secretary did 'not think that we should consider the attitude of the Bolshevik Siberians.'[112]

The White House conference made it clear that intervention was *not* designed to establish an Eastern Front against the Germans. That was 'physically impossible.' Furthermore, the discussion of the basic 'proposition and program' made no reference to aiding the Czechs against either the German or the Austrian prisoners-of-war. That phrasing appeared only as part of the 'public announcement' to be made in conjunction with Japan, and in the section of the memorandum enumerating the conditions which Japan would have to meet.[113]

Neither was there any mention of German or Austrian prisoners-of-war, or of Bolsheviks as German agents, in Wilson's aide-memoire of July 17, 1918. Though the document has often been described as rambling, fuzzy, and even contradictory, the truth of the matter is that Wilson was both lucid and candid. He discounted intervention as a manoeuvre to restore the Eastern Front, 'even supposing it to be efficacious in its immediate avowed object of delivering an attack upon Germany,' as 'merely a method of making use of Russia.' That would not help the Russians escape 'from their present distress.' The Bolsheviks were responsible for that distress.

As far as Wilson was concerned, the purpose of intervention was 'only to help the Czecho-Slovaks consolidate their forces and get into successful cooperation with their Slavic kinsmen and to steady any efforts at self-government or self-defense in which the Russians themselves may be willing to accept assistance.'[114] The full significance of the word *only,* and of the phrase *Slavic kinsmen,* should not be missed. The *only* was a throwaway word for the simple reason that the Czechs supplied all that was necessary from the American point of view. For that reason, the *only* was directed at Tokyo and designed to specify American opposition to Japanese aggrandisement. In a similar vein, the phrase *Slavic kinsmen* was designed to reassure the Russians that the Japanese would be kept under control.

Since Wilson and other top American leaders knew the Bolsheviks to be radical social revolutionaries, and had repeatedly stated their opposition to them on that ground, the meaning of Wilson's aide-memoire should be clear. American intervention in Russia was a long-debated and long-delayed tactical move in support of the basic anti-Bolshevik strategy that had been established in December 1917. 'I don't think you need fear of any consequences of our dealings with the Bolsheviki,' he wrote to Senator James Hamilton Lewis on July 24, 1918, 'because we do not intend to deal with them.'[115]

Lansing added his explicit documentation a bit later. Absolutism and Bolshevism were the 'two great evils at work in the world today,' and the Secretary believed Bolshevism 'the greater evil since it is destructive of law and order.'[116] It was, indeed, the 'most hideous and monstrous thing that the human mind has ever conceived.' That estimate led Lansing in 1918 to recommend a course of action that was to plague western statesmen for at least two generations. 'We must not go too far,' he warned, 'in making Germany and Austria impotent.'[117]

*   *   *

VI
PRESIDENT WILSON'S LAST AGONY

President Wilson continued to aid anti-Bolshevik forces in Russia well into 1919. For that matter, the last American troops did not leave Siberia until April 1, 1920. During those years and months, Wilson avowed his concern not only with the radicals in Russia, but also with 'the dangers of Bolshevism' in the United States. 'It will be necessary to be very watchful and united in the presence of such danger,' he warned on the morrow of Armistice Day, 1918.

As for the difficulties which prevented intervention from attaining its objectives, both the President and Secretary Lansing left terse but sufficient comment. Wilson's explanation to Winston Churchill during a discussion of the issue at the Paris Peace Conference contained all the essentials. 'Conscripts could not be sent and volunteers probably could not be obtained. He himself felt guilty in that the United States had in Russia insufficient forces, but it was not possible to increase them. It was certainly a cruel dilemma.' Lansing made the same point to George Kennan in a 'personal and Secret' letter. 'I wish you to know that it was not lack of sympathy which prevented the employment of a large active force in Siberia. . . . We were bound hand and foot by the circumstances.'[118]

American intervention in Russia does not present the historian with an insuperable problem or an impenetrable mystery. It did not involve any dark conspiracy among American leaders. The record makes it clear that the action was undertaken to provide direct and indirect aid to the anti-Bolshevik forces in Russia. It was thus anti-Bolshevik in origins and purpose. The men who made the decision viewed the Bolsheviks as dangerous radical social revolutionaries who threatened American interests and the existing social order throughout the world. They did not consider them to be German agents, nor did they interpret the Bolshevik Revolution as a coup engineered by the imperial German government.

Despite their concern to defeat Germany and to check Japan in the far east, American leaders repeatedly refused to explore the possibility of attaining those objectives through collaboration with the Bolsheviks. *This was not a hypothetical alternative.* In spite of their theoretical doctrine, and the suspicion and hesitance it created in their minds, the Bolshevik leaders made persistent efforts to establish such cooperation. This flexibility created one of those turning points in history at which no one turned. The primary reason this opportunity was never exploited was because American leaders proved in action to be more doctrinaire and ideologically absolutist than the

Bolsheviks. What might have been can never be known, but it is clear the American leaders proved less concerned with those possibilities than with the preservation of the *status quo*. As had so often been the case in the past, the United States defined Utopia as a linear projection of the present.

The only central question that remains unanswered about intervention concerns Wilson's personal authorisation for the official publication of the infamous Sisson Documents, which purported to prove that the Bolsheviks were German agents. Neither the British government nor the American State Department accepted the documents as proof of that allegation. Both therefore refused to publish the material. The President bears sole responsibility.

This becomes even more impressive when it is realised that *Edgar Sisson himself discounted the documents as proof that the Bolsheviks were German agents*. He said this explicitly on February 19, 1918, in a cable to George Creel, his superior in the Committee on Public Information. 'These are wild internationalists,' Sisson explained, 'who not only in the beginning but until lately were willing to have German support for their own ends of Revolution. Germany thought she could direct the storm but the storm had no such intention.'[119]

One can only wonder, since no documentary evidence has ever been found, if Wilson knew of and read this dispatch which was transmitted through the State Department. It would certainly help to know; for, early in March, the President privately and personally ordered Sisson to proceed straight to Washington without any further discussion of the documents he had purchased in Russia. We do know that Lansing refused to accept and publish the material under the seal of the Department of State, and that Sisson was an angry man when he left his confrontation with the Secretary at the end of the first week in May. And we know that Lansing later called Sisson 'a dangerous person' in a warning about dealing with him in connection with official business.[120]

Finally, of course, we know that Sisson prevailed upon Wilson to publish the forgeries. He did so behind Lansing's back, and despite the Secretary's explicit opposition. It is possible but unlikely, that Sisson simply persuaded the President that the documents were genuine. Wilson's own estimate of, and attitude towards, the Bolsheviks belies such an explanation. And while it is conceivable, it is highly improbable, that the decision hinged upon some personal matter between Wilson and Sisson.

Thus the evidence points towards the conclusion that Wilson underwrote the publication of the documents as a way of rationalising his decision to intervene against the Bolsheviks despite his commitment to the principle of self-determination. The President had been intensely aware of that dilemma from the outset of the crisis, and it had caused him great torment and anguish. But he had ultimately intervened. Yet, knowing Wilson, it seems extremely unlikely that the overt act resolved the personal and ideological agony. And so, perhaps as a last effort to ease that terrible pressure, the President acquiesced in Sisson's insistent pleas. If such was the case, then it was an appropriate curtain for the tragedy of intervention.

VII
THE CONSEQUENCES IN THOUGHT AND ACTION

American intervention in the Bolshevik Revolution initiated the cold war. Wilson and Lenin personified a fundamental confrontation between the established free market-free men conception of the world and the most far-reaching critique and challenging alternative that it had ever encountered. The Bolsheviks were in reality calling for an end to economic man and his replacement by the whole human being. Marx viewed economic organisation as a means whereby men could free themselves to realise their potential and not, as in the philosophy of classical liberalism, as the basis for defining and fulfilling their manhood. In an ironic way, American leaders took Leon Trotsky's most famous proposals for effecting that change and used them as guidelines for developing their negative response. They embarked upon a strategy of permanent counter-revolution and adopted the tactics of neither peace nor war.

This fundamentally negative response to the Bolshevik Revolution had many consequences, intellectual and psychological as well as economic and political, for the Soviet Union, the United States, and the rest of the world. Intervention seriously damaged the Russian economy *beyond the extent it would have suffered from the revolution per se*. It intensified, enlarged, and extended the civil war, and thereby increased the material and human costs of the revolution. And the subsequent and sustained American antagonism significantly added to the difficulties and the costs of rehabilitation and further development. The famine relief programme, and the modest trade revival of the 1920s, no doubt helped the Russians; but they needed the help so desperately because of the way intervention had deepened their troubles, and those actions did not in any sense compensate for the earlier costs.

Intervention also had a vital and sustained effect on the attitudes and feelings of the vast majority of an entire generation of Soviet leaders. The experience served in the first place to verify their broad, theoretical analysis of capitalist behaviour. A crucial part of this involved their conclusion, apparent throughout the interwar years and particularly during the late 1930s, that Americans who criticised the policy of the United States and tried to change it constituted a minority that could not be counted upon to succeed. This attitude was very probably more consequential than the more general reinforcement of their distrust of the capitalist establishment, for it led the majority of Soviet leaders to rely almost exclusively upon their own efforts, and to discount the argument of a minority of their colleagues that changes could be generated in western behaviour through collaboration and agreements to protect (and develop) their mutual interests.

Finally, and as suggested by these two effects, intervention confronted Soviet leaders with the ultimate choice of abandoning their revolution or of seeing it through on the basis of their own resources. It has often been argued during the cold war that the course of Soviet development was predetermined by Lenin's ideas; if not, indeed, by the logic of Marx's own thought. This kind of extreme determinism provides a convenient basis for anti-Soviet propaganda, and for justifying various western policies; but it is also dangerous, for it leads either to a fatalistic acceptance of nuclear war or to an equally dismal acquiescence in perpetual tension and strife. Less centrally, but nevertheless significantly, it also places those who use it in the peculiar—and at times ludicrous—posture of men who use the premises and logic of determinism to justify the inability of ostensibly free men to act in accordance with the logic of free will.

The argument is also wrong. The Soviets have not been (and are not today) unique specimens who function as robots programmed by men long since dead. They are men who have sought to attain their inherently very difficult and demanding objectives in an environment made vastly more formidable and hostile as the result of intervention and the related, sustained antagonism. It is possible to argue that mere mortals *cannot* realise *any* utopia, including the Marxian vision, and that *any* effort to do so will ultimately produce some form of despotism before the people decide to settle for considerably less. But it is neither logically nor morally possible to make that argument exclusively in connection with Marx, Lenin and their successors.

Adam Smith and John Locke (and even Lord Keynes) also promised grand results, and the United States has fallen far short of fulfilling their visions despite its particularly favourable circumstances. Yet the people who assert that the Russian failure is inherent in the ideas of the Soviet leaders are usually quick to explain and excuse American failures by reference to special difficulties. Very often they point to *outside* factors as the cause of all the trouble. If the argument is valid *in any degree* for the United States, then it is relevant *in an extensive degree* for the Soviet Union. The point can be grasped, perhaps, by considering the results of intervention by the British, the French, and central European nations in the United States during the Civil War and the era of Reconstruction; and then stopping to realise that there was no such development that can be used to explain the large gap between the rhetoric of the North and the performance of the North. To say that failure was inherent in the ideas of the abolitionists and other opponents of slavery is the equivalent of saying that failure was inherent in the ideas of the leaders of the Bolshevik Revolution—yet no American critic of the Soviets has been heard making that argument about his own country.

The decision to build socialism in one country, which evolved very directly out of the experience and the consequences of intervention, was very costly and very painful for the Russian people. But it was not the course that Soviet leaders preferred, and they followed it only because they had no alternative except abdication. The inability to step down when confronted with circumstances that promise grave difficulties in honouring one's ideas, however, is hardly peculiar to Soviet leaders. If western nations had acted on that basis, they would have promptly retreated from their expansion into the rest of the world long before the issue of intervention in Russia ever arose. The west can hardly complain, therefore, that Soviet leaders refused to hand over their *own* country in the face of a choice defined for them by outsiders. And it is extremely disingenuous, if not simply self-righteous and moralistic, for the west to evade its share of re-sponsibility for the painful consequences of intervention in Russia by recourse to a false syllogism that it declines to apply to itself.

In a typically ironic consequence of such action, however, the results of intervention were at least as serious and far-reaching for the United States (and the rest of the west) as for the Soviet Union. The direct and indirect costs have been considerably greater than it might appear. In order to mount and sustain intervention, material resources and manpower were taken from actual or potential invest-ments that would have been far more rewarding and creative. The goods and brains could have produced far more positive consequences in Cuba or Mexico, in defeated Germany or devastated France, or even in Russia and the United States (in the rehabilitation, say, of the two railroad systems).

These economic costs became even greater in subsequent years as the consequences of intervention began to pyramid. The significance of the trade and investment possibilities that were lost between the wars can be recognised, if not fully computed, by considering the benefits that were gained by the few Americans who circumvented or defied the official restrictions and limitations. Or even more effectively, perhaps, from the trade that developed between Germany and the Soviet Union. By the end of the Great Depression, moreover, the political consequences of intervention (and the outlook that had produced it) began to increase these economic costs in dramatic fashion.

For, even if it is argued that the war with the Axis would have come despite better relationships with Russia, the actual isolation and antagonising of the Soviets fantastically compounded the costs of that conflict in men and resources. The relationship between intervention and the attack on Pearl Harbor, for the Japanese as well as the Russians, for example, is only the most dramatic illustration of the way that the American attitudes and actions of 1917–20 affected later events. For Japan could only afford to launch a war with the United States because the risks had been significantly decreased by the lack of a meaningful relationship between America and the Soviet Union. And the war with Japan, fought without such ties, led directly to a further deterioration of relations and the subsequent nuclear arms race that extended the earlier misallocation and waste of resources for another generation.

The various and increasing economic costs, and particularly those after 1920, were intimately related to the intensification and consolidation of the outlook and attitudes that produced intervention, and which the practice and experience of intervention hardened into an intellectual dogma and an emotional bloc. The key to understanding this crucial process lies in realising that the foreign policy of the United States in the 20th century evolved during the last quarter of the 19th century, and was largely established and even codified by 1900. President Wilson had participated in the latter part of that dialogue and fully shared the premises that guided it and accepted the formulation that it produced.

The major statement of this policy, in the Open Door Notes of 1899–1900, was cast in industrial terms, and was composed and promulgated by leaders who represented (and symbolised) the triumph of industrial over commercial power in the American metropolis, as well as industry's victory over the agricultural sector of the political economy. Those leaders were primarily concerned with free access to foreign markets for manufactured goods and equal opportunity to exploit investment opportunities, and with similar conditions for obtaining industrial raw materials.

But the basic statement of the principles of the policy and its fundamental development, had been the work of the surplus-producing commercial agrarians that composed the majority of the population between 1861 and 1898. They had even provided, during the late 1870s and early 1880s, the first and primary formulation of the frontier thesis which asserted the need of expansion in order to sustain prosperity and freedom at home; an idea that metropolitan intellectuals and businessmen later adopted, refined, and then promulgated with great energy. In the broader sense, moreover, the industrial leaders learned the logic and the argument of overseas economic expansion from the example and the agitation of the agriculturalists, and hence the policy can be fully understood only through an examination of their original formulation.

The post-Civil War agrarians were not subsistence farmers. They were surplus-producing commercial farmers who thought and lived within the framework of the market-place. At a very early date, moreover, they became deeply involved in overseas markets. Exports pulled them out of the depression caused by the onset of the Civil War and out of the major depression of the 1870s, provided them with five years of extraordinary prosperity between 1878 and 1883, and largely determined the extent and duration of their periodic well-being after that time. As a result, they agitated vigorously and constantly for an expansion of their overseas markets and for a strong, nationalistic foreign policy.

Through cultural inheritance and the application of their own intellects, moreover, these men knew and accepted the philosophy of classical liberalism as stated by Adam Smith and John Locke. They understood the logic that called for an expanding market-place to sustain prosperity along with political and social freedom, and were committed to the equation that linked the free market with free men in a reciprocal and causal relationship. This outlook made them anti-colonial expansionists. They wanted markets, but they thought it both dangerous and immoral to invade and overpower, and then establish direct rule over, other societies. They were responsible for preventing the annexation of Cuba, and they very nearly scored a similar victory in the struggle over what to do with the Philippines. In the course of that defeat, however, they forced the annexationists so thoroughly on the defensive that the strategy of American expansion was formulated in the basic terms of the free market-free men philosophy that they had militantly advocated between 1860 and 1899.

The victory over the annexationists had the unfortunate result, however, of reinforcing the strong propensity inherent in the philosophy to equate non-colonial expansion with non-imperial expansion, and to infuse its advocates with the happy confidence that they were expanding without harmful consequences for anybody. This was unfortunately not true. The vast economic power of the United States imposed structural limits as well as operational controls on the societies that it penetrated, even though native leaders continued in many instances to hold formal power and authority. In equating non-colonial expansion with non-imperial expansion, therefore, Americans overlooked or discounted the very real imperialism they were practising.

From the outset of the 20th century, and to a significant degree under Wilson's leadership between 1912 and 1918, Americans came to believe that their expansion carried nothing but freedom and economic improvement to other peoples. To some extent, of course, those improvements were exported along with the controls. Cuba, for example, did benefit from the change in overlords. And similar limited gains resulted from American expansion into other countries. But the combination of American rhetoric about freedom and the progress generated by American economic power served to intensify the desire and the determination of such peoples to act upon the free market-free men philosophy for themselves.

The Bolshevik Revolution manifested and symbolised this desire and determination at the broadest level, and in addition challenged the central premise which asserted that the operation of the free market would produce free men. *In failing to meet that challenge by honouring the principle of self-determination in dealing with the Bolshevik Revolution, Wilson and other Americans began the corrupting and dangerous practice of equating freedom with similarity to the United States.* This meant that the policy of the Open Door became more and more restrictive and confining—for the United States as well as for other nations. It progressively closed the door to thinking about, as well as acting upon, creative alternatives to intervention designed to preserve the American definition of freedom.

People who did not use their freedom to accept and act on the free market-free men philosophy became increasingly defined and dealt with as *objects—things*—to be manipulated, and if necessary physically removed, in order that the true way could prevail. And, in the minds of Americans, every disruption of the *status quo* became a threat that they could not afford to ignore. Intervention thus became a way of life. By the end of World War II, when the Bolsheviks renewed their challenge at a time when many societies had become determined to exercise the right of self-determination in ways that were different from The American Way, the United States had carried this process of reducing people into things so far that it used nuclear weapons on the grounds that such action was the most humane way of defending and extending freedom.

Small wonder, then, that the United States found it necessary to mount an intervention every time a society tried—or even seemed to be trying—to use its freedom and its right of self-determination in ways that challenged the free market-free men dogma. Kennedy in

Cuba and Johnson in Vietnam were merely later manifestations of the process that Wilson had initiated in 1917. It is true that dogmas can be unfrozen, and that high priests can rediscover and act on their principles. But it seems more likely that less war and more welfare can be attained more easily and at less cost by quietly abandoning the philosophy of the free market-place in favour of a commitment to a cooperative human community.

REFERENCES

1. Wilson to Lansing, February 7, 1917: *National Archives of the United States of America,* Record Group 59, Decimal File No. 763.72/3261½. Hereafter cited by file number, save in instances involving another record group.
2. Lansing to Wilson, March 1, 1915: 793.94/240.
3. Lansing to Wilson, February 7, 1917; Wilson to Lansing, February 9, 1917: all documents filed as 763.72/3261½.
4. These and many of the following quotations come from copies of the President's speeches and articles filed on the *Wilson Mss.* Hereafter they will be cited by date only. These specific remarks come from addresses on May 23, January 3, and August 7, 1912.
5. Wilson, speech of May 23, 1912.
6. Wilson, speeches of September 4 and 9, 1912; also see his remarks of March 4, 1913.
7. Here see Wilson, 'The Reconstruction of the Southern States,' originally published in January 1901 and reprinted in *The Public Papers of Woodrow Wilson,* ed. R. S. Baker and W. Dodd (New York, 6 vols, 1925–7), I, pp. 389, 393–5 and Wilson, *A History of the American People* (New York, 5 vols, 1902), V, pp. 265, 274–5, 292 and 294–6.
8. Wilson, remarks of December 14, 1914: *Papers Relating to Foreign Relations of the United States, 1914,* Washington, 1924, p. 14. These volumes are hereafter cited as *FR.*
9. Wilson, as quoted by A. S. Link, *Wilson the Diplomatist,* Baltimore, 1957, p. 15.
10. Wilson, public statement of March 11, 1913: *Wilson Mss.*
11. Wilson to W. B. Hale, November 16, 1913: *Wilson Mss.*
12. Wilson, remarks as printed in an interview with S. G. Blythe published as 'Mexico: The Record of a Conversation with President Wilson,' *Saturday Evening Post,* Vol. CLXXXVI, May 23, 1914, p. 4.
13. Wilson to Tyrrell, November 22, 1913: *Wilson Mss.*
14. Wilson, Circular Statement to American Representatives Abroad, March 18, 1913: 893.51/1356a; and also see the remarks by Bryan, after-dinner speech of January 26, 1914, before the American Asiatic Association, reported in the *Journal of the American Asiatic Association,* Vol. XIV, February, 1914, p. 12.
15. Here see, in sequence: Wilson's memorandum to Japan, March 12/13, 1915: *FR 1915,* 104–111; Wilson to Bryan, February 25, 1915: 793.94/240; and Wilson to Bryan, April 14, 1915: 793.94/294½.
16. On these points first consult H. S. Notter, *The Origins of the Foreign Policy of Woodrow Wilson,* Baltimore, 1937, pp. 542–3, 81–2, 278; then Wilson's speeches of September, 1908, and October, 1909, *Public Papers,* II, pp. 54–5, 140–1; and finally his speeches of September 8, 1908, and May 23, 1912, in *Wilson Mss.*

17. Lansing, 'Private Confidential Memorandum on the Russian Situation and the Root Mission, August 9, 1917': *Lansing Mss.*

18. 'Memorandum on Strategy of the Present War. Prepared at the Army War College, October 17, 1917 ... Appendix II: Possible Line of Action Through Russia': *Lansing Mss.*

19. Lansing to Baker, November 7, 1917: *Lansing Mss.*

20. *New York Times*, November 10, 1917.

21. *Ibid.*, November 17, 1917.

22. *Ibid.*, November 12, 1917.

23. D. R. Francis, *Russia From the American Embassy, April, 1916 – November, 1918*, New York, 1921, pp. 173-7.

24. Summers to Lansing, November 26, 1917: 816.00/736.

25. *War Memoirs of David Lloyd George* (London, 6 vols, 1936), V, p. 2565.

26. House to Wilson, November 28, 1917: *Wilson Mss.*

27. Lansing to Francis, December 1, 1917: 861.00/1008a.

28. *War Memoirs of Robert Lansing*, New York, 1935, pp. 331, 339-43. See also the relevant material in the *Lansing* and *Wilson Mss.*

29. *War Memoirs of Lansing*, p. 345; R. S. Baker, *Woodrow Wilson. Life and Letters* (Garden City, 8 vols, 1937-8), II, p. 391.

30. Lansing to Francis, December 6, 1917: 861.00/796a.

31. Wilson, War Message of December 4, 1917: *Wilson Mss.*

32. *The New Democracy: Presidential Messages, Addresses, and Other Papers (1913-1917) by Woodrow Wilson*, ed. R. S. Baker and W. Dodd, New York, 1926, II, p. 3.

33. Colcord to Wilson, December 6, 1917; and Wilson to Colcord, December 6, 1917: *Wilson Mss.*

34. Moser to Reinsch, November 17, 1917: 861.00/963.

35. Reinsch to Lansing, December 6, 1917; and Lansing to Reinsch, December 8, 1917, both filed as 861.00/769.

36. Reinsch to Lansing, December 15, 1917: 861.00/822; and on later developments see J. A. White, *The Siberian Intervention*, Princeton, 1950.

37. Lansing, 'Memorandum on the Russian Situation, December 7, 1917': *Lansing Mss.*

38. Summers to Lansing, December 6, 1917: 763.72/8033.

39. Lansing to Wilson, December 10, 1917 (enclosing Summers' dispatch of December 6): 861.00/807a.

40. Lansing, Desk Diary entry of December 12, 1917: *Lansing Mss.*

41. Lansing, *ibid.;* and McAdoo to Lansing, December 12, 1917: 861.00/804d.

42. Lansing to Wilson, December 12, 1917, enclosing Lansing to Poole (sent December 13, 1917 as 763.72/820a); and Wilson to Lansing, December 12, 1917: both filed as 861.00/804d.

43. Lansing to Crosby, Confidential, December 12, 1917: 861.00/804d.

44. G. F. Kennan, *Russia Leaves the War*, Princeton, 1956, p. 178.

45. Lansing to Crosby, Confidential, December 12, 1917: 861.00/804d.

46. Judson to War College Staff, December 17, 1917: Record Group 120, File No. 10220-D-58; and see Lansing's Desk Diary entries for this period.

47. Francis to Lansing, December 24, 1917: 861.00/864.

48. Lansing, Desk Diary entry of December 26, 1917: *Lansing Mss.*

49. Lansing, 'Memorandum of an Interview with Japanese Ambassador Sato, December 27, 1917': 861.00/877½.

50. Summers to Lansing, December 29, 1917: 861.00/894; and Caldwell

to Lansing, January 1, 1918 (sent on to Wilson): *Wilson Mss.*

51. Francis to Lansing, December 31, 1917: *Lansing Mss.*

52. Miles, 'Memorandum for the Secretary of State, January 1, 1918': 861.00/935½.

53. Wilson to Lansing, January 1, 1918: 861.00/935¼.

54. Wilson to Lansing, January 20, 1918: *Lansing Mss;* Lansing to Daniels, January 3, 1918; and Lansing to Wilson, January 2, 1918, both in *Wilson Mss.*

55. A letter from William Bullitt, enclosing a 'Memorandum on the Momentary Hostility of the Bolsheviki ... [to the] German Government, January 3, 1918' (763.72119/1269½), which suggested the possibility of some kind of short-run collaboration with the Bolsheviks, created a flurry of activity inside the Department. See Phillips to Lansing, January 4, 1918: 763.72119/1269½. It should be kept in mind, however, that Bullitt reaped the labours of Judson and Robins, whose argument along similar lines had been reaching the Departments of State and War, and the White House, for approximately six weeks. Lansing was correct in worrying about Bullitt in terms of an increasing influence of the other men.

56. Lansing, Desk Diary entry of January 4, 1918: *Lansing Mss.*

57. C. Seymour (ed.), *The Intimate Papers of Colonel House,* New York, 1928, III, p. 331; Walling's article in the *New York Times,* January 14, 1918. Kennan's handling of this matter of the anti-Bolshevik nature of Wilson's 14 Point Speech contains some of the tightest and best analysis he has offered as an historian.

58. Lansing to Jusserand, January 16, 1918: 861.00/945; Polk to Wilson, January 18, 1918: 861.00/977–998; and Polk to Morris, January 20, 1918 (action dispatch: 861.00/945).

59. Gompers to Wilson, February 9, 1918; Wilson to Gompers, January 21, 1918: *Wilson Mss. The Papers of Samuel Gompers,* Manuscript Division, Wisconsin State Historical Society, Madison, Wisconsin, also contain considerable material on the anti-Bolshevik position taken by Gompers.

60. Wilson to Williams, February 6, 1918: *Wilson Mss.*

61. Other indications of Wilson's struggle with the dilemma can be followed in Page to Lansing, January 15, 1918: *Papers of Ray Stannard Baker,* Library of Congress, a dispatch enclosing a suggestion by Grant Smith (in Denmark) that the United States act as a kind of unofficial agent for the allies to initiate exploratory talks with the Bolsheviks. The reaction to this can be found in Lansing to Wilson, and Wilson's reply, both of January 20, 1918: *Baker Mss.*

62. Lansing to Wilson, February 15, 1918: *Wilson Mss.*

63. Francis to Lansing, February 5 (received the 7th), 1918: 861.00/1064. The disturbed remarks by Miles appear on the dispatch and were sent on up the line. Actually, Francis was also being influenced by American Army Officers Keith and Riggs. Both men concluded that the Bolsheviks were in power to stay, and that the United States should help them resist the Germans. Riggs added, quite accurately, in his report of January 28, 1918, that the Bolsheviks were inclined towards such collaboration with the United States. See also Keith, 'Military Report of January 28, 1918': both filed in Record Group 165:F6497–367.

64. Lansing to Francis, February 14, 1918: 861.00/1064.

65. Lansing, 'Memorandum to the British Embassy, February 8, 1918': 861.00/1097; and Lansing to Page, February 13, 1918: 861.00/1066.

66. Lansing to Page, February 13, 1918: 861.00/1066. In this dispatch Lansing himself emphasised the meaning of the word *now* by explaining

that the United States 'has not lost hope of a change for the better to be brought about without foreign intervention.'

67. Trotsky to Murmansk Soviet, March 1 and 2, 1918: quoted in Strakhovsky, *Origins of American Intervention,* p. 29, and in his *American Opinion,* p. 59. Also see Kennan, *Russia Leaves the War,* p. 491.

68. This material on Sadoul is drawn from sources in the National Archives; and, more recently, from conversations with Harvey Goldberg who has had access to manuscript sources in France. Also see the present author's *American-Russian Relations,* New York, 1952, pp. 133–5, 140–1.

69. Miles, 'Dept. of State Confidential Periodical Report on Matters Relating to Russia, No. 9, February 19, 1918': *Lansing Mss.*

70. Lansing's comment is on a copy of the dispatch reporting the French proposal that Phillips sent to Lansing on February 19, 1918: 861.00/1125. Lansing took this document to Wilson for their discussion.

71. Materials as noted in Note 69 above.

72. Francis to Lansing, March 26, 1918: 862.20261/74. See also the dispatches filed by Riggs, some of which are quoted by Strakhovsky, *Origins of American Intervention,* p. 89, and *American Opinion,* p. 55.

73. Wilson, Message of March 10, 1918, to the Congress of Soviets: *Wilson Mss.*

74. Also see, on this point, Lansing to Wilson, February 27, 1918: 861.00/1165½ a and b.

75. Lansing to Wilson, February 27, 1918: *Wilson Mss.*

76. Lansing to Page, February 27, 1918: 861.77/307.

77. Lansing to Wilson, February 27, 1918: 861.00/1165½.

78. Sharp to Lansing, February 28, 1918: 861.00/1173; and an even earlier, direct awareness of these matters documented in Lansing to Wilson, February 27, 1918. Also see Jusserand to Lansing, March 12, 1918: 861.00/1676.

79. Lansing to Wilson, February 27, 1918: *Wilson Mss.*

80. Polk to Lansing, in a letter of March 5, 1918, reviewing the events of February 28 and March 1, 1918: 861.00/1246.

81. Reinsch to Lansing, February 21, 1918: 861.00/1138; Lansing to Page, February 24, 1918: 861.00/1136½; Reinsch to Lansing, February 24, 1918: 861.00/1136½; and Summers to Lansing, February 23, 1918: 861.00/1154.

82. Wilson, draft telegram handed Lansing on March 1, 1918: 861.00/1246.

83. Polk to Lansing, March 5, 1918: 861.00/1246.

84. Polk to Lansing, March 15, 1918: 861.00/1285. This is another review of the events of February 27–March 1, 1918, written for Lansing's information.

85. Wilson, Circular of March 5, 1918: *Wilson Mss.* This was sent to Japan as 861.00/1246 at 4 p.m.

86. Long to Reinsch, March 14, 1918: *Papers of Paul S. Reinsch,* Wisconsin State Historical Society, Madison.

87. Lansing, 'Memorandum of March 18, 1918': *Lansing Mss;* and, particularly, Lansing to Wilson, March 19, 1918: *Wilson Mss.* The latter document carries as enclosures a number of telegrams from Knight and others on the scene in Siberia.

88. Lansing to Wilson, March 24, 1918: 861.00/1433½.

89. Wilson to Lansing, March 22, 1918: *Wilson Mss.* The President repeated his judgment when returning Lansing's letter of March 24. Lansing's notation on the document reads as follows: 'This was returned

to me 3/26/18 by the President who said he quite agreed but did not think the situation yet warranted change of policy.' These notations added to various documents by the protagonists seem generally to have been ignored by most students of intervention.

90. Masaryk to Crane, April 10, 1918: *Wilson Mss;* Reinsch to Lansing, April 10, 1918: 861.00/1571; Reinsch to J. V. MacMurray, April 29, 1918: *Reinsch Mss.*

91. 'Report of Colonel Speshneff, March 9, 1918'; W. S. Drysdale to Reinsch, March 19, 1918, April 10, 1918; all in *Reinsch Mss.*

92. For example, see Ruggles to War College Staff, April 7, 1918: 861.00/1730½; and his report on April 8, 1918, on his conference with Trotsky of April 8; RG 179: 1240/23. Then consult Francis to Lansing, February 26, 1918.

93. Francis to Lansing, May 11, 1918: *FR, Russia, 1918,* I, p. 526.

94. Lansing to Sharp, April 23, 1918: 861.00/1674.

95. Lansing to Wilson, May 16, 1918: 861.00/1894½; Wilson to Lansing, May 20, 1918: 861.00/1895½.

96. See *American-Russian Relations,* pp. 147–50, 152–3.

97. First consult, on the question of general economic aid, Lansing to Morris, May 22, 1918: 861.00/1819; a dispatch which suggests that the American plan of intervention involved, from an early date, a decision to act unilaterally once the time for action had arrived. This is further borne out by Lansing's response to the request to transport Belgian and Italian troops. In the end, of course, this was the way American intervention was handled. Then see Wilson to Lansing, May 20, 1918 (enclosing Reinsch's dispatch), and Lansing to Wilson, May 21, 1918 (enclosing Miles, 'The Military Advance of Semenoff, May 21, 1918'): all in *Wilson Mss.*

98. W. Wiseman to Sir R. Drummond, May 31, 1918: *Papers of Sir William Wiseman,* Yale University Library. This is a long, detailed account of an hour-long conversation with the President.

99. Kennan to Lansing, May 26, and Lansing to Kennan, May 28, 1918: *Lansing Mss.*

100. Page to Lansing, May 28, 1918: 861.00/1901.

101. 'Agreement of Allied Ambassadors, May 29, 1918. Confidential': RG 159:800/1918.

102. Reinsch to Lansing, May 30, 1918: 861.00/1900.

103. Lansing to Francis, June 1, 1918: 861.77/402.

104. Lansing to Page, June 4, 1918: 861.00/1901; and Lansing to Francis, June 4, 1918: 861.00/1955.

105. Long to Lansing, June 7, 1918: 861.00/2008.

106. Lansing to Wilson, June 13, 1918: 861.48/614 3/4a.

107. Reinsch to Lansing, June 13, 1918: 861.00/2014; Major D. P. Barrows, 'Memorandum of April 7, 1918,' and especially Drysdale to Reinsch, June 25, 1918: all in *Reinsch Mss.* Also see Moser to Lansing, June 10, 1918: 861.00/1996; Caldwell to Lansing, June 12, 1918: 861.00/2040; same to same, June 14, 1918: 861.00/2021; and Lansing to Morris, July 2, 1918: 861.00/2169.

108. Wilson to Lansing, June 17, 1918: 861.00/2145½; Poole to Lansing, June 12, 1918: 861.00/2053, sent on to Wilson by Lansing, June 19, 1918: 861.00/2053.

109. Wilson to Lansing, June 19, 1918: 861.00/2148½.

110. Wilson to Baker, June 19, 1918 (enclosing a memorandum dated June 17, 1918): *Wilson Mss.*

111. March, 'Memorandum' to Baker, June 24, 1918: *Wilson Mss.*

112. Lansing to Wilson, June 23, 1918: *Wilson Mss;* Lansing to Morris, July 2, 1918: 861.00/2168; and Lansing, 'Memorandum on the Siberian Situation, July 4, 1918': *Lansing Mss.*

113. Lansing, 'Memorandum of a Conference at the White House in Reference to the Siberian Situation, July 6, 1918': *Lansing Mss.* Also see Abbott to Wilson, July 10, 1918: *Wilson Mss.*

114. Wilson, Aide-Memoire of July 17, 1918: *Wilson Mss.*

115. Wilson to Lewis, July 24, 1918: *Wilson Mss.*

116. Lansing to Root, October 28, 1918: *Lansing Mss.*

117. Lansing, 'Memorandum on Absolutism and Bolshevism, October 26, 1918': *Lansing Mss.*

118. Lansing to Kennan, 'Personal and Secret,' February 2, 1920: *Papers of George Kennan,* Library of Congress; Wilson, remarks to the meeting of the Big Five on February 14, 1919: *FR, Paris Peace Conference, 1919,* Washington, 1943, III, pp. 1042–4.

119. Sisson to Creel (drafted by Sisson), sent from Russia as Francis to Lansing, February 19, 1918: 1918 Correspondence, Confidential, Dispatch No. 2388.

120. Lansing, remarks of February 27, 1919: *FR, Paris Peace Conference, 1919,* XI, p. 80.

The World War and the Cold War

JOHN BAGGULEY

ANY assessment of the events and conflicts which followed the armistice of 1945 will depend in the last analysis on an appreciation of the conduct of the war which preceded it.

One such appreciation has long been with us. It reflects with dismay upon the 1930s, regrets the passage of a shameful deal at Munich, and has not forgotten the tragedy of the French defeat. It notes the plight of Britain in September 1940, isolated, withdrawn, and threatened from the air, and recalls with pride the conduct of the few. Its recollections thereafter take on a beleaguered air: the attack on Russia, the onslaught at Pearl Harbor, and the expansion of the Axis empires until nearly all of Europe and East Asia had been subdued. Only with great difficulty, according to this view, with extensive sacrifice, and the mobilisation of vast resources, were the Germans driven out of Africa, out of Sicily and southern Italy, and the return to France secured. The triumphs of those days are brought to mind: the greatest invasion ever launched from the sea; the defeat of the German armies in the west of France, the drive towards Berlin; concurrently, on the eastern front, the continued withdrawal of the German armies, and, in the Pacific, the dislodgement of the Japanese from their island forts.

It was then that tragedy occurred. The wartime alliance, never firm despite the liberal aid to Russia, dissolved, and the patient, cautious efforts of the allies to build a lasting peace, to destroy the roots of Fascism, to revive the democratic form of government, were set at nought. Partly from a misplaced obsession with security, oblivious, apparently, of what the United Nations might undertake, and partly from motives of a grasping and expansive nature, the Soviet Union refused to withdraw from areas which force of arms had won. That nation feigned, while implementing the very opposite, the maintenance of representative government; imposed, on nations with long traditions of independence and free relations with the west, a most brutal social system; and was prevented, by military and political alliance amongst the threatened nations, from encroaching yet further into Europe.

But if it can be shown that the European war was not a general conflict of the nations, was, rather, a Soviet-German war, with

76

British and American action on the periphery alone; if it can be demonstrated that the notion of spheres of influence and exclusive dealing was as firmly entrenched in Washington and London as it was in Moscow, and turned, indeed, on explicit understandings between the powers, then the Soviet attempt to secure a zone in east and south-east Europe in 1945 would take on a very different aspect. Seen in that light, the drive to remove the Soviet influence from these areas would no longer appear as acts in furtherance of peace and justice, but rather as the at times perilous and short-sighted breach of agreements brought into being by the war. From the standpoint of this alternative, revised, approach, the discord and hostility arising after Yalta were less the signal of a western firmness in the face of Soviet aggression, than an indication of the acrimony naturally occurring when two of those who had agreed to divide the continent of Europe—the United States and Britain—attempted to deprive the third party of its share.

This essay is concerned to present a revised approach to the clash of 1945, to set out the facts and arguments which, jointly apprehended, define the reality of the war; to indicate how the course of military affairs, when combined with natural interests and traditional directions of concern, impinged upon the construction of the peace; to contribute a brief analysis of how the peace was won and lost. It begins with the initial set-backs of the war, with the defeat of Poland and of France.

I

The badly equipped and ill-trained Polish forces could not long withstand the invasion which marked the advent of the war. No one expected them so to do; but there was considerable surprise in military circles, when the French, in turn, proved brittle. The German victory of 1940, taking in the precipitate expulsion of the British from the Lowlands and culminating in the partial occupation of France, was widely attributed to the superiority in number and in firepower of the German armour, to the ruthless machinations of a savage Fuehrer. This verdict has long since given way to more cautious truth: that, at the military level, the Germans, having no particular superiority, save in the air, had yet more skilfully assessed the factors of mobility and economy of force; and that, at the wider, strategic level, the course of their diplomacy, drawing on no fund of goodwill and but small coincidence of view, had shown a greater understanding of statecraft in the east.

The military victory was of the simplest. The German armour, gathered in concentrated form, punched holes in French defences whose not inferior armour was thinly spread[1]; its mobility drove across the allied rear in sweeps which divorced the allied armies and defences from their sources of direction and supply. The bulk of the beleaguered armies, save those units crushed before the Belgian border, had hardly seen engagement, yet their flanks were turned, their life-lines cut. The British, their position soon untenable, fled for the sea.

They regrouped around Dunkirk, while the German panzer forces, reaching a line a short distance to the south and west, held their march, as the result of Hitler's active intervention, for two vital days. The moment of victory passed, the British reembarked.[2] The French, not seeking to prolong the war by last-ditch stands and hurried reassessments, produced not the miracle of the Marne, but a swift and appropriate surrender.

Such victories are not produced in days and weeks. The peculiarities of the blitzkrieg, the use of armour and airpower in coordinated, concentrated form, were based on extended reflection and debate. At a time when the French, for instance, had neglected the development of tanks and self-propelled artillery, and had chosen to spread such forces thinly along their lines, the Germans had gathered theirs in strike, or panzer, divisions, which, breaking through at several points, might join like pincers to trap unwary forces retained in line. Again, while the Royal Air Force saw its role in the long-range bombing of industry and housing, spreading panic and dislocation in the rear, the Luftwaffe was principally designed to give direct support in armoured, mobile war.

Behind the military success, the diplomatic. The departure from the Disarmament Conference, the negotiation of the Anglo-German Naval Agreement, and the unchallenged decision to rearm, prepared the way for the return to military strength, while the political and territorial restraint on German power established at Versailles—the separation of Austria from the Reich, the creation of a string of independent states in eastern Europe—was systematically dissolved. The Nazi-Soviet Pact of August 1939 was the final stroke against the Versailles system. The non-aggression treaty embodied in the Pact presaged the end of Polish independence, free from the interference of the only power at hand, and opened the way, in time, for further expansion towards the east. The promise of peace between the Soviet Union and Germany, however temporary it might prove to be, fulfilled the ambition of all who pursued a forward German foreign policy: to avoid military engagements in both east and west.

Neither signatory to the Nazi-Soviet Pact trusted the intentions of the other; neither, in one sense, had any alternative but to sign. The successful revision of the Versailles Treaty and the restoration of Germany to its principal place in east and central Europe demanded that the enemies of change should not band together but should be picked off one by one. Britain, France, Poland, the Soviet Union and Czechoslovakia, all had stood by while Austria was annexed, the first three had confirmed the destruction of the fifth, and now it was the turn of Poland. The emptiness of the British guarantee to Poland, given in early 1939, was appreciated nowhere more clearly than in Moscow, where policy was trapped between a profound distrust of Britain's inclinations and the desire not to oppose the might of German power alone. It was an unsprung trap. Britain and France could offer nothing concrete in support of eastern Europe, and the defence of Poland would be borne by Soviet power alone. And given the anti-Soviet tendencies of British policy, the encouragement lent to Polish fractiousness, the drawing out of negotiations as though to avoid conclusion, as well as the wider Soviet fear of a European alliance directed against itself, Germany offered the most that might be attained: a treaty of neutrality and the limitation of German gains in Poland and the Baltic.[3] However hostile the ambitions of the Germans, however temporary the truce, the Pact protected the interests of the Soviet Union and allowed the further consolidation of its defences. During the two years of its operation, the Pact permitted the continued construction of the Soviet military apparatus, the further development of industry beyond the Urals, far from the likely scenes of conflict; and gave an opportunity, not oversuccessfuly exploited, to fortify yet farther to the west.

The fall of France brought sudden instability to the European balance. The Soviet attempt to call in France and Britain to redress the power of Germany had clearly failed, and other counters, more sure and certain, were drawn and played. Two weeks before the final French surrender, the Soviet armies deprived Lithuania, Latvia and Estonia of their independence, and in the south, Rumania of its Bessarabian province. These moves were not welcomed in Berlin: Lithuania, the most westerly of the Baltic states, had originally been assigned to Germany's sphere of influence, while Rumania's vital oilfields were now more clearly threatened. Nevertheless, such action could not be unexpected in a troubled Europe, and instant counter-action might have prejudiced the winding-up of operations in the west.

That winding-up took longer than expected. Conditions for the French were easily settled—the occupation of those areas vulnerable to invasion, much help for German economic needs—but the British proved intractable. Despite the elimination of their continental ally, despite the loss of arms and reputation at Dunkirk, no conditional détente, surrender, or even significant negotiations seemed in the offing. The mutual end of city bombing was placed on offer; and was refused. Attempts to start negotiations came to nothing.

Hitler had been placed in a dilemma. Should he, ignoring the unconquered islands to the west, return to the major field of forward policy, and prepare for actions in the east; or should he first reduce the British Isles? His decision was not long in coming. He was un-prepared, politically and militarily, to invade these islands. The dissolution of the British Empire would bring no advantage to the Reich,[4] while the continued independence of Great Britain held no great danger for the German cause. He became convinced that the only British hope of victory, of defeating Germany on the continent, was without foundation.[5] The German navy, too, was quite unready to deliver troops across the Channel.[6] At a series of conferences be-tween July 29 and 31, 1940, Hitler and his principal advisers re-viewed the military situation and decided, for some time to come, the future of the war. On July 31 he announced the definite intention to attack the Soviet Union not later than the following spring; actions from the air might be launched in the interim against Great Britain, and even, in the event of their success, an invasion undertaken:

> The air war will start now and will determine our ultimate relative strength. If the results of the air war are not satisfactory, invasion preparations will be stopped. But if we gain the impression that the English are being crushed and that the air war is, after a certain time, taking effect, then we shall attack.[7]

Hitler's distaste for landings in the British Isles was strengthened, shortly afterwards, when the navy continued to press its opposition; in final form, a landing was envisaged, as Jodl put it, 'if it is a question of finishing off an enemy already defeated in the air war.'[8] But there could be no question of a German army fighting its way up the beaches and across the fields: either action from the air would be successful, or decision would be postponed.

The major problems were now of timing and of preparation. Hitler's disposition inclined to speedy action in the east, but the more careful spirits on his staff counselled delay and caution. They had, initially, advised against the operation, but the certainty with which they pressed their point of view was undermined by their confidence that the Soviet Union might, if necessary, be defeated. In December 1940, the invasion date was set for May 15, 1941, and in accordance with this directive, military and diplomatic concentration on the east increased. Pressure continued in the Balkans to attach the independent states more closely to German, rather than Soviet, lines of policy, and the military build-up gathered pace: western Europe was drained of forces and supplies and the strengthening of the army deprived the Luftwaffe, as was perpetually the case, of that priority in production without which a decision against the RAF could not be achieved.[9]

The decision to invade the Soviet Union was perhaps the most important one that Hitler made. During the months of plans and preparations, other operations were only set in motion insofar as they contributed to the coming battle; and in the years of invasion and defeat, it was to this theatre that the overwhelming portion, measured in manpower and supplies, of the German effort was devoted. It was here that the Wehrmacht was principally engaged and eventually ground to pieces. Between the fall of France and the Normandy invasion, other theatres were at best a small distraction, and, after the landings of 1944, a real threat, perhaps, but still of secondary importance.

Thus, in the months before the start of BARBAROSSA, the invasion of the Soviet Union, the growing concentration in the east did not preclude due consideration for schemes in other theatres, but the degree of organisation and supply required for so large an operation limited what might practically be done. Direct action in southern Europe had been considered, but the inability to satisfy both Spain and Vichy France with each other's North African possessions, and the diffidence of General Franco, held up a German drive southwards through Gibraltar. Planning for that operation was abandoned in December 1940; one of its companions, an attack on the middle east through Palestine or Syria, had been dropped a month before.[10] Operation SEELOEWE, the invasion of the British Isles, had been cancelled in October. Further defeat in Africa seemed imminent, indeed, the British secured a victory in December, but Hitler was not excessively concerned, though recognising that the delivery of some modern matériel might be necessary to prevent the fall of Mussolini.[11]

Operations against Great Britain accorded with this pattern. However bitter the action in the air, whatever implication for Britain's future was held in store, the Battle of Britain formed a secondary sphere of German operations. The Battle took place in the autumn of 1940, when the decision to concentrate on the Soviet Union had already been made; it was an attempt to bring Britain to terms by an easy route, by capturing superiority in the air. A certain lack of success was unfortunate, in German eyes, but could only postpone decision for a year or so. And when the Battle was called off, it was not because the German air force was in complete defeat, though it had clearly suffered some reverse, but because the relevant squadrons were needed for a more important theatre, for the impending Soviet-German war. One historian has concluded, indeed, that 'there can be little doubt that the fact that Hitler was already making plans for the attack on Russia, even before the Luftwaffe began its large-scale operations against Britain, must have affected the prosecution and therefore the outcome of the Battle of Britain, and, of course, the prospects for Operation "Sea Lion".'[12] At sea, of course, the submarine effort against Britain's trade remained, another option which, like the action in the air, might bring victory without invasion.

The problems facing Britain were not of a defensive kind alone. The decision had been taken to reject the German offer of negotiations, to continue the struggle towards some eventual victory, and it was considered politically impossible, in these circumstances, to remain entirely on the defensive. But the desire for victory seemed to outrun the military capability for its achievement. The armies of the Reich in Europe appeared invulnerable, even could a force be landed, and attention was therefore focussed on those other avenues of war, the blockade at sea, strategic bombing from the air, and peripheral, attritive operations on the land.

The control of the sea had two traditional facets: not only might the trade and communications of Great Britain be safeguarded in time of war, and supply and direction of an expeditionary force ensured, but the Royal Navy might also deprive the enemy of his sea connections. With the declaration of war, the coast of Germany was sealed by naval action and there was some optimism that, given the needs of an economy at war, that country might be brought near to collapse. Calculations were made of the shortages induced in its economy, of the lack of oil and rubber and other raw materials—but the widespread substitution of synthetics, the concealed imports through the Soviet Union, and access to the oilfields of Rumania, changed the nature of the situation. Germany seemed less near to ruin than had been hoped. Even so, relentless pressure, if indecisive itself, might facilitate the return to Europe.

In a memorandum of 1940, written in anticipation of the fall of France, the British Chiefs of Staff had given 'air-attack on economic objects in Germany and on German morale'[13] an equal place with the sea blockade as the two principal methods of inflicting pressure. In September of that year Churchill indicated the essentially offensive, and even decisive, role that the first might play:

> The Navy can lose us the war, but only the Air Force can win it. Therefore our supreme effort must be to gain overwhelming mastery in the air. The Fighters are our salvation, but the Bombers alone provide the means of victory. We must therefore develop the power to carry an ever-increasing volume of explosives to Germany, so as to pulverise the entire industry and scientific structure on which the war effort and economic life of the enemy depend, while holding

him at arm's length from our Island. In no other way at present visible can we hope to overcome the immense military power of Germany, and to nullify the further German victories which may be apprehended as the weight of their force is brought to bear upon African or Oriental theatres.[14]

Perhaps the fighters did offer 'salvation' at that time, when the Battle of Britain was being fought, but the continued manufacture of the Spitfire delayed both the opening of the Second Front in Europe, and the development of an effective bombing policy. Production was 'indissolubly welded' to the Spitfire, as one dissident general complained,[15] and the very short range of that aircraft lent weight to Churchill's objections to a second front: it confined the area of planning for an amphibious attack across the Channel to a small and fortified section of the coast. This fact, as much as the absence of landing craft, powerfully assisted Churchill's arguments against invasion in 1942; but in permanently confining production to the short-range type of aircraft, the Prime Minister permitted the continuation of a condition which he was to cite so often as an intractable barrier to an operation which he disliked on other, more murky, grounds. The failure to develop a long-range fighter also hampered Bomber Command: its operations were confined to the nocturnal bombing of the German cities, a policy which, whatever objections may be raised on moral grounds, and however much it suited the prevailing outlook, had little enough effect on the outcome of the war. Time after time, as will be observed, the considerations of policy at the beginning of the war, the desire for quick results and spectacular engagements, were allowed to dominate both priorities of production in the years to come, and the scope of long-term operations; were allowed, in fact, to prejudice the conclusion of the war in favour of a narrow advantage for the present.

While the fighters guarded the shores of Britain, the bombers could carry the war to the heart of Germany. But how might the bombs most witheringly be applied? Some made the suggestion that the destruction of German industry would have the most effect, while others urged an assault upon the dwellings of the German working class. The first real attempt to use Bomber Command in its intended strategic role began in January 1941 against the German oil industry, and was continued in July, August and September in attacks against the railway marshalling yards in the cities—either the railway system would be crippled, or the errant bombs would shatter the surrounding houses.[16] The most optimistic assessments were made of what was being done. In July Churchill said:

We have now intensified for a month past our systematic, scientific, methodical bombing on a large scale of the German cities, seaports, industries, and other military objectives. We believe it to be in our power to keep this process going, on a steadily rising tide, month after month, year after year, until the Nazi regime is either extirpated by us or, better still, torn to pieces by the German people.[17]

The truth was very far away. The shortage of modern bombers, the absence of long-range fighter protection, and the strength of the German air defence system, made any but night-time attacks impossible and an inability to find and bomb scheduled targets under such conditions brought the failure, in practice, of the necessarily precise attacks on industry. The effect on German oil production in 1941, according to the most reliable investigations carried out, was 'scarcely discernible', and attacks on railway yards were hardly more successful, only 15 per cent of the aircraft, on average, coming within five miles of their intended target.[18] No great destruction was wrought in 1942 and 1943. Oil production steadily increased until the spring of 1944, and the output of war munitions grew by leaps and bounds —by more than three hundred per cent between the beginning of 1942 and the summer of 1944.[19] It was not until the latter date that strategic bombing had significant effect, when the speed and capability of the new American bombers, the reduced potential of the Luftwaffe after three years' fighting on the eastern front, and the appearance, at last, of American fighters capable of operations over Germany, changed the balance of advantage. Accurate daytime assaults on German industry and transportation were now possible. Oil production, for instance, dropped precipitously: from 662,000 tons per month in the first four months of 1944, to 422,000 tons in June, 260,000 tons in December, and 80,000 tons in March 1945.[20] Aircraft production, after reaching an all-time peak in July 1944, thereafter rapidly declined.[21]

These successes were not gained in addition to, but instead of, victories on the land; and were obtained at too late a date to affect the outcome of the war. The concentration of Britain's effort on the production of bomber aircraft, and the channelling of manpower into the RAF, meant a proportionate lessening of the resources that might be applied to the training and equipment of an army more pertinent to Germany's defeat. Thus in March 1944, on the eve of the long-delayed invasion across the Channel, the British Secretary of State for War estimated that there were as many workers 'engaged on making heavy bombers as on the whole Army programme'. Even at this late date, the country was still devoting 40 to 50 per cent of its war production to the RAF alone.[22] Yet, as we have seen, this mighty effort, originating early in the war, had had no appreciable effects on German war production; and the great successes after the spring of 1944 came too late to affect the outcome of, and put only the finishing touches on, a war that was already being won upon the land—on the Soviet-German front.

The strategy of the First World War was thus abandoned early in the Second. No longer would a British army fight its way, yard by yard, towards Berlin; the strategic bomber would play the major part in the offensive. Small and well-equipped land forces might still be deployed, however, at sensitive, peripheral points around the Axis territories, and especially in areas vital to Britain's trade and empire. The constant attrition of the German effort as forces were dispersed to meet every conceivable invasion, the aid and encouragement rendered to the disaffected rising in revolt, and the overall destruction of industry and morale that Bomber Command would wreak, might bring the fall of Germany without a costly, central confrontation with the Wehrmacht. In Churchill's phrase, the soft underbelly, rather than the armoured other portions, of the German animal would be engaged.

The Mediterranean abounded in such sensitive points. Churchill had considered at the beginning of the war that a series of swift and striking victories there would have 'a most healthy and helpful bearing upon the main struggle with Germany.'[23] After the fall of France, schemes were examined and prepared for recovering French North Africa from its Vichy rulers, but the other, eastern end of the Mediterranean seemed to offer even more significant successes. The defence of Egypt and the middle east, and the expulsion of the Italians from their Libyan colony, would bring concrete economic and strategic advantage. The oil supplies of the middle east would be safeguarded, Suez, cross-roads between east and west, secured, and the Italian army, never as capable as its German ally, would be destroyed. The pressure on Italy, if pursued, might bring that country's defection from the war, the conquest of Italy, the British Chiefs of Staff informed their American counterparts in August 1940, being a strategic aim of the first importance.[24] Were land operations against the Germans, then, unnecessary to achieve decision? The British Chiefs held that they hoped for a serious weakening in the morale and military efficiency, if not a total collapse, of Germany, before the British army delivered its *coup de grâce*.[25]

The eastern Mediterranean also offered room for setbacks. The German concentration on the Balkans in the winter of 1940–1, the prelude to BARBAROSSA, brought hasty and precipitate response. Churchill had long hoped to recruit the Turks and Yugoslavs to the British cause, but it was with the Greeks that anti-German operations were finally undertaken. The superior German forces, however, drove the British landing force back into the sea. Equipment, planes and ships were lost, and, not unconnected with the diversions to the

Balkan theatre, General Wavell's forces in North Africa suffered some defeat.

The failure of the Greek campaign seemed not to discredit the principles which underlay it. Not long after that defeat, Churchill described for President Roosevelt his own conception of how the war might best be waged. In 1942 and 1943, an augmented programme of strategic bombing should be set in motion, together with intensified blockade and propaganda measures, in the hope that such assault might evoke an opposition, or even a collapse, in Axis countries. But plans should also be made 'for coming to the aid of the conquered populations by landing armies of liberation when opportunity is ripe.'[26] It was the policy of wait and see, of easy choices and leisurely exploitation: Britain's land forces would remain upon the side-lines until that uncertain time when Bomber Command, and such other enemies as Hitler might attract, had cracked the German will to fight, and encouraged subject Europe to rise against its rulers. Then, and only then, numbers of armies, and each one necessarily small, therefore, would land around the edges of the Axis territories, to take advantage of the situation.

The policy of engagements at peripheral, sensitive points, as it worked in practice, in North Africa, Greece and Italy, far from draining the Germans of their resources and will to fight, hardly affected their concentration on the eastern front; and far from providing the possibility of Germany's defeat, took up a large proportion of British, and later United States, resources in areas where success or failure could have little bearing on the final victory or defeat. The early British actions in Libya and Egypt served to make impossible a second front in western Europe; and in encouraging extended efforts in the Mediterranean, Churchill permitted the continuation of a condition which he was so forcefully to cite as a bar to operations in more decisive theatres of the war. At the time of his message to Roosevelt described above—and when the Red Army was suffering grave defeats at German hands—nearly half of British military production was being directed to North Africa.[27] The commitment to that desert, and to plans against possible German drives through Spain, was such that when, at the outbreak of the Soviet-German war, Stalin asked for immediate action in the west, it was soon discovered that such action could not be greater than the damage a few hundred men might do, disembarking from motorboats across the Channel.[28] The events leading up to this request from Stalin will briefly be examined.

Germany's failure to honour the economic obligations of the Nazi-Soviet Pact, its continued penetration of south-east Europe and Finland, and the hasty Soviet occupation of the Baltic states brought a growing deterioration of relations, a deterioration smoothed over in the winter of 1940–1, perhaps, but breaking through the surface once again. The haste with which the Pact was signed had precluded a careful delimitation of respective spheres of influence: a Soviet interest in Rumanian Bessarabia had been indicated, and a German 'disinterestedness' proclaimed,[29] but whether the Soviet claims were limited to Bessarabia, and whether Germany had disavowed an interest in the rest of south-east Europe was not entirely clear. Unmistakable, however, in Soviet eyes, were German transgressions in areas vital to the Soviet Union. The intervention of German diplomacy in a territorial dispute between Hungary and Rumania, the award, without consultation, of tracts of the latter's territory to the former, the subsequent engineering of a pro-German government in Bucarest, and the adhesion of Bulgaria to the Tripartite Pact, brought solemn warnings from the Soviet Union.[30] But the pressure continued. Efforts were made to draw Yugoslavia into the German orbit, and their eventual failure brought on the intervention of the Axis armies. That intervention, brief, bitter, and effective, nevertheless caused a slackening of the German build-up on the Soviet border; delay seemed now inevitable, and the invasion was postponed from May 15 to June 22, 1941.

The direction of the German invasion turned on an appreciation of the capacities of the enemy; its form and timing on the fruits of German military experience. The concentration of Soviet industry and raw materials, their location in areas adjacent to the western border, and the dependence of the modern war economy on their continued preservation, would make the traditional Russian strategy of withdrawal impossible. Since the Soviet government would necessarily seek to defend these areas, an attack in their direction would coincide with that other aim of strategy: to engage and eliminate the main forces of the enemy. Three lines of attack, then, were prepared: in the south, towards the Ukraine and the Donets basin; in the centre, towards the Moscow complex; and in the north, towards the Baltic states and Leningrad, whose fall would not only represent a major loss of industry and raw materials, but also a severe hindrance to the Soviet fleet. A surprise attack, concentrations of armoured forces, and deep, pincer-like movements across Soviet territory, not directly assaulting the towns and fortified positions, but outflanking and surrounding them, would bring successes like those attained elsewhere; the Soviet Union would soon cease to exist. There was no doubt that the Red Army could be crushed before the winter.

The invasion was a great success. Despite the bare equality of the forces in the north and centre, and the Soviet preponderance in the south, the objectives planned for the early part were soon attained. German intelligence on July 8 reported that, of the 164 infantry and 29 armoured divisions with which the Red Army had begun, 89 of the former and 20 of the latter had been totally or largely destroyed.[31] Until these shattered divisions could be reorganised, Soviet forces would be reduced to a shell. Only a month after the crossing of the border, Smolensk, 220 miles from Moscow, was practically surrounded, Uman and Kiev, the keys to the eastern Ukraine and the Dnieper basin, were under siege, and areas south of Leningrad had fallen into German hands.[32]

The success of the first stage, however, contrasted unfavourably with the difficulties and dissensions which were to follow. Two major lines of action were proposed. The first, favoured by the German High Command and the commanders in the field, was to use the whole strength of the forces in the centre for the attack on Moscow. The defence of the principal city and capital of the country, the repository of the very essence of national life, would surely attract the principal efforts of the Soviet authorities; and it would be in this theatre that decision might be achieved. To Hitler, this opinion seemed too narrowly based. It was less on Moscow than on the industrial areas of the south of Russia, the basins of the Dnieper and the Donets rivers, that the Soviet effort depended; their capture would not only deprive the enemy of his industries, it would bring immediate benefit to the economy of the Reich. The debate continued, in one form or another, from the end of July until the early weeks of September, and was settled along the lines of Hitler's Directive of August 21:

> The most important aim before the onset of the winter is not the capture of Moscow but the seizure of the Crimea and the industrial and coal regions of the Donetz, and the interception of Russia's oil route from the Caucasus. In the North Leningrad is to be cut off and a junction effected with the Finns. Only after these operations have been completed will forces be available for a renewed offensive on the Central front.[33]

The evils of delay, from the German point of view, were aggravated by the other developments of July. Whereas, at the beginning of that month, Halder, the German Chief of Staff, had confided to his diary that the Russian campaign had been won,[34] his opinions a month later had undergone a substantial transformation:

> The whole situation makes it increasingly plain that we have underestimated the Russian Colossus. . . . At the outset of the war we reckoned with about 200 enemy Divisions. Now we have already counted 360. These Divisions indeed are not armed and equipped according to our standards, and their tactical leadership is often

poor. But there they are, and if we smash a dozen of them, the Russians simply put up another dozen.[35]

The qualities of the Red Army had begun to show themselves. Units cut off from the rear had in many cases bitterly resisted the German onslaught, while a number of them had entrenched themselves in positions suitable for attack on the German flanks and rear. Armoured divisions caught between the pincers now began to show a capacity to absent themselves from the trap. Most serious of all, intelligence estimates were having to be revised: the Soviet armies, as Halder pointed out, were not limited to the 200 divisions accounted for at the beginning of the war, for numbers continued to appear whose existence had not been indicated. It now appeared that the size of Soviet industry, its geographical location, and the success with which it had been transferred beyond the Urals, were less favourable to the German invasion than had originally been supposed. Pessimism grew among the German leaders that the very conditions which they had endeavoured to avoid, the bogging down of the German war machine in endless, costly reductions of powerful defences, with few sudden encirclements and annihilations, were the order of the day. Perhaps the war might not be over before the winter.

II

If the German High Command, with its thorough planning, its patient observation, and its comprehensive system of intelligence, had underestimated the capabilities and determination of the Soviet forces, how much greater, then, were the errors in the west. British intelligence clearly expected the war to last only a few months at the outside,[36] and in Washington, the day after the invasion began, the Secretary of War, Henry Stimson, advised the President of the estimate of his Department: 'Germany will be thoroughly occupied in beating Russia for a minimum of one month and a possible maximum of three months.'[37] Clearly, if the Soviet Union were close to military collapse, the diversion of materiel to that theatre would be a waste of time and effort, and it was with such thoughts in mind that Harry Hopkins, Roosevelt's personal representative, left for Moscow in late July.[38] The recovery of the preceding days had put Stalin in confident mood, and, while stressing the need for munitions and raw materials, he spoke of the imminent stabilisation of the front.[39] Hopkins reported his impressions to the President when the latter met Churchill off the Newfoundland coast in early August.

The British had hoped that this meeting of the two heads of government presaged some more active American commitment to the war: such hopes were disappointed, but the meeting did afford an opportunity to secure agreement on the political bases of the post-war peace, and to consider the overall strategy of the war. The political agreement, the so-called Atlantic Charter, included direct or indirect reference to Roosevelt's Four Freedoms, freedom from want, from fear, freedom of religion, and of information; and the eight points of the Charter made clear the support of the signatories for that system of international relations based on respect for freely-determined national boundaries and national self-determination, on free trade and economic collaboration. After 'the final destruction of the Nazi tyranny,' and pending the establishment of a permanent system of security, the Charter called for the forcible disarmament of those nations whose actions threatened the peace of the world; such disarmament, Roosevelt's chief adviser was later to reveal, was to be carried out by the United States and Britain, no great opinion being held of the power or significance of the Soviet Union in the postwar world.[40]

It was in accordance with the spirit of the Charter, and with its specific clauses, that wartime pressure from the Soviet Union, and, in part, from Britain, for the delineation of boundaries and the assignation of forms of government in east, south-east and central Europe was constantly opposed by the United States; such delineation and assignation not conforming, it was held, with the promise to eschew territorial changes and forms of government imposed from without. Remembering the unfortunate effects rendered by the publication of the secret treaties of World War I, and not unaware of the influence in electoral terms of the many millions of Americans of central and east European extraction, the United States resisted any suggestion of a carve-up of territory or an imposition of boundaries and governments. In this, it often found itself in dispute with the Soviet Union and Great Britain, both of whom, for various reasons, were unwilling to leave the solution of the problems of boundaries and constitutions until the end of hostilities. Communications and missives flowing eastward across the Atlantic constantly reiterated this theme. Representatives of Britain and the Soviet Union could hardly meet together without receiving copious American advice. Thus, for instance, just before Pearl Harbor and the coincidental first visit of Anthony Eden to Moscow, the United States Secretary of State wrote that 'it would be unfortunate were any of these three governments to express any willingness to enter into commitments regarding specific terms of the postwar settlement. . . . Above all, there must be no secret accords.'[41]

In a letter which the Secretary of State wrote to President Roosevelt early in 1942, two justifications of the American position were advanced. The first was that if the principle of entering into agreements about postwar frontiers was admitted before the peace conference, the consequent mutual suspicion and intrigue would weaken the unity and strength of the alliance. The second was that if the British were to enter into such agreements with American approval, then the latter government would be hard put to resist additional Soviet demands, and 'There is no doubt that the Soviet government has tremendous ambitions with regard to Europe. . . .'[42] The Secretary of State thought that, while he could sympathise fully with Stalin's desire for the protection of his western borders against future invasions, 'this security could best be obtained through a strong postwar peace organisation.'[43]

The harmonies of the political agreement reached in the Atlantic Charter received no echo in the military conversations of the period. At the Atlantic Conference itself, and in the months preceding the entry of the United States into the war, the British Chiefs of Staff presented the main lines of their strategy for comment by their American counterparts. That comment was overwhelmingly critical: the Americans had little confidence in the attempt to wear down Germany by intensive air bombardment, and by operations at sensitive points along the periphery of the Axis empires.[44] As the United States Chiefs of Staff, in effect, pointed out in September, 1941: 'It should be recognised as an almost invariable rule that wars cannot be finally won without the use of land armies.'[45] And the notion that a substitute for large land armies might be found in small mobile forces backed by a widespread subversive movement was even less favourably received. The Americans would give no comment on these matters 'because they appear to lack definition sufficiently clear to form a basis for practical campaign plans.'[46] Just before the Conference, Hopkins had delivered the American estimate of the particular pressures then being applied in the middle east: there the British had an indefensible position; and they were making too many sacrifices to maintain it. At any moment the western Mediterranean might be sealed, the Suez Canal blocked, and the Germans might concentrate a sufficient superiority of air and armoured forces to overwhelm the British armies.[47]

The bricks which the critics had so scornfully rejected were soon to form the cornerstones of policy. The principal activities of American forces in the European theatre, until the summer of 1944, coincided exactly with what Churchill most strongly advised—the assault on Axis forces in peripheral theatres of the war. In choosing to fall in with British plans for North Africa, culminating in the

Anglo-American landings in December 1942, Operation TORCH, President Roosevelt acted against the strongest counsel of his military advisers. Six months before the landing, his Secretary of War declared with all his conviction that

> The one thing Hitler rightly dreaded was a second front. In establishing such a front lay the best hope of keeping the Russian Army in the war and thus ultimately defeating Hitler.... German success against Russia, whether fast or slow, would seem to make requisite not a diversion from BOLERO [the American build-up in Britain for a cross-Channel operation] but an increase in BOLERO as rapidly as possible.[48]

General Marshall and Admiral King threatened to carry opposition to the landings in North Africa up to the point of resignation.[49] In July, Marshall and the Navy Commander-in-Chief informed the President that the landings would be 'indecisive', would prevent any operation in Europe in 1942, and would curtail, if not make impossible, such an operation in the spring of 1943. In their opinion, the failure to act in Europe in 1942 would mean an avoidance of the American commitment to the Soviet Union.[50] Eisenhower, who was to command in both French North Africa and Europe, felt that he would prefer to cross the Channel rather than open a new front in North Africa, for the latter, he believed, would 'not materially assist the Russians in time to save them.'[51]

The decision to land in Africa in December 1942 was the result of two decisions, military in form but political in essence. 'Mr Churchill and his advisers categorically refused to accept the notion of a cross-Channel invasion in 1942. Mr Roosevelt categorically insisted that there must be *some* operation in 1942. The only operation that satisfied both of these conditions was TORCH.'[52] To President Roosevelt, continued concentration on the European theatre, the rebuttal of growing pressures for diversion to the Pacific, and, above all, the cultivation of the offensive spirit, that sense of national effort which alone could guarantee successful participation in the war, demanded that military action soon be undertaken.

The defeat of the Axis forces in North Africa inflicted no crushing blow on the German armies, diverted no divisions from the eastern front, and brought no new opportunities for the prosecution of the war. A handful of German divisions had been engaged, but the overall effect, the landings having revealed the allied hand, was to permit the Germans to move their forces from west to east. Stalin complained that, after the landings, 27 German divisions had reinforced the Soviet-German front, an estimate which, in the face of Churchill's less gloomy estimate, he was later to increase; but Churchill could not disagree that, in the early months of 1943, substantial German forces had been moved from west to east.[53] Churchill was to grumble that the western allies were 'playing about' with six German divisions while the Russians were facing 185.[54] Not only did success in North Africa lead to no very important consequences, no freshly opened avenue to Berlin, but also the commitment to that theatre carried with it, in the long term, the concentration of future planning on what might best be implemented from there, rather than on what might have most effect on the decision of the war. Sicily and Italy appeared inviting, and the way was open for that slow and costly crawl up the leg of Italy, that endless battling from hill to hill, which was to make so slight an impact on the German effort, and caused so great an attrition of western energies and resources.

The landings in North Africa, once made, prevented a major second front in 1943. The equipment necessary for that theatre and the struggle for the Mediterranean was quite removed from what the invasion of France required, and the concentration of production on the former meant the drastic lowering, in practice, of relative priority for the latter. By January 1943 ·the construction of landing craft in the shipyards of the United States, and the production of field artillery shells in Britain, both prerequisites for large-scale land warfare in France, were substantially reduced; and their manufacture would not reach the 1942 levels again until 1944.[55] And for most of 1943 the shipping required for the African operation helped limit the despatch of allied matériel to Murmansk to less than a third of the levels of 1942.[56] That limitation, together with the failure to launch a second front, had significant and unfortunate effect on the course of western-Soviet relations.

The scale of Soviet efforts against the Germans on the eastern front, the heavy sacrifices of soldiers, civilians and material resources, the constant threat, indeed, to the integrity of the Soviet Union itself, led Stalin to urge the western allies to greater efforts in their theatres of the war. His requests were met with a constant pattern of reply: a quiet refusal to launch a second front, plus a promise that such relief would not be long in coming. On two occasions, though, in 1942, commitments of a more or less specific character were given, whose non-fulfilment led to a worsening of relations. On May 29, during his visit to Washington, Molotov, the Soviet Foreign Minister, asked for a straight answer to the question of an Anglo-American landing in Europe; and Roosevelt appended his signature to a statement that 'full understanding was reached with regard to the urgent tasks of creating a Second Front in Europe in 1942.'[57] And in London, a week before, Churchill had informed Molotov that the current western plans for 1943 contemplated 'the landing of a force of up to

a million and a half United States–British troops on the Continent.'*
When, in May 1943, it was impossible to hide the fact that a second
front would not be launched that year, Stalin withdrew his
ambassadors in Washington and London.

It was Churchill, rather than Roosevelt, who had most strongly
opposed a second front in France: the quality of the German forces
there, the strength and extension of the coastal fixed defences, and
the limited military resources of Great Britain, would lead, he
claimed, to military disaster. In September 1941 Churchill told his
ambassador in Moscow that the coast of France was 'fortified to the
limit, and *the Germans still have more divisions in the West than
we have in Great Britain*',[58] and he wrote to Stalin explaining that
in view of the commitments on the sea and in the air, Britain 'can
never hope to have an army or army munition industries comparable
to those of the great Continental military Powers.'[59] In August 1942
he spoke of nine 'first line' German divisions across the Channel.
These claims were generally without foundation. The shores
of France in the west and south were not really defended, but
merely protected, along interminable, sparsely manned fronts;
the fortifications, in the words of their commander, were a 'propaganda bluff' to deceive the world.[60] Contrary to what British
intelligence maintained, throughout 1942 and 1943 the German
army in the west was always extremely pressed for manpower and
equipment, and by the autumn of 1942 the point was reached
where there were hardly sufficient troops for seizing the unoccupied
parts of Vichy France.[61] Contrary to Churchill's claim, and
in general accordance with Stalin's assertion, in August 1942,

---

* 'The Hinge of Fate', *New York Times,* October 21, 1950. Trumbull
Higgins comments on Churchill's statement thus: 'This statement, so
damaging to Mr Churchill's argument [that the west never promised to
launch a second front in 1943, and that Stalin's anger in that year was
quite unjustified], has been removed from the bound version of *The Hinge
of Fate,* published in the United States, pp. 335–42.' (*Winston Churchill
and the Second Front, 1940–1943,* New York, 1957, p. 234.) In exploring
the alleys of Churchill's policy, and in pointing the direction for further
research, Trumbull Higgins has done valuable work.

Meeting Stalin in Moscow in August 1942, Churchill writes: 'But, as
Mr Stalin knew, they were preparing for a very great operation in 1943.
For this purpose a million American troops were now scheduled to reach
the United Kingdom at the point of assembly in the spring of 1943, making
an expeditionary force of twenty-seven divisions, to which the British
Government were prepared to add twenty-one divisions.' (*Hinge of Fate,*
p. 430.) Stalin was due for a disappointment, and Churchill complained
to Ismay in March 1943 how 'very conscious' he felt of the 'poor contribution the British and American Armies are making in only engaging perhaps a dozen German divisions during the greater part of this year. . . .'
(*Ibid.,* p. 832.)

that there was not a single German division in France of any value, a United States Army historian has concluded from German sources that, after May 1942, 'it was made a matter of policy that the west should be permanently garrisoned only by troops who because of various disabilities could not be used in the hard fighting in Russia.'[62] Their quality further declined in 1943.[63] Had the allies landed in southern France in 1943 they would have met with practically no resistance.[64] Nor were the British forces as weak as was suggested. In aircraft, trucks, tanks, self-propelled guns, and several other types of armaments, British production was greater than that of Germany in 1940, 1941 and 1942.[65] In the autumn of 1941 Britain was diverting a million men into the RAF from the United Kingdom alone, and was maintaining the great force of over 32 field divisions in garrison at home; for 1942 it was organising a total strength, including Empire units, of an estimated 99 divisions throughout the world. For all the stress on poor training and equipment, the Red Army was fighting on much worse terms.[66]

From early 1941 until the Normandy landings of June 1944, the entire strength of the British Empire and Commonwealth engaged between two and eight divisions of the principal Axis power, Germany. During all but the first six months of the same period, the Soviet Union withstood, contained, and eventually repulsed, an average of about 180 German divisions. And the western effort was, for the most part, squandered in a secondary theatre of the war. An average of 12 divisions of the western allies took two-and-a-half years to force back about the same number of Axis divisions from Egypt to the north of Italy, a distance of some two thousand miles, over terrain bereft of good communications and endowed only with a frequency of highly defensible positions—over terrain, that is, entirely unsuited to the kind of mechanised offensive that had proved so effective in other theatres of the war.[67] The fall of Africa and of Italy offered neither industry and raw material, nor a launching-ground for new attacks. At the end of the war, when the German armies in Italy had surrendered, they did so not because decision had been arrived at in that theatre, but because the German armies and the German rear had collapsed from assaults elsewhere. And even had the surrender in Italy preceded that collapse, the course of the war could not have been substantially different, for the whole of the Alps had still to be traversed. As Eisenhower later wrote, speaking of the plans of 1942: 'While conceivably Italy might readily be eliminated as an enemy, the heart of the opposition was Germany— an Italian collapse would not be decisive. The difficulty of attacking Germany through the mountainous areas on her southern and south-western flanks was obvious . . .'[68]

III

The failure of the western allies to play a powerful part in the defeat of the German armies had significant effect on the course of western-Soviet relations. The refusal to invade Europe in 1942, and the constant postponement of a second front thereafter, consolidated the feeling in Moscow that it was through the Soviet effort alone that Germany had been defeated, and that the security of the Soviet borders, the erection of barriers to future invasions by the Germans, would depend on what the Soviet Union might unilaterally perform. Gradually, the basis of future conflict was created, a conflict between that system of security in which the states of Europe reverted to their prewar form, with prewar styles of government and foreign policy, under the umbrella of a refurbished League of Nations, and that system which, abandoning the prewar shape of Europe, created barriers to further aggression and invasion by committing the governments of eastern Europe to policies favourable to the Soviet Union, and the governments of western Europe to policies acceptable to the United States and Britain. The singlemindedness with which the Soviet Union sought tangible guarantees against further German incursions, through the creation of a sphere of influence in east and south-east Europe, was paralleled only by the tenacity of purpose with which the United States and Britain sought, in the name of democracy and self-determination, both to establish an equivalent sphere in the west and south, and, this having been achieved, to prevent the Soviet Union from consolidating control in its own allotted zone.

It gradually became clear that the United States was unable to agree on the practical aspects of the guarantees which, in theory, it recognised as desirable. The American government was conscious both of the scale and extent of the destruction wreaked by the Germans on this and on previous occasions, and of the role which the small powers of eastern Europe had played in providing the highway for such invasions. Its palliatives centred round the demilitarisation of Germany, the establishment of governments friendly to the Soviet Union in east, and certain parts of south-east Europe, the redrawing of certain boundaries by mutual agreement at a postwar peace conference, and the creation of an international organisation through which measures to combat future aggression might be concerted. But the conflict between these provisions and the other aims of American policy—the reestablishment of a Versailles system of independent nations with social and economic systems of their own choosing, the resuscitation, in fact, of the capitalist and western-orientated regimes of the prewar period—was not resolved, in Soviet eyes, in a manner which would effectively prevent further German adventures. To the Soviet government, the effective demilitarisation of Germany meant both the end of militarism and the control of the economic and social base that had brought it into being; the establishment of governments friendly to the Soviet Union in eastern Europe precluded the possibility of those persons and political parties participating in government which had been previously hostile to the Soviet Union and were presently opposing the redrawing of frontiers. And the international organisation, it was undoubtedly felt, however desirable in principle, might offer guarantees no more certain than those provided by the League of Nations.

A considerable difference emerged between the policies which the United States urged upon its allies and those which it came in practice to adopt. In its published view, the challenge of the postwar world lay in the reestablishment of peace and security, especially in those areas which had been the occasion of conflict. To that end, a rapid return was envisaged to the system of independent nations, representative governments, and liberal trading relations, which was seen as the ideal form of national life. Peoples finding themselves under the domination of fascist parties and regimes should be liberated therefrom, and, with the exception of the suppression of these anti-social groups, be permitted to set up their own elected governments. The crushing of fascism and the prevention of its recurrence could be achieved by the use of allied troops and measures of coercion, but in the long run the peace of the area, the American government suggested, could be secured only by a world system representative of all the nations, dedicated to the solution of international problems by peaceful means, but containing within its structure a mechanism by which the great powers, with the help and agreement of the smaller nations, might, in the event of aggression or threat to the peace, take appropriate action and inflict condign punishment. In a phrase, by an organisation along the lines of what came to be called the United Nations. And any boundary problems that remained after the creation of representative governments could be solved by negotiations between the powers concerned.

A particular irony in the history of this period, in the clash between different outlooks on the problems of security, lies in the fact that it was not the Soviet Union which was first able to put into practice its ideas on the structure of government in the liberated areas. Many months before Soviet troops had set foot in any part of east or south-east Europe, the conquest of North Africa and the surrender of Italy presented an occasion on which the intentions and dispositions of the United States and Britain might be put to the test. It was in Italy, indeed, where some of the difficulties of applying fine-sounding generalities about representative government and liberal democracy came up against the concrete realities of the situation.

The crisis of confidence following the loss of Libya and the invasion of Sicily brought a new government to power in Italy, a change impelled less by a great and popular outburst against Fascism and all its agents than by a realisation on the part of Italy's rulers of the dangers to which Mussolini's policy had led. The demise of Mussolini was a mere palace revolution, instigated by royalist army officers and prominent Fascists, his place being taken by General Badoglio, the conqueror of Abyssinia. However narrow the basis of Badoglio's power, however suspect his political principles, he could be represented by the allies as the embodiment of political legitimacy, and the adhesion of the king and his government to the allied cause appeared to bring with it the loyalty of those units of the armed forces not in German hands.

In the negotiations leading to the Italian armistice, in the administration of Italy during the two years following that event, the influence of the Soviet Union was substantially excluded, and, no less significantly, less attention was paid to the demands of the Italian people, voiced through their parties and their press, than to the conservation and extension of allied—and particularly British—prerogatives in the area.

The negotiations for an Italian surrender and for the governmental arrangements of that country were in the hands of Britain and the United States alone. Stalin's attempt to lend his voice to the question of the armistice terms and the new administration came to nothing. His government was excluded from effective say in these and other matters. He was informed, if in desultory fashion, of the armistice negotiations, and, while not objecting to the terms envisaged, expressed dissatisfaction with the lack of real allied consultation. Taking up an earlier British suggestion, he wrote to Roosevelt and Churchill, then meeting in Quebec (August 1943), asking that a Military-Political Commission of representatives of the three allies be set up 'with the purpose of considering the questions concerning the negotiations with the different governments disassociating themselves from Germany'. It was not possible, he said, to tolerate the existing situation, in which the United States and Britain made agreements, and the Soviet Union was informed about them afterwards.[69] Under pressure, the United States and Britain agreed that such a commission might be formed, but were not willing to invest it with any substantial power. Whereas Molotov, in a note of September 25, suggested that the Commission should have the power to direct civil, and guide military, activities in the occupied territories (and the importance which he attached to its operations was instanced by his nomination of Vyshinsky as the Soviet member), the western allies would accept a liaisory and advisory body alone.[70] It was the views of the latter which prevailed. At the Moscow meeting of the Foreign Ministers in October, an Advisory Council was set up to observe Italian affairs: it had no power of issuing orders of any kind.[71]

The Soviet (and the French) desire to participate in the allied control of Italy was not satisfied by membership of the Advisory Council. The Soviet government claimed to be entitled to appoint its representative to the Allied Control Commission, the organ through which allied policy towards the Italian government was conducted. And although this claim was granted—nearly five months after the armistice—membership of the ACC hardly offered more hold on the reins of power than did a seat on the Advisory Council: the constitution of the ACC was such that, while its president, the allied commander-in-chief, received orders direct from London and Washington, the functions of the French and Soviet members were consultative.[72]

It was less in accord with the tenets of Italian self-determination that the policy of the allies was determined, than in conformity with the desire most speedily to terminate the war, and most effectively to maintain the long-term interests of Britain and the United States. The maintenance of allied military government for long periods in areas significant to military events, and the selection, for less essential areas, of an Italian government with strong links with previous Fascist administrations, the stifling, for as long as possible, of strong anti-monarchical tendencies, and the exclusion or frustration of the reforming elements in the north in their various Committees of National Liberation—Communists, Christian and Social Democrats, tended to determine the political, social and economic structure of postwar Italy; went far, in fact, towards retaining the conservative, clerical and anti-communist outlook which had formed the basis for previous, discredited Italian administrations, and which still exists today.

A good deal of allied direction of affairs in Italy was inevitable. The liberation of Italy was slow in progress, and general elections could not be held until two-and-a-half years after the early landings; the wartime chaos impeded formal consultation at any stage of the existing liberated area. But those informal thermometers of opinion, the political parties and the press, were generally ignored, and indigenous tendencies were subordinated to the long-term interests of the occupying powers. The official historian of allied military government has assessed its political achievements. In the first place, the recognition afforded by the allies to the king's government, in the early months after the fall of Mussolini, helped Italy 'to avoid many of the inconveniences caused by revolutions.' Again, in 1944, after some political freedoms had been restored, the vehement opposition of the renascent political parties, Christian Democrats and Communists alike, to the regime which had been placed upon them caused some political difficulties, and 'it is difficult to see how he [Badoglio] could have maintained his administration' but for the 'active support' of the Allied Control Commission. Finally, in the weeks immediately following the surrender of the Germans, 'there would appear to be little doubt that the establishment of Allied Military Government in the northern Regions did help to avoid very serious trouble, which at one time looked like amounting to a revolution.'[73] The point is not that an isolated seizure of power by communist workers was straightforwardly suppressed,[74] or that some portion of allied military government had no compunction in employing obvious Fascists, as long as they were efficient.[75] It is rather that, by maintaining in power a government of an extremely right-wing character for a long period against the wishes of every political party, by preventing the question of the monarchy from being decided until over two years after it had been raised, and by frustrating the reforming schemes of the Committees of National Liberation of the great northern cities, allied policy set Italian society on a path more in accord with allied—and particularly British—wishes than with the reforming, even revolutionary, disposition that had arisen with the fall of Fascism.

The Soviet Union had not interfered with the actions of the western allies. After the right of membership of the Allied Control Commission had been conceded, with the insubstantial 'consultative' role that that afforded, it had let events take the course dictated by Britain and the United States. Its two significant acts of policy were such, in fact, as to reinforce the position of its allies' nominees. In March 1944 Vyshinsky's successor made it clear that his government was anxious to establish diplomatic relations with Badoglio's; and that same month Togliatti, returning from his Moscow exile, broke the political boycott of the regime by offering his services to Badoglio and the king.[76] In all, the Soviet government appeared to have abandoned the Italian left, and to have gracefully accepted that Italy should lie within the western sphere of influence.

There was a real concern, in the west, that the future of east and south-east Europe, of Poland, Hungary, Rumania, Bulgaria, Yugoslavia and Greece, would be determined in accordance with the practice which had so successfully been established in Italy—that the power whose forces liberated the area, while paying lip service to the principles of allied cooperation, would actually come to supervise, for the foreseeable future, the political, social, and economic structure of the states therein. East and south-east Europe might fall irrevocably into the Soviet orbit. Before examining the steps that were taken to oppose this threat, however, the course of the war on the eastern front may briefly be outlined.

The German decision to concentrate on the southern front in the autumn of 1941, in accordance with Hitler's decision in August, precluded the reinforcement of the central front, but the consequent failure to capture Moscow was not compensated, from the German point of view, by the gains of the armies in the south. After the fall of Kiev, the Crimea and the Donets basin were overrun, but the drive towards the Caucasian oilfields was unsuccessful.[77]

In 1942, lacking the resources for operations on the scale of those of 1941, the concentration in the south continued; and was, for a time, successful. A break-through was achieved in the area of Kursk and Kharkov, and the German armies, wheeling south, moved down towards the oilfields. In six weeks, the more westerly oilfields, around Maikop, had been secured, and a plan was laid for an advance northwards which, engaging the rear of the Soviet armies covering Moscow, or striking at the new industrial base towards the Urals, might secure a rapid Soviet surrender. The forces providing this advance, reaching up as far as Stalingrad in the autumn, were the subject of a Soviet counter-attack which, launched from positions to the north and south, squeezed off von Paulus's 6th Army, the 4th Tank Army, and encircled 330,000 men.[78] This great victory, the turning point on the Soviet-German front, was achieved with equipment practically all of which was of Soviet manufacture, only a small number of western tanks, lorries and jeeps being used.[79]

The major German offensive of 1943 was launched near Kharkov in July. Within a week the German armoured divisions were seriously reduced; and the Soviet counter-offensive, while not at first making headway very fast, established a pattern which was to be continued throughout the war. The alternating strokes of the more powerful Soviet armies at points across a wide offensive front kept the scanty German reserves hurrying from sector to sector. By the end of September the Red Army had reached the Dnieper, and, in early January, the pre-war Polish frontier.

In 1944 the German front remained as wide as ever, and the continued shrinkage of the German, and the growing superiority of the Soviet forces, enabled the advance to be continued. By March Rumania had been entered and Hungary threatened; but the main offensive of the summer was launched, not from the great wedge in southern Poland, but across the central front, along the road to Minsk and Warsaw, which, being the best fortified sector of the

German front, had withstood repeated assaults in 1943. By the end of July the Soviet forces had penetrated the suburbs of Warsaw in the centre, had reached the gulf of Riga and threatened the borders of East Prussia in the north, and in the south were preparing a drive which took their armies to Yugoslavia and Bulgaria. German intelligence that December reported that 225 infantry divisions, and 22 armoured corps, of the Red Army had been identified on the front between the Baltic Sea and the Carpathians; the Anglo-American invasion of the continent, launched in June, was maintained by 37 divisions.[80]

The military realities spoke for themselves. The numbers and successes of Soviet troops in areas of east and south-east Europe more directly affected the future of these areas than could any number of allied advices or protestations, just as the absence of Soviet forces in the Mediterranean and western Europe was, or would soon be, decisive in the apportionment of control there. What could be done? Some, and they found major representation within the British government, maintained that a deal might be made whereby south-east Europe be divided into spheres of influence; that the preponderant interest of the Soviet Union in the future of Rumania, Bulgaria and Hungary be recognised, while the lesser interest of the western powers in those countries, and their preponderant interest in Greece, receive acknowledgement. There were others, and they were particularly influential within the American State Department, who urged a less flexible attitude. They were determined that none of these countries should fall irrevocably into the Soviet orbit, and they urged, therefore, that no recognition, whether verbal or in writing, should be given to a condition whereby the Soviet Union was afforded legitimate control. The difficulty was, and Roosevelt was quick to recognise it, that the Soviet Union was in a position to take over and arrange the administration of the area in any case; if no agreement were entered into, there was a real possibility that the interests of Britain and the United States would receive no recognition whatsoever. Under considerable pressure from Churchill, who was anxious to retain Greece within the western sphere of influence, and to have some say in the future of Hungary and the Balkans, Roosevelt agreed that a suitable arrangement might be set up for a three-month trial period.[81] The State Department was not immediately informed.

Four months later in October 1944, an even more elaborate Anglo-Soviet agreement was negotiated. 'Let us settle about our affairs in the Balkans,' Churchill proposed to Stalin in Moscow in October, and the two agreed to acknowledge a 90 per cent Soviet influence in Rumania in exchange for an equal degree of British influence in Greece. In addition, the influence of the Soviet Union was defined as 80 per cent in Bulgaria, 80 per cent in Hungary, and 50 per cent in Yugoslavia.[82] Churchill had thus recognised varying degrees of Soviet predominance in Rumania, Bulgaria and Hungary, in exchange for a free hand in Greece and joint responsibility in Yugoslavia; and Roosevelt's ambassador, Averell Harriman, who had observed the negotiations, raised no objections to what was being done.[83]

It was in Greece that these arrangements were first put to the test. It became clear, late in 1944, that a 90 per cent British responsibility in the area might be interpreted as the right to impose a government against the clearly expressed wishes of a nation; to reimpose a royalist regime whose army had proved hostile to its claims, and whose people, *The Times* was later to report, were four-fifths against the king's return.[84] The British authorities ordered the disbandment of ELAS, the military wing of the anti-Fascist popular movement EAM, which, Anthony Eden admitted, controlled seventy-five per cent of the resistance forces,[85] declined to punish quislings and collaborators, and reformed the National Guard with officers trained by the Nazis. The ensuing war, fought between the British and the resistance forces who had both fiercely opposed the Nazis and liberated Athens from the departing Germans, was imbued with the spirit of Churchill's message to his military commander: that the Greek forces should be deprived of their control of Athens 'with bloodshed if necessary.'[86] Only when EAM had been crushed, its leaders and thousands of its members jailed, exiled or shot, and the government, including all the machinery of intimidation, placed firmly in rightist hands, were elections permitted. Yet after thus breaking a popular opposition, Churchill felt himself able to announce that he had but one principle for the liberated countries: 'Government of the people, by the people, for the people, set up on a basis of free and universal suffrage election, with secrecy of the ballot and no intimidation.'[87]

Not one word of reproach emerged from Moscow in this period. Stalin was carefully adhering to the agreements which he had signed with Churchill, and was, from September onwards, putting into effect his part of the bargain. The terms of the armistice agreements negotiated with Rumania, Bulgaria and Hungary expressed the predominance of the Soviet Union in those areas. The Soviet commander, who was to be chairman of the Allied Control Commission in each instance, was granted the same almost unlimited authority which the earlier Italian armistice had granted to the west. In Rumania, the terms of the armistice were to be executed 'under the general direction and orders' of the Soviet High Command, acting on behalf of the allied powers, until the signing of a peace treaty;[88] while in Bulgaria and Hungary, reflecting the reduced percentages secured by Churchill, the armistice terms permitted a vague increase in western representation on the Commissions after the German surrender, and up until a peace treaty had been negotiated.[89] Just as in the case of Italy and Greece, the initial shape of the administration within the Soviet sphere of influence went far towards retaining in those countries governments amenable to the liberating forces.

The division of Europe which received endorsement in the Churchill-Stalin discussions of 1944, and which was effected in all the countries of south-east Europe, was no hastily conceived or temporary condition. It has been claimed that the percentage division was designed only for the duration of the war,[90] but there is no evidence that Churchill reached such an understanding with Stalin. On the contrary, it was in order permanently to protect the position of the British in Greece that the deal had been promoted, and on a number of occasions after Germany's defeat, Churchill acknowledged the continuing obligations of the undertaking.[91]* Nor did the United States disown, or fail to understand, what was being done. President Roosevelt and his advisers were fully conscious of the significance of their actions,[92] and endorsed the transformation of the general understanding into the terms of the armistice agreements for Hungary, Rumania and Bulgaria.†

IV

The division of south-east Europe on the basis of traditional interests and immediate military achievements was continued in texts emerging from the Yalta conference of February 1945. No serious challenge was made to the arrangments described above, but there were other, more sensitive European countries, whose future could not be decided with any such unanimity: the future, that is, of Germany and Poland.

One historian has written that, at Yalta,

> The Polish question was a dishevelled presence in every conference hour. It was discussed in the private talks which Churchill, Stalin, and Roosevelt had with one another; in the group meetings of the

* Churchill referred to the 50–50 deal in Yugoslavia in negotiations with Stalin, June and July, 1945.

† There is some substance to the claim, perhaps, that in these countries, and in contrast to events in Greece, no attempt was made in the early stages to set up governments of a particularly communist or radical complexion; the test of their suitability to the Soviet Union was their attitude to continuing 'friendship' with that country, rather than a similarity of political and social structure. Some liberal and conservative elements passing this test of friendship were allowed to function and take part in government.

Foreign Ministers; and at all but one of the plenary sessions. It became the testing ground between the West and Communist Russia —between two conceptions of security.[93]

Two issues divided east and west: first, what the frontiers of Poland should be, the answer to which had considerable bearing on the second, who was to govern Poland.

The immediate subject of altercation about the frontier between Poland and Russia was the so-called Curzon Line. The Curzon Line had been suggested at the Paris Peace Conference of 1919 as the just and equitable boundary between the countries; it was based on historical, ethnographic and economic grounds. Both the British and American governments of the time had recognised its suitability, and the latter had urged the fractious Poles to remain behind the line. However, the defeat inflicted by Poland upon the Soviet Union in the war of 1920–1 enabled the former to acquire vast tracts of territory long forming part of western Russia, whose inhabitants were by no means preponderantly of Polish affiliation.

A number of considerations impelled the Soviet Union to demand the return of territory lost in 1921. The Polish administration of the area between the wars was universally admitted to be atrocious, and its population, the majority of whom where not Polish, had been persecuted and exploited. More than justice was at stake, however, for there was also the question of Soviet defence. Stalin had referred to this in his first wartime message to Churchill in 1941: 'It is easy to imagine that the position of the German forces would have been many times more favourable had the Soviet troops had to face the attack of the German forces, not in the regions of Kishenev, Lwow, Brest, Kaunas and Viborg, but in the region of Odessa, Kamenets Podolski, Minsk and the environs of Leningrad.'[94] The return to the Curzon Line would not secure the full benefit granted by the territory secured in the Nazi-Soviet Pact, but it would nevertheless make a substantial contribution to Soviet defence. Stalin expressed his government's determination in the matter, and his own inability to compromise, when he remarked at Yalta that he could hardly return to Moscow and face the people if they could say that he and Molotov had been less sure defenders of Russian interests than Curzon and Clemenceau.[95]

The refusal of the Polish government, in exile in London, to make any concession in the matter of their eastern frontier had far-reaching effects on the attitude of the Soviet Union. The latter could hardly permit a nation whose territorial integrity and political attitudes were so vital to its defence to come under the sway of a government whose predecessor's foreign policy, in the words of a Soviet historian, 'boiled down to the encouragement of any and all anti-Soviet schemes,' and whose present statements expressed the most implacable hostility to, in Soviet eyes, the most reasonable demands—demands accepted as legitimate, in principle, by both Churchill and Roosevelt.[96]

The question of the Polish frontiers was the subject of a good deal of negotiation as the war progressed. It was recognised in Britain that the claims of the Soviet Union to the areas lying to the east of the Curzon Line could not be resisted, and that some form of compensation, a slice of Germany's pre-war eastern territories, perhaps, might be granted to Poland in its stead. The case for this reforming, for the wholesale shift of Poland to the west, was less clear in the United States, and the importance of the Polish vote in the 1944 elections, as well as other, more general, considerations, prevented Roosevelt from lending his agreement. Thus when the British Foreign Secretary had informed the President of the Soviet claims, in March 1943, the latter maintained a certain reticence. He said that the Great Powers would have to decide what territories Poland was to get, for he had no intention of bargaining with the Poles; and on hearing of the Soviet demand for territory up to the Curzon Line, he agreed that Poland might receive East Prussia in the west.[97]

At the Teheran Conference in November 1943 Roosevelt's fears for the Polish vote again prevented detailed discussion of the Polish frontiers, but the President did admit that he would like to see the eastern borders moved further to the west, and the western border moved even to the River Oder.[98] The non-discussion of outstanding issues in eastern Europe, however, was a luxury which the west could ill afford during the Red Army's continuing advance, and Churchill and Stalin took up the matter by themselves. Churchill returned to London with a Curzon Line-to-Oder River formula for Poland's frontiers, which he put before the exile government there. His own views he expressed to the House of Commons in February 1944: 'I cannot feel that the Russian demand for a reassurance about her Western frontiers goes beyond the limits of what is reasonable or just.'[99]

Britain was concerned, not with boundaries alone, but also with the composition of the postwar Polish government. It hoped to see, at the end of hostilities, the administration of that country in the hands of elements drawn from the exile, London, government, whose friendship with the west was not in doubt. How might this aim of policy be reconciled with the repeated assurance to the Soviet Union that a government hostile to its interests would not be permitted to recur? Essentially, by persuading the exile government to accept the boundaries outlined above, and by pressing on the Soviet government the view that such a gesture of goodwill fulfilled the test of friendship. The force of Churchill's diplomacy, then, was to convince the London Poles of the need to recognise the Curzon Line, and to convince the Soviet Union that the London government was not hostile to its claims; for if the Soviet government came to believe that the exile government would not accept what even Churchill and his advisers thought was reasonable and just, the way was clear for its veto to be placed against the London government, and for it to heed those Poles of more friendly inclination.

The attitude of the London Poles was not helpful in this matter. Their government was willing to accept any quantity of Germany in the west, but would not agree to concessions in the east. Thus, in the summer of 1944, having at last gained an interview with Roosevelt, their prime minister and perhaps most reasonable representative, Mikolajczyk, maintained an unrelenting inflexibility. When the President suggested a free and independent Poland, with frontiers running from a modified Curzon Line to the River Oder, Mikolajczyk replied that Russia had no more right to half his country than it had to that portion of the United States from the Atlantic to the Mississippi.[100] This refractory passion for what was essentially Russian territory served to confirm Moscow in its view that the London government was incapable of forming friendly relations with the Soviet Union and was not, therefore, acceptable as the government of Poland.

The intransigence of the London Poles received some encouragement in Washington's equivocation. The hostility with which the State Department viewed the Soviet claims, and the unwillingness of the President to declare his hand before the 1944 election, seemed to presage a degree of American diplomatic support by the operation of which alone, in the face of Soviet anger and persistent British pressure, the cause of the London Poles might hope to be upheld. Following his success in the November elections, however, Roosevelt was quick to state his views: he endorsed the position which Churchill had been pressing.

The refusal of the Poles to accept the boundaries which had been offered placed them in a very vulnerable position. As the war developed, as the Red Army moved nearer to, and then across, the territory of prewar Poland, the need for an administration with a degree of popular support able and willing to keep order in the liberated territories, to supervise areas behind the Soviet lines, became a matter of practical necessity; and the continued intractability of the London government, its hostility to the Soviet Union, removed it from consideration. Stalin had in part supported the claims of the so-called Lublin Poles, men who, fleeing from Poland during the period of semi-Fascist rule, or after its military defeat, had set up a government in Moscow whose claims were intended to rival those of the London government. Their friendliness to the Soviet Union was not in doubt—their existence was partly due to the actions of that country—and their political complexion was decidedly more radical than that which prevailed in London. When the Soviet attempt to get the agreement of the London Poles to the Curzon Line was finally abandoned, it was to the Lublin group that the administration of the country liberated from the Germans was entrusted. The western allies had not, however, abandoned their support for the London Poles, and the champions of those from London, and those from Lublin, were to discuss, and attempt to solve, the problems of the postwar government at Yalta in February 1945.

The problem of Germany was discussed only in general terms before the Yalta Conference. At Teheran in 1943 the three heads of state had agreed that Germany should be de-Nazified and dismembered, but on the extent and nature of the dismemberment there were differences of opinion. Roosevelt suggested dividing Germany into seven parts, Churchill suggested its division into two, and Stalin expressed no opinion either way. The matter was not accorded any great priority.[101]

The breach of the German frontiers by American troops in the autumn of 1944 made the clarification of policy a necessity, but discussion within the United States administration had already revealed differences between the Treasury, under Henry Morgenthau, and the War Department, under Henry Stimson. The Treasury suggested that, apart from diversions of German territory to Poland, Russia, Denmark and France, the Ruhr should be internationalised, and the rest of Germany divided into two independent states. Heavy industries should either be removed for reparations or destroyed. Nothing should be done to sustain the German economy, which would in future have a primarily agricultural character. Morgenthau was convinced that unless this plan were carried out, the Germans would one day recommence their aggressive schemes.[102] Stimson's opposition to this plan derived from his view of the basis of a satisfactory postwar peace. He hoped for a settlement which would involve no burden of debts, no barriers to the internal trade of central Europe, no politically independent and economically helpless 'successor states'.[103] This worthy vision implied contentious policy prescriptions, and Stimson was quite consistent in opposing the division of Germany, and in supporting the retention by Germany of much of its industry and commerce. As the Yalta Conference approached, Morgenthau's plan was losing support within the government, perhaps, but it was in accord with the directions which he had laid down that Roosevelt set out to negotiate the American position.

At Yalta the division of Europe into spheres of influence was given a legitimacy with which the unilateral actions of the different powers had been unable to endow it. The preponderance of Soviet power in east and south-east Europe, and that of Britain and the United States in the Mediterranean, western Europe, and the Pacific, themselves the result of different degrees of military commitment and achievement, as well as of differing traditions and concerns of foreign policy, were given recognition. There was a good deal of bargaining over those countries in which the claims of the west and the Soviet Union were in competition, as in Poland, but the compromises that eventually emerged reflected the balance of forces which existed and the progress which had already been made towards acceptable solutions.

This limited but stable solution to the problems of the world was achieved not instead of, but in spite of, an adherence to the principles of the Atlantic Charter. For although the signatories agreed that the return to peaceful conditions in the liberated areas would be achieved 'by processes which will enable the liberated peoples to destroy the last vestiges of Nazism and Fascism and to create democratic institutions of their own choice,'[104] and although interference in the affairs of these areas would be permitted only to the concerted action of the three Great Powers, the challenge that more concrete words and measures might have made to the accepted spheres of influence was deliberately rejected. The State Department had suggested, before the Conference, that western influence in the Soviet sphere might be reestablished only if democratic governments were promoted and free elections held; it urged a general 'Declaration' of intent, and real machinery for its implementation.[105] Roosevelt, while accepting with reluctance a modified version of the Declaration, struck out the provisions tending to establish an agency by which the broad ideals might be implemented;[106] and made no attempt to reconsider the specific conditions of the armistice agreements which had been signed—agreements which reserved, in fact, the major responsibility for the affairs of certain countries in south-east Europe to the Soviet Union. This, as has been seen, was less the rude rejection of the claims of freedom than the mere recognition of obligations to an ally who, in turn, had renounced his claims to areas within the western sphere of influence.

A compromise was found for Poland. After considerable argument over the terms by which the various groups of Poles should be known, and in what way, if at all, the Lublin government should be altered (the details need not concern us), the outcome was that the 'Provisional Government which is now functioning in Poland', that is, the Lublin Poles, should be 'reorganised on a broader democratic basis with the inclusion of democratic leaders from Poland itself and from Poles abroad.' The government which emerged from this reorganisation would be pledged to hold 'free and unfettered elections as soon as possible on the basis of universal suffrage and secret ballot. In these elections all democratic and anti-Nazi parties shall have the right to take part and put forward candidates.'[107] The new Russian-Polish boundary would follow, with slight digressions, the Curzon Line.

The position taken up by President Roosevelt towards the German question was along the lines proposed by Henry Morgenthau; a harsh peace treaty was envisaged, with the permanent reduction of the power of Germany in Europe. The advice of Henry Stimson, that the division of that country, its impoverishment and de-industrialisation, if proceeded with, would create a source of future hatred, appears to have been discounted; and the Yalta signatories agreed to take 'such steps, including the complete disarmament, demilitarisation and dismemberment of Germany as they deem requisite for future peace and security.'[108] The future of Germany was further clarified in the statement of the heads of state: 'We are determined to disarm and disband all German armed forces; break up for all time the German General Staff ... remove or destroy all German military equipment; eliminate or control all German industry that could be used for military production. ...'[109] It was agreed, in addition, that reparations in kind should be extracted, in the form of removals of capital wealth, requisition of goods from current output, and the use of German labour, the total value of which, and its distribution among the victims of German aggression, was to be decided at the meetings of a Reparation Commission to be held in Moscow.

The agreements signed at Yalta represented the greatest concessions that the western allies could obtain. Given the history of the war, the failure to launch a second front until the military need for it had passed, the gains and achievements of Soviet power could not be removed by diplomatic courtesies alone. As James F. Byrnes, adviser at Yalta and later Secretary of State, said: 'It was not a question of what we would *let* the Russians do, but what we could *get* them to do.'[110] The shape of Europe had been decided, and the Conference at Yalta served to give it recognition. In areas where agreements had been reached, these were confirmed; and in other, more contentious, areas, such as Poland, discord and disagreement were masked by compromise and ambiguity.

The weeks immediately following Yalta saw the continuation of these lines of policy. When the Soviet government intervened in Rumania to secure a change of government, Roosevelt and Churchill refused to do any more than suggest a consultation; that being rejected, they let the matter rest. The President did not think that the crisis in Rumania offered the 'best test case' of western-Soviet relations,[111] and, as the Prime Minister later pointed out: 'If I pressed him [Stalin] too much he might say, "I did not interfere with your action in Greece; why do you not give me the same latitude in Rumania?"... I was sure it would be a mistake to embark on such an argument.'[112]

V

The Yalta accords did not have the full support of the United States administration. A number of important officials in the State Department and elsewhere had opposed the division of Europe into spheres of influence; or, more correctly, wished to deprive the Soviet Union of its sphere in east and south-east Europe. The President and his immediate advisers had disregarded or rejected their advice. Henry Stimson was not at Yalta and the recently-appointed Secretary of State had but little influence. The recommendations and studies submitted by the State Department for the Conference were largely ignored,[113] and the most significant attempt made by that agency to reverse the general understanding on spheres of influence, by giving the Anglo-American members of the Control Commissions in south-east Europe real power, was quickly squashed.

Opposition to the President's policy within the administration was not held back by personal considerations alone. Quite apart from Roosevelt's belief that cooperation with the Soviet Union was a valid course for policy, two other, more concrete factors checked those who urged a less flexible position. They were, first, the fear that a more determined policy might destroy the alliance against the Germans, and second, the concern that an immediate showdown might prejudice Soviet help in the war against Japan. The launching of a political initiative to reduce the Soviet hold on south-east Europe might precipitate a separate peace between Germany and the Soviet Union; and this fear had the very strongest impact, for, as has been seen, the preponderant role of the Soviet Union in the defeat of Germany, and the rather smaller roles of the United States and Britain, gave great benefits to the latter powers, not least in reducing casualties to relatively insignificant figures. And the defeat of Japan, at least until early 1945, appeared to demand not only the invasion of the homeland, with the bitter struggle that that implied, but also the reduction of the Japanese armies in East Asia. In this respect, Soviet help seemed important: if, at the end of the war in Europe, the Soviet Union declared war upon Japan, a most favourable military situation would then unfold.

Even before the death of Roosevelt (April 12, 1945) western-Soviet relations began to fray. The persistent attempts of Germany, even in defeat, to split the allies, had some effect: the removal of forces from the western theatre, where the British and the Americans continued easily to advance, and their addition to the eastern front, where the Red Army was engaged in bitter fighting, led to the suspicion, in Moscow, that the western allies were encouraging this development.*
Again, in March, conversations in Switzerland between British, American and German representatives appeared to imply a breach of the undertaking that no separate surrender talks would be convened, and seemed, to Stalin, to presage a shift of German divisions from Italy to the Soviet front. Roosevelt angrily denied the Soviet charges.†
More significantly the conflict over Poland had recommenced. The Soviet attitude was that those Poles who had signified their opposition to the Yalta accords, and in particular to the provision that the Curzon Line should form the Polish-Russian frontier, were, *ipso facto,* hostile to the Soviet Union, and could not, therefore, be considered as possible members of a Polish government. Since all the members of the exiled, London, government, including its former leader, Mikolajczyk, had placed themselves in that position, they could neither be considered for a place in the government nor be invited to Moscow for consultation with the relevant allied commission. By April 1, Roosevelt had come round to Churchill's view: that any Pole nominated by one of them should be invited to Moscow for consultation.[115] In his last message on the Polish question before the death of Roosevelt, Stalin conceded that any Pole might be consulted, but only if he publicly endorsed the agreements reached at Yalta; and in a closing paragraph he more openly mentioned the substance of the conflict—the preponderance of the Lublin Poles within the postwar government. He offered a similar ratio as had prevailed in Yugoslavia, a preponderance, in practice, of approximately four to one.[116]

With the death of Roosevelt, and the imminent defeat of Germany, two obstacles were removed to the adoption of a policy designed to

---

* In February 1945, 1,675 tanks and assault guns were despatched by the Germans to formations fighting in the east, as against only 67 to those in the west. (C. Wilmot, *The Struggle for Europe,* London 1952, pp. 663–4.)

† Contrary to western assertions at the time, the talks did go into the details of surrender terms, and came very near to what must be termed negotiations. The first notification which the Soviet government received spoke of the Germans arriving in Switzerland to discuss the surrender of the German armed forces in northern Italy.[114]

deny the Soviet Union its sphere of influence in east and south-east Europe, to exclude, indeed, that country from the area; and the accession of a new President, untrained in foreign affairs, ignorant even of the development of the atomic bomb, opened the way for advisers within the State and War Departments and the Moscow embassy to press their counsels. To them, the agreements negotiated at Yalta, two months before, gave the Soviet Union too great a role in Europe and the far east, a role which they wanted to reduce. The American ambassador in Moscow, Averell Harriman, returning to Washington for consultations, found, and reinforced, a hardening attitude to the Soviet prerogatives. To Truman he argued that the west was facing 'a barbarian invasion of Europe': the extension of Soviet control over neighbouring countries meant the death of freedom and the extinction of their independent foreign policies. But the situation was not irretrievable. The United States could have its way on important matters, could secure Soviet concessions, without crippling American-Soviet relations, for the Soviet Union needed help in reconstruction, and would depend for credit on the United States.[117]

The men with whom Harriman consulted had, in general, reached the same conclusion: a firm line with the Soviet government should now be taken. The State Department was fully in accord: Acting Secretary of State Joseph Grew saw in the Soviet actions in Europe and East Asia a drive towards world domination, and recorded his opinion four weeks later that war was certain.[118] Secretary of the Navy James Forrestal, whose fear of Soviet intentions was later to appear as paranoia, was enthusiastically in favour of a tough approach.[119] The President's Chief of Staff agreed with the economic pressures Harriman had in mind, while Henry Stimson feared that too strong a pressure over Poland might cause a break in western-Soviet relations.[120]

At the new President's first meeting with a major Soviet figure, twelve days after the death of Roosevelt, some indication of the new, aggressive, attitude to the Soviet Union, the formal beginning, indeed, of the attempt to reverse the course laid down at Yalta, was given. A few hours before meeting the Soviet Foreign Minister, on his way to the opening meeting of the United Nations, Truman had called in his advisers for a final review of policy. It was on Poland that a showdown would be forced. Whatever the rights or wrongs of Soviet policy in that area (and Admiral Leahy, for one, believed that the Soviet government was acting within the terms of the agreement signed at Yalta[121]); the majority, including Leahy, agreed that the time for hard words and a firm attitude had been reached; that Molotov should be told that it was his country which was breaking the agreements.[122] Leahy later described the mood: 'The consensus of opinion . . . was that the time had arrived to take a strong American attitude towards the Soviet Union. . . .'[123] With this Truman was in complete agreement; he felt that the agreements with the Soviet Union so far had been 'a one-way street' and that he could not continue; 'it was now or never.' If the Russians did not care to cooperate with his plans 'they could go to hell.'[124] The President expressed the same view at the actual meeting with the Soviet Minister in language which was 'not at all diplomatic.'[125]

The final obstacle to those who wished to reverse the basis of the wartime agreements had been the question of Soviet aid in the war against Japan. Too hasty a showdown over European issues might prejudice Soviet action in Manchuria, which, tying down the Emperor's forces there, would facilitate the American invasion of Japan. By mid-April 1945, however, the military planners had concluded that Soviet intervention was no longer necessary, that the American air and naval forces could themselves prevent the reinforcement of the homelands from Manchuria. On April 24, the Joint Chiefs of Staff were advised that 'early Russian entry into the war against Japan is no longer necessary to make invasion feasible.'[126] There being no objection to this report, it was adopted on May 10.[127] With the change of view thus represented, all three barriers to the new policy had been dissolved: Roosevelt's personal inclinations, by his death, the need for an alliance against the Germans, by their surrender in early May, and the desire for Soviet help in the war against Japan, by an altered estimate of the military situation.

Two methods of influencing Soviet policy, of reducing its predominance in areas formerly assigned to it as a sphere of influence, were undertaken. The first stemmed from the belief that the parlous economic state of the Soviet Union, its need for western aid and credit, would make it amenable to western pressure. The practical form of this pressure, the precipitate cutting-off of Lend-Lease aid, failed to take effect. Soviet policy in Poland remained unchanged, Stalin insisting that there could be no agreed decision on the Polish question until the government functioning in Warsaw was accepted as the 'basis' for reorganised Polish government.[128]* The second attempt to influence the Soviet Union was bound up with the position of the allied troops in Germany. The course of the war on the western front had allowed the Anglo-American forces to pass

* Public opinion was roused by the abrupt manner in which aid was cut off, and Truman substituted a modified order, which, in fact, accomplished much the same purpose. Truman has never disclaimed responsibility for the substance of the action, and it is clear that he was thoroughly informed of the impact of the measure on the Soviet Union.[129]

beyond the previously-agreed demarcation line in Germany, the line which still divides Germany today. Churchill pressed first Roosevelt, then Truman, to delay the withdrawal of forces until certain problems in central Europe had been settled, and the latter, at first indecisive, eventually agreed; the new President even suggested a joint message to Stalin linking the troop withdrawals to the solution of the problem of the control of Austria (April 26).[130] In Austria, however, it was the Soviet forces whose position was advantageous, and the western tactics were easily countered: Stalin would not permit the allied control of that country to be established until the British and American forces in Germany were withdrawn. At the beginning of May, complete deadlock was in sight, and Churchill began to urge that the troops be held in position even if Stalin gave way on the Austrian issue; he wrote to Eden on May 4:

> We have several powerful bargaining counters on our side...*the Allies ought not to retreat from their present positions to the occupational line until we are satisfied about Poland, and also about the temporary character of the Russian occupation of Germany, and the conditions to be established in the Russianised or Russian-controlled countries in the Danube valley, particularly Austria and Czechoslovakia, and the Balkans.*[131]

By the middle of May, the deadlock was complete. Truman continued to maintain the American forces in position, and Stalin continued to refuse joint control arrangements in Austria. To those advisers who had urged a firm line on the President, there now seemed no way out, save an immediate conference of the heads of state at which these matters might be thrashed out. That the meeting should be convened as soon as possible was the import of their advice, and to this Churchill lent his weight. He has explained the urgency with which he viewed the matter.

> The main reason why I had been anxious to hasten the date of the meeting was of course the impending retirement of the American Army from the line which it had gained in the fighting to the zone prescribed in the occupation agreement.... Now, while the British and American Armies and Air Forces were still a mighty armed power, and before they melted away under demobilisation and the heavy claims of the Japanese war—now, at the very latest, was the time for a general settlement.[132]

The President did not accept this counsel. His two perhaps most influential advisers were now asking for delay. Henry Stimson, his ageing, authoritative Secretary of War, believed that, far from delay being dangerous, it was positively helpful to the American position: it was his judgment that the atomic bomb, once developed, would add great power to American diplomacy, and that no major issue should be decided before the bomb's role could be accurately assessed.[133] James Byrnes, Truman's nominee for Secretary of State, became no less convinced of the bomb's potentialities; it was he who had first informed the new President of the significance of the atomic project, and the bomb, he explained, might well put the United States in a position to 'dictate' its own terms at the end of the war.[134]

Truman began to refuse requests for an immediate conference with Stalin. Whereas Churchill believed that a meeting was of paramount importance before the western military strength had disappeared, and continued to press this point of view,[135] Truman sought for time: time to forestall a unilateral Soviet solution to the Polish problem, time in which the atomic bomb, the key to heightened western influence, might be tested and demonstrated. The despatch of Harry Hopkins to Moscow was the immediate solution to the problem of delay.

Hopkins was well known as the associate of Roosevelt, was on friendly terms with the Soviet leaders, and might be expected to give the impression in Moscow of a genuinely accommodating approach to the problems of western-Soviet relations. The alteration in American policy, the reversal of tendencies for an immediate showdown with the Soviet Union, was further indicated by the failure to consult the British government, the concealment of the trip, until it was planned and ready, from the State Department, and the continuation of the plan in the face of the solid opposition of both of them.[136] Meeting Stalin at the end of May, Hopkins was able to smooth the course for further negotiations on the Polish issue by making some concession: the Lublin Poles might form the basis of the postwar government. In return, some Poles from London might be admitted, and the new, provisional government would be committed to free elections.

The need to wait until the atomic bomb had been tested and demonstrated was the controlling factor on American diplomacy throughout the summer. The meeting at Potsdam of the heads of state was twice postponed to permit such demonstration, but, despite the accelerated work on the development of the bomb,[137] it became clear, by the end of June, that the bomb could not be tested until mid-July, nor used until early August; could not be demonstrated to the world, that is, until some days after the meeting had taken place. However, once the President knew that the test in New Mexico had been successful (and of this he was informed the day before the first session of the conference on July 17), he was able to present the full range of American demands without, at this stage, revealing the strength available to support them. Those demands centred on an evacuation by the Soviet Union of its sphere of influence. Truman asserted that the Yalta obligations had not been fulfilled; a reorganisation of the governments of Rumania and Bulgaria to include representatives of all democratic elements, and the holding of free elections, was immediately required. Stalin complained to Churchill that he was not meddling in Greek affairs, and it was unjust of the Americans to put forward such demands.[138]

The change in American policy is also revealed in the negotiations on the German problem. At Yalta, harsh terms for Germany had been agreed upon, under which that country would be held accountable for the damage and destruction that had been done. Reparations would be extracted, not on a residual basis, in which other economic priorities would have first call on the available resources, but according to the principles of immediate compensation, the deleterious effect of large withdrawals on the German economy being regarded as of secondary importance. Roosevelt had committed himself to a figure of 20 billion dollars as the basis for discussion on reparations, 50 per cent of which would go to the Soviet Union.[139] In the spring and early summer, however, a different policy took its place. Henry Morgenthau, the proponent of the 'harsh' policy, had been asked to resign, and emphasis was now placed less on the extraction of reparations than on the creation of a strong economy for Germany. In June the American representative on the Reparations Commission withdrew his agreement to a fixed reparations figure, a position confirmed at Potsdam, where Secretary of State Byrnes suggested that the Soviet Union might content itself with what could be extracted from its own zone, plus a small transfer from the western zones.[140] Byrnes linked this offer with two other, extraneous, issues, and told Molotov that 'we would agree to all three or none and that the President and I would leave for the United States the next day'.[141]

And so the conference proceeded. Truman and Byrnes revealed the full extent of the American demands, Stalin and Molotov, not aware of the significance of the weapon soon to be revealed, countered with the repetition of their long-held positions, and deadlock ensued. The President was by no means dismayed, and was eager to leave; his decision of July 23 to end the conference quickly was taken before serious consideration of the main issues in dispute had been undertaken. These issues might be settled in further meetings of the foreign ministers—after the weapon had been demonstrated against Japan.

The decision to use the atomic bomb against Japan was not based on military calculations alone. Indeed, it was those closest to the problems of securing the Japanese defeat whose opinions were either least sought after or ignored. General MacArthur, Supreme Commander of the Allied Forces in the Pacific, was only informed of the weapon five days before its use; his advice was not invited.[142] Admiral Leahy, the Chairman of the Joint Chiefs of Staff, considered, two months before Hiroshima, that the Japanese had already been 'thoroughly defeated' by sea blockade and conventional bombing, and were ready to surrender.[143] Admiral King, Commander-in-Chief, US Fleet, had advised on many occasions that the naval blockade would, in time, starve the enemy into submission, without expending thousands of American lives in a land invasion.[144] The Commanding General of the US Army Air Forces also thought that Japan could be defeated by air assault and blockade, without an American invasion.[145] And General Marshall, representing the Army, gave it as his opinion, in June, that the impact of the promised Russian invasion of Manchuria on the already hopeless Japanese 'may well be the decisive action levering them into capitulation....'[146] The body principally concerned with the use of the atomic bomb, the Interim Committee, had but one military member, who had himself seen only administrative command, and its advisers, in the words of one of them, '... didn't know beans about the military situation in Japan. We didn't know whether they could be caused to surrender by other means or whether the invasion was really inevitable.'[147]

The decision to use the atomic bomb had been made at higher, political level: not in order to defeat Japan with the minimum expenditure of American lives, but in order to induce a Japanese surrender before the forthcoming Soviet invasion of Manchuria had time to take effect. If an immediate surrender could be obtained, the control of Japan in the postwar world, and predominant influence in the Pacific and East Asia, would pertain to the United States alone, untrammelled by Soviet claims to influence. The sudden surrender of Japan, moreover, would underline the immense, atomic, power now at American disposal.

The use of atomic weapons against Japan in early August 1945 had significant effect on the course of European affairs. A new determination of the United States to impose its solutions on the problems of that continent appeared, and correspondingly, and for a time, a new willingness of the Soviet Union to yield. In Germany, Eisenhower and Khukov established amicable relations, and free enterprise, free trade, free travel and free political activity were promoted in the Soviet zone.[148] In Poland, western correspondents were granted unrestricted access, and there seemed every prospect of free elections being held. In Hungary, elections were postponed at the request of the United States, and, when held, were free of intimidation; the Communist Party suffered a defeat. But when the pressure continued, when the attempt was made to reduce the influence of the Soviet Union, to remove its sponsored governments in Rumania and Bulgaria—in defiance of the Churchill-Stalin deal, the armistice agreements and the decisions at the Yalta Conference— concession could go no further, and a new Soviet rigidity appeared. At the London Conference of Foreign Ministers in September, the deadlock was complete: it was impossible even to agree upon a protocol to record the failure.

*   *   *

The twelve months ending in September 1945 had seen the very greatest concentration of diplomatic effort on the affairs of Europe. It was the western powers, however, who had made the running: in the latter half of 1944, with the Italian precedent behind and the countries of western Europe falling safely into western hands, Britain had taken the initiative in the division of south-east Europe, and then engaged in energetic action to safeguard its sphere of influence; and the United States, increasingly confident in world affairs, conscious of the power at its disposal, had set out in early 1945 to secure a division yet more favourable to the west, to push the Soviet Union out of the sphere of influence to which it had been previously assigned. The pressure of the United States, determined, intensive, and supported by the threat of force, met with insignificant success; and in the period of soured relations, amidst the hostility and recriminations with which the later 1940s were imbued, the line of demarcation became hard and fast, an iron curtain as Churchill (and before him Goebbels) had described it. Soon, in the Soviet sphere, moderation was abandoned, the opposition was crushed and the logic of a sphere of influence was carried to the limit. In western and southern Europe too, the governments of the liberated countries initially placed in office, and continually encouraged and supported by the western powers, were soon deprived of any pro-communist complexion which they might once have had. The division of Europe took on a permanent appearance, which twenty years were not lightly to remove.

In the Pacific, no such difficulties could arise. The United States alone supervised the armistice and the postwar administration of Japan; the Pacific islands were taken over by the United States, and have effectively remained in its possession ever since. The chairman of the Senate Foreign Relations Committee described his country's policy in that area in 1945:

> ... If we are in possession of an island which we have conquered from Japan at the cost of blood and treasure we can remain in possession of it, if it is within a strategic area, until we consent to have it go under trusteeship, and when we do agree that it go under

trusteeship, we have the right to stipulate the terms upon which it will go there.... Under our conception, all we have to do is to hold on to them [the Pacific islands] until such time as we need to give them up. I do not think we would want to give them up if they are in strategic areas.[149]

A recipe, one might think, sufficient to justify the Soviet predominance in the strategic areas of east and south-east Europe.

REFERENCES

1. R. Challener, 'The Military Defeat of 1940 in Retrospect', *Modern France,* ed. E. M. Earle, Princeton, 1951, pp. 410–13.

2. An account of the Battle of Dunkirk, and of the German miscalculations, may be found in H. A. Jacobsen, 'Dunkirk 1940', *Decisive Battles of World War II,* ed. Jacobsen and Rohwer, New York, 1965.

3. A. J. P. Taylor has indicated the lack of real alternatives open to the Soviet Union in August 1939: *The Origins of the Second World War,* London, 1961, pp. 262–3.

4. General Franz Halder, *The Halder Diaries,* Infantry Journal, Washington, 1950, IV, p. 117, entry for July 13, 1940.

5. *Fuehrer Conferences on Naval Affairs, 1941,* Admiralty ed., London, 1947, p. 12, entries for January 8–9, 1941.

6. *Fuehrer Conferences on Naval Affairs, 1940,* Admiralty ed., London, 1947, pp. 69–70, entry for July 19, 1940.

7. *Fuehrer Conferences ... 1940,* US ed., Vol. IV, pp. 9–12, quoted in J. M. A. Gwyer and J. R. M. Butler, *Grand Strategy,* III, Part 1 by J. M. A. Gwyer (*History of the Second World War. UK Military Series,* ed. J. R. M. Butler), HMSO, London, 1964, p. 55.

8. *Fuehrer Conferences ... 1940,* Admiralty ed., pp. 81–5; Jodl, quoted in J. M. A. Gwyer, *op. cit.,* p. 56.

9. Karl Klee, 'The Battle of Britain', Jacobsen and Rohwer, *op. cit.,* p. 91.

10. *Fuehrer Conferences ...* Admiralty ed.: *1940,* p. 112; *1941,* p. 4.

11. *Halder Diaries,* entry for January 16, 1941.

12. Klee, *op. cit.,* p. 91.

13. Quoted in Gwyer, *op. cit.,* p. 27.

14. W. S. Churchill, *The Second World War,* II (*Their Finest Hour*), London, 1949, pp. 405–6.

15. Lt-Gen. Sir F. Morgan, *Overture to Overlord,* London, 1950, p. 51.

16. Gwyer, *op. cit.,* pp. 32, 35.

17. *The Unrelenting Struggle. War Speeches by the Rt Hon. Winston S. Churchill,* ed. C. Eade, London, 1942, p. 191.

18. *United States Strategic Bombing Survey* (cited hereafter as *USSBS*), *Oil Division: Final Report,* 2nd ed., Washington, January 1947, p. 18; Gwyer, *op. cit.,* p. 36.

19. *USSBS, Oil Division, loc. cit.; USSBS, Overall Economic Effects Division: Effects of Strategic Bombing on the German War Economy,* Washington, October 1945, p. 275.

20. *USSBS, Oil Division, op. cit.,* pp. 22–3.

21. *USSBS, Overall Economic Effects Division, op. cit.,* p. 148.

22. Maj.-Gen. J. F. C. Fuller, *The Second World War 1939–45. A Strategical and Tactical History,* London, 1948, p. 230.

23. Churchill, *The Second World War,* I (*The Gathering Storm*), London, 1948, p. 325.

24. J. R. M. Butler, *Grand Strategy*, II, London, 1957, pp. 342–4.
25. M. Matloff and E. Snell, *The War Department. Strategic Planning for Coalition Warfare, 1941–2 (The United States Army in World War II*, ed. K. R. Greenfield), GPO, Washington, 1953, pp. 23–4.
26. Churchill, *Their Finest Hour*, p. 223.
27. R. E. Sherwood, *The White House Papers of Harry L. Hopkins*, I (*September 1939–January 1942*), London, 1948, p. 316.
28. Gwyer, *op. cit.*, p. 95.
29. R. J. Sontag and J. S. Beddie (eds.), *Nazi-Soviet Relations 1939–41*, Department of State, Washington, 1948, p. 78.
30. *Ibid.*, pp. 270–1, 277–9.
31. *Halder Diaries*, VI, p. 210, entry for July 8, 1941.
32. *Ibid.*, pp. 264–5, entries for July 21 and 22, 1941.
33. Quoted in Gwyer, *op. cit.*, pp. 103–4.
34. *Halder Diaries*, VI, p. 196, entry for July 3, 1941.
35. *Halder Diaries*, VII, Part 1, p. 36, entry for August 11, 1941.
36. Gwyer, *op. cit.*, pp. 89–90; Sherwood, *op. cit.*, pp. 304–5.
37. Sherwood, *op. cit.*, p. 303.
38. *Ibid.*, p. 317.
39. *Ibid.*, pp. 329–41.
40. H. A. Notter, *Postwar Foreign Policy Preparation 1939–45* (Publication 3580, *General Foreign Policy Series 15*, Department of State), Washington, 1949, p. 50.
41. C. Hull, *Memoirs of Cordell Hull*, London, 1948, II, p. 1166.
42. *Ibid.*, pp. 1168–9.
43. *Ibid.*, p. 1170.
44. M. S. Watson, *The War Department. Chief of Staff: Prewar Plans and Preparations (United States Army in World War II)*, Washington, 1950, pp. 400–10.
45. *Ibid.*, pp. 407–8.
46. Quoted in Gwyer, *op. cit.*, p. 143.
47. Sherwood, *op. cit.*, p. 314.
48. H. L. Stimson and McG. Bundy, *On Active Service in Peace and War*, New York, 1947, pp. 419–23.
49. H. A. DeWeerd, 'Marshall, Organiser of Victory', *Infantry Journal*, Washington, LV, 1 Jan. 1947 (cited in Higgins, *op. cit.* (p. 94 above), p. 152).
50. E. J. King and W. M. Whitehill, *Fleet Admiral King. A Naval Record*, London, 1953, p. 189.
51. H. C. Butcher, *Three Years With Eisenhower*, London, 1946, p. 9.
52. Stimson and McG. Bundy, *op. cit.*, pp. 425–6; M. Matloff, *The War Department. Strategic Planning for Coalition Warfare, 1943–4 (United States Army in World War II)*, Washington, 1959, pp. 13–14.
53. Churchill, *The Second World War*, IV (*The Hinge of Fate*), pp. 667–72.
54. *Ibid.*, Appendix C, p. 832, Memos of March 3 and 4, 1943, Prime Minister to Ismay.
55. Higgins, *op. cit.*, pp. 166, 183–4; R. M. Leighton and R. W. Coakley, *The War Department. Global Logistics and Strategy, 1940–3 (United States Army in World War II)*, Washington, 1955, pp. 682–6; H. D. Hall, *North American Supply*, London, 1955, pp. 357–8.
56. Higgins, *op. cit.*, p. 180.
57. Sherwood, *op. cit.*, II, pp. 581–2.
58. Churchill, *The Second World War*, III (*The Grand Alliance*), p. 409. Churchill's italics.

59. *Ibid.*, p. 414.

60. Von Runstedt, quoted in Von Blumentritt, *Von Runstedt*, London, 1952, p. 161; see also pp. 158–60, 122, 127; B. H. Liddell Hart, *The Other Side of the Hill*, London, 1948, p. 245.

61. Von Blumentritt, *op. cit.*, pp. 135–8, 144–7; *cf.* R. Ingersoll, *Top Secret*, London, 1946, p. 72.

62. G. A. Harrison, *The European Theatre of Operations. Cross-Channel Attack (United States Army in World War II)*, Washington, 1951, p. 141; Churchill, *The Hinge of Fate*, p. 431 (cf. Von Blumentritt, *op. cit.*, pp. 131, 177–81); Liddell Hart, *op. cit.*, p. 241.

63. Harrison, *op. cit.*, pp. 146–7.

64. Von Blumentritt, *op. cit.*, pp. 168–74.

65. *USSBS, Overall Economic Effects Division, op. cit.*, p. 6.

66. Churchill, *The Grand Alliance*, Appendix J, pp. 765, 453.

67. Higgins, *op. cit.*, pp. 186–7.

68. D. D. Eisenhower, *Crusade in Europe*, London, 1948, p. 51.

69. H. Feis, *Churchill. Roosevelt. Stalin. The War They Waged and the Peace They Sought*, Princeton, 1957, p. 172.

70. *Ibid.*, pp. 183–95.

71. C. R. S. Harris, *Allied Military Administration of Italy 1943–1945 (History of the Second World War*, ed. Butler), London, 1957, p. 116.

72. Harris, *op. cit.*, p. 117.

73. *Ibid.*, pp. 382–3.

74. *Ibid.*, p. 37.

75. *Ibid.*, p. 92.

76. *Ibid.*, pp. 141–3.

77. A good, brief account of the campaign on the eastern front will be found in B. H. Liddell Hart, *The Soviet Army*, London, 1956, pp. 100–26.

78. Alexander Werth, *Russia At War, 1941–45*, London, 1964, p. 542. (A German source gives a rather smaller figure: W. Görlitz, 'The Battle for Stalingrad, 1942–43,' Jacobsen and Rohwer, *op. cit.*, p. 243.)

79. Werth, *op. cit.*, p. 496.

80. Liddell Hart, *The Soviet Army*, p. 122; Eisenhower, *Crusade in Europe*, p. 317.

81. Hull, *op. cit.*, p. 1455.

82. L. Woodward, *British Foreign Policy in the Second World War*, London, 1962, pp. 307–8; Churchill, *The Second World War*, V (*Triumph and Tragedy*), pp. 198–204; Hull, *op. cit.*, pp. 1455–8, Sherwood, *op. cit.*, II, pp. 825–6.

83. Feis, *op. cit.*, pp. 449–51.

84. *The Times*, London, April 17, 1945.

85. House of Commons, April 5, 1944: 398 *House of Commons Debates*, 5s, p. 1978.

86. Churchill, *Triumph and Tragedy*, p. 252.

87. House of Commons, January 18, 1945: 407, *House of Commons Debates*, 5s, p. 398.

88. Armistice with Rumania, September 12, 1944, Article 18; *A Decade of American Foreign Policy. Basic Documents, 1941–49*, Senate Committee on Foreign Relations, Washington, 1950, p. 485; Feis, *op. cit.*, pp. 415–16.

89. Armistice with Bulgaria, October 28, 1944, Article 18; *A Decade of American Foreign Policy*, p. 485; Armistice with Hungary, January 20, 1945, Article 18; *A Decade of American Foreign Policy*, p. 497.

90. Churchill, *Triumph and Tragedy*, p. 204.

91. *Ibid.*, pp. 488, 550.
92. Feis, *op. cit.*, pp. 415–17.
93. *Ibid.*, p. 521.
94. Churchill, *The Grand Alliance*, p. 342.
95. Feis, *op. cit.*, p. 253.
96. G. Deborin, *The Second World War. A Politico-Military Survey*, ed. I. Zubkov, Moscow, 1964, p. 54.
97. Feis, *op. cit.*, pp. 122–3.
98. *Ibid.*, p. 285.
99. February 22, 1944. 397 *House of Commons Debates*, 5s, p. 698.
100. S. Mikolajczyk, *The Rape of Poland. Pattern of Soviet Aggression*, New York, 1948, p. 60.
101. P. E. Mosely, *The Kremlin and World Politics. Studies in Soviet Policy and Action*, New York, 1960, p. 137.
102. Feis, *op. cit.*, pp. 367–8.
103. Stimson and McG. Bundy, *op. cit.*, p. 567.
104. Yalta Conference, Protocol of Proceedings, Declaration on Liberated Europe. *A Decade of American Foreign Policy*, p. 29.
105. *Foreign Relations of the United States: The Conferences at Malta and Yalta 1945*, US Department of State, Washington, 1955, pp. 97–108.
106. *Postwar Foreign Policy Preparation 1939–1945*, US Department of State, Washington, 1949, p. 394.
107. Statement by the three heads of state, Part VI, Poland, quoted in E. R. Stettinius, *Roosevelt and the Russians. The Yalta Conference*, London, 1950, Appendix, pp. 299–300.
108. *A Decade of American Foreign Policy*, p. 30.
109. Statement by three heads of state, Part II, quoted in Stettinius, *op. cit.*, p. 296.
110. Quoted in C. E. Black, 'Soviet Policy in Eastern Europe', *The Annals of the American Academy of Political and Social Science*, May 1949, p. 155.
111. J. F. Byrnes, *Speaking Frankly*, London, 1947, p. 53.
112. Churchill, *Triumph and Tragedy*, p. 369.
113. Byrnes, *op. cit.*, p. 23; J. C. Crew, *Turbulent Era. A Diplomatic Record of Forty Years, 1904–1945*, London, 1953, II, p. 1444.
114. See *Correspondence Between the Chairman of the Council of Ministers of the USSR and the Presidents of the USA and the Prime Minister of Great Britain During the Great Patriotic War of 1941–1945*, Moscow, 1957 (London, 1958), II, p. 297; Feis, *op. cit.*, pp. 585–94; G. Alperovitz, *Atomic Diplomacy: Hiroshima and Potsdam*, New York, 1965, pp. 258–9; *New York Times*, July 14, 1964.
115. Churchill, *Triumph and Tragedy*, pp. 371–2; Stalin, *Correspondence . . .* pp. 201–4.
116. *Ibid.*, pp. 211–13.
117. H. S. Truman, *The Memoirs of Harry S. Truman*, I (*Year of Decisions* 1945), London, 1955, pp. 73–4. Elsewhere, Harriman wrote of the 'enormous plans' for industrial expansion, which the Russians wanted the USA to finance (W. Millis (ed.), *The Forrestal Diaries. The Inner History of the Cold War*, London, 1952, p. 57).
118. Alperovitz, *op. cit.*, p. 26; J. C. Grew, *Turbulent Era. A Diplomatic Record of Forty Years, 1904–1945*, London, 1953, II, p. 1446.
119. *Forrestal Diaries*, pp. 65–6.
120. Truman, *op. cit.*, pp. 80–2; *Forrestal Diaries*, p. 65.
121. Truman, *op. cit.*, p. 81; *Forrestal Diaries*, p. 66.

122. Truman, *op. cit.*, p. 82; *Forrestal Diaries*, p. 66.

123. W. D. Leahy, *I Was There*, London, 1950, p. 411.

124. *Forrestal Diaries*, p. 65.

125. Leahy, *op.cit.*, p. 413.

126. *The Entry of the Soviet Union into the War against Japan: Military Plans, 1941–1945*, US Department of Defense, Washington, 1955, p. 67.

127. *Ibid.*, p. 68.

128. Stalin, *Correspondence*... II, p. 232.

129. See Alperovitz, *op. cit.*, pp. 35–9.

130. Truman, *op. cit.*, p. 133; Churchill, *Triumph and Tragedy*, pp. 450–1; Stalin, *Correspondence*... II, pp. 337–8; Feis, *op. cit.*, pp. 633–5.

131. Churchill, *Triumph and Tragedy*, p. 439. Churchill's italics.

132. *Ibid.*, p. 522.

133. Truman, *op. cit.*, pp. 90–1; Alperovitz, pp. 49–61. The closing pages of this essay are indebted to the light which Alperovitz has thrown upon the diplomacy of mid-1945, and the effect of the atomic bomb upon it.

134. Truman, *op. cit.*, p. 90.

135. Churchill, *Triumph and Tragedy*, pp. 520–4; Stalin, *Correspondence*... I, pp. 360–3. Note the desperate tone of Churchill's message of June 1: '... I consider that July 15th, repeat July, the month after June, is much too late for the urgent questions that demand attention between us.... I have proposed June 15th, repeat June, the month before July, but if that is not possible why not July 1st, July 2nd, or July 3rd?' (*Ibid.*, p. 362.)

136. Woodward, *op. cit.*, p. 512; Truman, *op. cit.*, p. 178.

137. Truman, *op. cit.*, p. 345; *In the Matter of J. Robert Oppenheimer. Hearings before Personnel Security Board, April 12-May 6, 1954*, US Atomic Energy Commission, Washington, 1954, pp. 31–3.

138. Churchill, *Triumph and Tragedy*, p. 550.

139. *Foreign Relations of the United States: The Conferences at Malta and Yalta 1945*, US Department of State, Washington, 1955, p. 983.

140. *Foreign Relations: Conference of Berlin (Potsdam) 1945*, US Department of State, Washington, 1960, I, pp. 522–3.

141. *Ibid.*, II, p. 510; J. F. Byrnes, *op. cit.*, p. 85.

142. F. Knebel and C. Bailey, *No High Ground. The Inside Story of the Men Who Planned and Dropped the First Atomic Bomb*, London, 1960, pp. 73, 142.

143. Leahy, *op. cit.*, pp. 449, 513–14.

144. King and Whitehill, *op. cit.*, pp. 382, 389.

145. W. F. Craven and J. Cate, *The Army Air Forces in World War II*, V (*The Pacific: Matterhorn to Nagasaki, June 1944 to August 1945*), Chicago, 1953, p. 749.

146. *Conference of Berlin*, I, p. 905.

147. *In the Matter of J. Robert Oppenheimer*, p. 34.

148. Alperovitz, *op. cit.*, p. 201.

149. *Hearings on the Charter of the United Nations, July 9–13*, Senate Foreign Relations Committee, Washington, 1945, p. 315.

A Conservative Critique of Containment

Senator Taft on the Early Cold War Program

HENRY W. BERGER

I

FOR the past twenty years American foreign policy has been conducted essentially along ideological and practical lines established by the Truman Doctrine in 1947. The content of that message made quite clear the international outlook developed by key United States policy-makers after World War II. In delivering his address on 'the gravity of the situation,' President Harry Truman declared 'that it must be the policy of the United States to support free peoples who are resisting attempted subjugation by armed minorities or by outside pressure.'[1] The President thus initiated a far-reaching policy which ultimately involved military, political and economic programs by the United States throughout the world on behalf of 'freedom, economic stability, and orderly political processes,'[2] or, in less ideological terms, to maintain the social, political and economic *status quo* within the western orbit.

Though certain limited aspects of this postwar outlook had appeared before 1947 in American actions in China, south-east Asia and Iran, it was the Truman Doctrine and the events surrounding the Greek-Turkish crisis (the immediate reason for the President's declaration) which signalled the larger and more permanent policy. The message thus became the basic formula for future United States commitments abroad.

The significance of the Doctrine was three-fold. First, it bypassed the United Nations and announced a unilateral American approach to matters considered vital to United States interests. Second, it proclaimed the now familiar containment thesis against radicalism in general and communism in particular.* Third, it invoked the domino

* George Frost Kennan, author of the famous 'containment' article in *Foreign Affairs*, XXV, July 1947, pp. 566–82, opposed the tone and the specific recommendations of the Truman Doctrine message when he saw it. His own views appear to have been an attempt at a somewhat more

theory, though not by that specific name. If Greece 'fell,' it was argued, the middle east and Europe would then be in danger. 'It is necessary only to glance at the map,' declared the President, 'to realise that the survival and integrity of the Greek nation are of grave importance in a much wider situation. If Greece should fall under the control of an armed minority, the effect upon its neighbor, Turkey, would be immediate and serious. Confusion and disorder might well spread throughout the entire Middle East. Moreover,' Truman added, 'the disappearance of Greece as an independent state would have a profound effect upon those countries in Europe whose peoples are struggling against great difficulties to maintain their freedom and their independence while they repair the damages of war.'[3]

There is little doubt that those making policy at the time realised the considerable importance of both the crisis and the official response to it. It was not just an abstract fidelity to freedom which governed the American decision to extend its power and influence abroad. The definition of American domestic security was enlarged to the world arena. 'If we falter in our leadership,' warned the President to Congress, 'we may endanger the peace of the world—and we shall surely endanger the welfare of our nation.'[4] Senator Arthur Vandenberg, a leading Republican from Michigan and chairman of the Senate Foreign Relations Committee, announced bipartisan support for the policy precisely on grounds of American security. 'The independence of Greece and Turkey must be preserved, not only for their own sakes but also in defense of peace and security for all of us.'[5]

The sense of crisis in these terms was also keenly felt in the State Department. Joseph Jones, a diplomatic officer who played a major role in the drafting of both the Truman Doctrine and Marshall Plan addresses, revealed his own thoughts on the matter some two weeks before Truman's message to Congress in a letter to William Benton, Assistant Secretary of State for Public Affairs.[6]

'There are many signs that the world is approaching this year the greatest crisis since the turn in the tide of the war in November 1942,' he wrote. 'It is primarily an economic crisis centered in Britain and Empire, France, Greece, and China. . . . If these areas are allowed to spiral downwards into economic anarchy,' warned Jones, 'then at best they will drop out of the United States orbit and try an independent nationalistic policy; at most they will swing into the Russian

---

limited response to the Soviet Union. Kennan actually wrote the *Foreign Affairs* piece in 1946 *before* the Truman Doctrine was conceived. It of course became a key document which American policy-makers used as they saw fit to justify or rationalise their acts *after* 1947. See Kennan's recent testimony on the containment policy and his role in fashioning it in *The Vietnam Hearings*, New York, 1966, esp. pp. 129–35.

orbit. We will then face the world alone. What will be the cost, in dollars and cents, of our armaments and of our economic isolation? I do not see how we could possibly avoid a depression far greater than that of 1929–1932 and crushing taxes to pay for the direct commitments we would be forced to make around the world.'

The Truman Doctrine seemed to Jones as well as to others in the State Department to provide the instrument to prevent the catastrophe he feared. Jones of course approved the contents of the message he had helped to draft and he saw it as a definitive benchmark in the way American foreign policy functioned. 'It seemed to me as though it marked our passing into adulthood in the conduct of foreign affairs,' he concluded.

II

The forceful manner and speed with which the Truman administration acted during the Greek-Turkish crisis and the bipartisan support which the Doctrine received were indeed impressive developments. But the message and the policy were not without domestic critics and sceptics. Historians have tended to neglect such critics and have chosen instead to emphasise the favourable consensus towards the policy or have dismissed the opposing arguments as either pro-communist or isolationist in nature. This is a misleading judgment.

There were a number of Americans who took issue with the world-wide commitment which the Doctrine represented and who vigorously objected to the unilateral American approach which simply ignored the United Nations and which correctly forecast the future permanent tendency of this kind of action by the United States. Newspaper columnists Walter Lippmann and Marquis Childs stressed these points in their written editorials.[8] Journalists Stewart Alsop and Anne O'Hare McCormick expressed considerable concern about the possibility of war with the Soviet Union and warned of continuing crises as a result of the American policy, while Robert Conway, foreign correspondent for the *New York Daily News,* called the royalist regime which the United States was supporting in Greece one of the most repressive in history.[9] Many of these same sentiments were, of course, echoed by former Secretary of Commerce Henry A. Wallace who demanded a drastically reformed Greek social and political system as a condition for United States assistance.[10]

Criticism of the Truman Doctrine, however, was by no means limited to Wallace and members of the press. There were also expressions of doubt and opposition from within the United States Congress and such criticism came from both liberal *and* conservative politicians. Senator Claude Pepper (Democrat, Florida), the eloquent dissenting Southerner, declared that the Truman Doctrine was in complete defiance of the United Nations and that the authoritarian nature of the existing governments of both Greece and Turkey left the whole argument of assistance for freedom seriously open to question.[11] Pepper's critique was repeated in even stronger terms by congressmen such as Senator George Malone, conservative Republican from Nevada, the even more conservative Harry Byrd, Democratic Senator from Virginia, Senator Edwin Johnson (Democrat, Colorado), and Representatives George Bender (Republican, Ohio), John Folger (Democrat, North Carolina), John A. Blatnik (Democrat, Minnesota), Adolf Sabath (Democrat, Illinois), Adam Clayton Powell, Jr (Democrat, New York) and Chet Holified (Democrat, California).[12] Each of these men, along with other congressional figures, declined to support the appropriations for the Truman programme.[13]

But one of the most important critics of the President's foreign policy in Congress was the influential Senator from Ohio, Robert A. Taft. A leading contender for his party's presidential nomination four times between 1940 and 1952 and most certainly the chief Republican conservative in Congress, Senator Taft emerged as a leading opponent of American foreign policy. Even though he voted in the end for the Greek-Turkish appropriations, the Ohio Senator raised significant questions about the Truman Doctrine at the time and came increasingly thereafter to object to the broader policy which followed. His was, in fact, a classic conservative critique of the containment policy.

Senator Taft has often been regarded as an isolationist in American foreign relations. That characterisation is distorted and misleading. It is understandable however that such an image of Taft has existed. Because the term 'internationalist' in recent American history has come to mean support of commitments abroad, alliances with other nations such as the North Atlantic Treaty Organisation (NATO), the South-East Asian Treaty Organisation (SEATO), and the Baghdad Pact (CENTO), and positive efforts to exert American power overseas, many who deviate from that definition are regarded as isolationist or neo-isolationist. Hence Senator Taft was so labelled.[14] In reality he was neither. For in fact he did not oppose *all* American commitments abroad, *all* alliances with other nations, or the extension of *all* American power beyond the United States. What he did was to question quite frequently the assumptions and objectives which policy-makers held about America's actions in the postwar world and thus the *way* the United States engaged in overseas activities. Because of his apprehensions about these matters, he was often cast in the role of negative critic and this did much to create the image of isolationism with which he is associated.

Senator Taft's first reaction to the proposed Greek-Turkish aid bill came on March 12, 1947, the day of the President's speech. Taft indicated approval for relief loans to Greece and Turkey but raised important questions about the President's request to send armaments and military missions to Greece. He remarked that this might be an attempt to 'secure a special domination over the affairs of these countries' and that such action 'was similar to Russia's demands for domination in her sphere of influence. If we assume a special position in Greece and Turkey,' he warned, 'we can hardly longer reasonably object to the Russians continuing their domination in Poland, Yugoslavia, Rumania, and Bulgaria.'[15]

Only six months earlier, in September 1946, Henry A. Wallace, then still Secretary of Commerce (and a political opponent of Taft), had provoked a crisis in the Truman administration when he opposed American attempts to deny a Soviet sphere of influence in eastern Europe. 'On our part,' Wallace admonished, 'we shall recognise that we have not more business in the *political* affairs of Eastern Europe than Russia has in the *political* affairs of Latin America, Western Europe, and the United States. . . . Whether we like it or not, the Russians will try to socialise their sphere of influence just as we try to democratise our sphere of influence.'[16]

Senator Taft did not then agree with Wallace's definition of spheres of influence which would result in Soviet control over eastern Europe, but neither did he agree that the United States ought to assume hegemony over Greece and Turkey. To him it seemed that such a course of action represented a double standard of conduct by the United States. Moreover, he asked whether the policy might not provoke a war with the Soviet Union. 'I want to know,' he inquired, 'what our top military people think of the possibility that Russia will go to war if we carry out this program, just as we might be prompted to go to war if Russia tried to force a Communist Government on Cuba.'[17]

By the time the aid bill came to the Senate floor for a vote a month later, Taft announced that he would support the programme in its entirety. This he did because of his belief that the national interest was at stake, because he hoped the measure would be a limited, temporary action, because he was apparently satisfied that war would be avoided, and because he believed that President Truman had virtually committed the country to the program before Congress had even acted on it. Indeed, the commitment was more than rhetorical on the part of administration officials. It was announced on March 19, a week after Truman's address to Congress, that a naval-air task force would visit the ports of Greece and Turkey in the spring.[18] On April 11, Taft made a lengthy statement on the President's aid requests. 'I intend to vote for the Greek and Turkish loans,' he affirmed, 'for the reason that the President's announcements have committed the United States to this policy in the eyes of the world, and to repudiate it now would destroy his prestige in the negotiations with the Russian Government, on the success of which ultimate peace depends.'[19]*

Taft made it quite clear, however, that he did not view the aid program as a permanent institution, quickly separated the economic loans from the military assistance, and indicated his approval of both as a contribution to peace. 'In so far as the loans are for reconstruction and rehabilitation,' he remarked, 'we are only doing what we have done elsewhere. In so far as they help preserve order, I think they must be justified as a means of maintaining the status quo during the period while the basis for peace is being worked out.'[20]

In giving his qualified support to the program, the Ohio Senator was not acting under any illusions about the nature of the Greek government which was then engaged in widespread civil war. Taft wrote later that 'in Greece we moved in with overwhelming support for the Greek Government, even though it at first had strong reactionary tendencies.'[21] The regime to which the United States offered support in the cause of freedom was a right-wing monarchy which had established the Metaxas Fascist dictatorship before World War II. Recognition of this fact in addition to his belief that the Truman proposals should not constitute permanent involvement prompted Taft to advise that the United States 'withdraw [from Greece] whenever a Government representing the majority of the people requests us to do so, and whenever the United Nations finds that action taken or assistance furnished by it makes the continuance of our assistance undesirable.'[22]

III

In the years which followed the Truman Doctrine, the United States extended its activities abroad. As it did so, Senator Taft increasingly took issue with specific policies and for a variety of reasons. His alternatives were not always clear and at times were even contradictory. Yet a set of rather well-defined ideas about American society and about foreign policy constituted the core of his criticisms. His expressions also revealed an acute awareness of the connection which

* The negotiations with the Russians to which Taft referred were the Big Four Conferences of Foreign Ministers in Moscow, March and April 1947 to arrange peace treaties for Germany and Austria.

policy-makers made between domestic and foreign policy. Taft's critique was also made on that basis.

The Ohio Republican strongly believed in what he often called 'the American way of life.' He was convinced that the strength and vitality of the American system depended upon a free economy, political democracy, and the preservation of national independence. Liberty was the touchstone of the political economy which he felt the nation ought to perfect and protect at home. By doing this the United States would become an influential exemplar to the world.

Given this confidence in the system, it is hardly surprising that Senator Taft insisted that the resolution of America's problems had to be made in America and was concerned that the United States might undertake obligations overseas which would evade those problems or compromise the system itself. He was especially fearful too that such obligations would result in an excessive tax burden for the American people in order to pay for increased foreign expenditures. This would not only mean a larger federal government, which he opposed, but would also risk domestic economic and political freedom.

These aspects of Taft's domestic philosophy influenced his view of foreign affairs. Consequently the Senator opposed many foreign policy measures and voiced strong reservations about others which he reasoned might increase chances for depression, war or private and public oligarchy. It was these fears which explain more than anything else Taft's attitude about postwar American foreign policy and why he appeared as a critic of the policies which came after the announcement of the Truman Doctrine.

In view of Taft's firm belief in the strength of the American system at home, it is not difficult to understand why he opposed such measures as reciprocal trade agreements and why he issued warnings about foreign loans and economic investment by the United States abroad. He did so on the grounds that the home market was the key to American prosperity, and because he was unconvinced that foreign trade and investment increased employment (as argued so vehemently by the proponents of reciprocity).[23] He strongly suggested that it was a reliance upon the export of capital that had contributed heavily to the depression of 1929. At that time, he pointed out, an abnormal export market had been stimulated by private credit, and then observed that government credit was creating a similar situation in the present with the danger that another crisis would result.[24]

Taft was also concerned that private or public expansionist policies might assume the economic and political characteristics of imperialism. Such a development, he believed, would undercut the example that America should present to the world, and might also lead to war.

Taft was particularly concerned about the latter possibility, because wars wasted economic and human resources, increased the concentration of power in the hands of government, severely limited individual liberty, and tended to produce crises from which the system might never recover.[25]

Taft's concern about excessive economic investment overseas reflected his moral and philosophical dislike of imperialism and, more importantly, his fear that imperialism would result in conflict. Such economic expansion, he explained in 1949, would constitute a threat to peace because it was 'likely to build up hostility to us rather than any genuine friendship. It is easy to slip into an attitude of imperialism and to entertain the idea that we know what is good for other people better than they know themselves. From there it is an easy step to the point where war becomes an instrument of public policy rather than the last resort to maintain our liberty.' This, he insisted, was alien to the American way of life.[26]

Because Taft feared the domestic consequences of war, he persistently argued after World War II that the United States 'cannot and should not go to war with Russia.' He also maintained that the preservation of peace was a necessary condition for the success of foreign policy objectives.[27] Because of this Taft said that he could support the Marshall Plan of economic aid to Europe only if it did not risk the start of a war. He warned that the proposed aid would leave the United States open to charges of interference and imperialism.[28] For that reason he advised that aid should be confined to specific needs, sent to areas where it would accomplish a specific purpose, and that it should be given with the understanding that it was the countries themselves which would have to achieve their economic salvation.[29]

Taft justified support for the Marshall Plan only because he felt that it was in the American tradition to assist others in time of deprivation, and because the assistance 'might help us in the battle against Communism.'[30] He admitted that the risks (and the charges) of imperialism and war had to be taken in light of the communist threat, but he added that the whole theory behind the Marshall Plan rested upon the assumption that the Russians did not contemplate aggressive war.[31]

This statement was a significant aspect of Taft's foreign policy. He believed that the struggle against communism was ideological rather than military. While opposing further extension of Russian power into Europe, Taft came to accept a Soviet sphere of influence in eastern Europe and opposed military action against Russia when the Czech coup occurred in 1948. 'I know of no indication,' he said, 'of Russian intention to undertake military aggression beyond the sphere of influence which was originally assigned to them. The situation in Czechoslovakia was indeed a tragic one,' he acknowledged, 'but Russian influence has dominated there since the end of the war.'[32] He openly attacked the military hysteria over the Czech situation which surrounded the debate on the Marshall Plan. 'There's no sense in our having voted the Marshall Plan if there is going to be a war. All this was based on the assumption of peace.' The real contest with Russia, he asserted, was an ideological one. 'That's why I supported the Marshall Plan.'[33]

Senator Taft reiterated these views on various other occasions, and the debate on the North Atlantic Pact of 1949 and the subsequent dispatch of American troops to Europe in 1951 served to dramatise his views. He argued that such acts accentuated Russian fears of encirclement by the west, and warned that such fears might well provoke the Soviet Union into aggression. He again denied that Russia was already committed to military conflict with the west. On the contrary, he maintained that the Atlantic Pact would lessen the chances for peace. 'I cannot vote for a treaty which, in my opinion, will do far more to bring about a third world war than it will ever maintain the peace of the world.'[34] 'We must proceed on the assumption that war is possible, but that peace is also possible,' he explained. 'We must establish a system which we can maintain for 5 or 10 years without turning this country into a garrison state, abandoning all the other ideals of life and surrendering all the freedoms which have made America what it is today.'[35]

It was obvious that Taft's concern for the economic well-being of the United States was an element in his opposition to the kind of military obligations he envisioned as implicit in the Atlantic Pact. He argued that 'our economic health is essential to the battle against Communism and ... arms should be sent only to a country really threatened by Russian military aggression.'[36] If nations invested heavily in arms they would decrease their standard of living. Countries 'must choose between guns and butter,' he said.[37]

As an alternative policy, Taft emphasised a military defence posture based on air and sea power. This argument was based on his belief that such an alternative would be less likely to provoke war than massed armies. 'We wish to find the policies which will deter Russia from military aggression,' he countenanced, 'and at the same time will not be so provocative themselves as to give Russia a sound reason for such aggression.'[38] He joined this strategic concept to a proposal that the United States issue a warning to the Soviet Union, in the style of the Monroe Doctrine, that the United States would respond militarily *if* the Russians attacked western Europe.[39]

*   *   *

IV

Senator Taft's views on Asia seemed at first glance contradictory to his position vis-à-vis Europe. He seemed to assume a more militant stance with respect to military involvement there and seemed to be prepared to take stronger measures on behalf of American interests. Taft considered Asia a vital area to the security of the United States because of its economic resources and its strategic importance. He considered Asia more important to the peace of the United States than Europe, and was concerned about the advance of communism there because conditions were very unstable and ripe for radical revolutions which he certainly opposed. He also felt that the defeat of Japan in World War II and the collapse of China to the communists had destroyed the balance of power which had heretofore existed in that region between those two countries and the Soviet Union. He attacked the Roosevelt administration for allowing Russia to acquire 'wide interests in Manchuria and the best half of Korea, to say nothing of the Kurile Islands and the Japanese half of Sakhalin.'[40]

Taft had supported Chiang Kai-shek in China and was bitterly disappointed at the defeat of the Nationalist regime and at what he termed the failure of the Truman administration to give more vigorous assistance to Chiang. Such a policy of extended American aid would seem to have conflicted with Taft's many concerns about American involvement abroad. He himself reflected the dilemma when he refused to advocate the use of American ground forces in China.

After the fall of China, and the retreat of Chiang Kai-shek to Formosa, Taft insisted that 'we should take steps to see that the Communists do not cross over into Formosa and I would use the Navy to keep them out if necessary.'[41]

Although Taft's position seemed more defensive than offensive in this last regard, he was not opposed to American material assistance to the Chinese Nationalists in efforts by them to regain control of the mainland 'so long as it does not involve the use of American troops on the mainland.'[42] When asked if he did not believe that such an action might not bring Russia into war, Taft answered, 'Absolutely not. What does Russia care about a local war in Communist China? I should think they [the Russians] would be so much more concerned about American air bases in Turkey and Norway and Britain, which they regard as a direct threat against Russia itself. There's no threat to Russia in a civil war in South China.'[43]

When the Korean War began in June 1950, Senator Taft supported American intervention but insisted that the President's action in sending troops into Korea 'was a usurpation of authority in the making of war.'[44] He chastised the Truman administration for not making it clear to the communists earlier that an attack on Korea would mean retaliation by the United States—just as he advocated similar warnings to Russia with respect to Europe.[45] The extent to which Taft was willing to risk all-out war in Asia in order to stop the communists became clearest in his approval of American air attacks on Manchuria and South China after the Chinese communists entered the Korean War. He was fully aware that bombing Manchuria and China 'might bring Russia into the war. But it's a risk to take if we're to bring the war to a close in Korea.' In any event, he argued *and* rationalised that the United States had done many things in Europe—such as the establishment of the Atlantic Pact and the arming of Germany—'which the Russians may regard as threatening their security. I cannot see that any bombing of China without invasion can be regarded in any way by Russia as an aggressive move against Russia itself, or a reason for war.'[46]

In the final analysis, however, it is important to understand that Taft did not view the communist threat as primarily military in nature. He was far more concerned with what he considered the ideological threat of communism and urged the nation to respond to this challenge. 'I do believe we should oppose any Russian aggression,' he had said in 1947. 'We should not make any concessions to the Russians on vital matters. Of course,' he then pointedly remarked, 'I am optimistic that they [the Russians] are far more concerned in spreading their ideology than in utilising their military force. I am hopeful that we don't face a war.'[47]

V

In retrospect, several aspects of Senator Taft's critique of postwar American foreign policy are very relevant. Particularly important was his assessment of Soviet intentions vis-à-vis western Europe as opposed to the official version offered to the American public. The notion of a poised Russian military force ready to spring upon a defenceless western Europe following World War II has been a cherished and established myth. Only the 'toughness' of the Truman Doctrine, the generosity of the Marshall Plan, and the prudent strength of NATO prevented the Russian offensive, or so goes the myth. Senator Taft, as has been shown, doubted the validity of this contention.

What is curious about the myth, however, is that *very few*, if any, responsible American officials actually believed in it at the time it was created. That this is so has been confirmed since by several historians and public figures. Among the historians, D. F. Fleming, William A. Williams, Gar Alperovitz, John Lukacs and David Horowitz have each argued persuasively that there was in fact no such Russian offensive threat to western Europe after the war, and several of these authors then offer the testimony of American policy-makers who held this same view at the time.[48]

Thus, Secretary of State James Byrnes (in office from July 1945 to late January 1947) doubted that the Russians intended a military or political threat beyond eastern Europe.[49] His judgment was shared by other officials such as John Foster Dulles, who was a member of the United States delegation to meetings of the Council of Foreign Ministers in 1946 and 1947, Secretary of Defense James Forrestal, and General Walter Bedell Smith, Ambassador to the Soviet Union.[50]

Perhaps most significant of all has been the verdict of George Frost Kennan who, it will be recalled, raised serious objections to the Truman Doctrine at the time it was pronounced. Kennan became increasingly aware that policies very often assume a life of their own and substitute a mythical reality for the truth. So it was with his own statement on containment, and he feared the awful consequences of the erroneous use which policy-makers had made of his 1947 analysis then and after.

Kennan's concern about this was first publicly revealed in the Reith Lectures delivered over the British Broadcasting Corporation network in England in 1956. He tried to puncture the myth concerning Soviet military intentions and criticised the 'over-rating of the likelihood of a Soviet effort to invade Western Europe.'[51] Still later, Kennan admitted that the myth of a Russian juggernaut after World War II was not believed by responsible officials.*

Indeed, several students of the period have concluded that many policy-makers were far less concerned about Soviet threats to western Europe and more interested in placing pressure upon the Russians to retire from eastern Europe.[52] Such a policy, it has been argued, intensified the cold war, and specific actions by the United States from 1945 to 1949 (e.g. the American approach at the Potsdam Conference, the abrupt cessation of lend-lease to the Russians, the Truman Doctrine, and the establishment of NATO) provoked Russian countermeasures such as a tighter hold over eastern Europe and in general escalated the prospects for a direct confrontation between the Soviet Union and the United States.[53]

It was precisely because Senator Taft feared the consequences of this trend that he had been critical of the specific American policies as they were being proposed and executed. But even more significantly

* See the quotation from Kennan's lecture at Geneva, May 11, 1965 on page 11 of this book.

Taft questioned the assumptions on which the policy was allegedly based. That it has *now* been conceded that these assumptions constituted a myth which has persisted, further illustrates Senator Taft's perception. It also reveals a central challenge to all Americans, in particular, in their world outlook. The challenge is to discard myths which have replaced realities and which have led not only to unworkable non-pragmatic solutions but which have also taken on an independent ideological existence, the consequences of which have resulted in increasing violence to cherished American principles and in more and more agonising political and military involvements.

REFERENCES

1. *The Congressional Record*, 80th Cong., 1st Sess., Vol. 93, Pt 2, March 12, 1947, pp. 1980–1.
2. *Ibid.*
3. *The Congressional Record, loc. sit.*
4. *Ibid.*
5. Arthur H. Vandenberg, Jr (ed.), *The Private Papers of Senator Vandenberg*, Boston, 1952, p. 343. Vandenberg's support was especially important at the time since the Republicans controlled the 80th Congress.
6. Jones has given his own account of the crisis in his book *The Fifteen Weeks*, New York, 1955. However, the letter to William Benton is not included in that account. The present reproduction of that document is from the *Papers of Joseph Jones*, Box 1, Jones to Benton, February 26, 1947, Harry S. Truman Library, Independence, Missouri.
7. *Papers of Joseph Jones*, Box 1, 'Memorandum for the File: The Drafting of the President's Message to Congress on the Greek Situation', March 12, 1947, Harry S. Truman Library.
8. Walter Lippman, 'The Bypassing of the UN', *New York Herald Tribune*, March 22, 1947, reprinted in *The Congressional Record*, 80th Cong., 1st Sess., Vol. 93, Pt 10, March 24, 1947, p. A1231; D. F. Fleming, *The Cold War and Its Origins, 1917–1950*, I, Garden City and New York, 1961, p. 452.
9. Fleming, *op. cit.*, pp. 452–3; Robert Conway, quoted in *The Congressional Record*, 80th Cong., 1st Sess., Vol. 93, Pt 3, p. 3732.
10. Henry A. Wallace, speech reprinted in *The Congressional Record*, 80th Cong., 1st Sess., Vol. 93, Pt 10, pp. A1064–5.
11. *The Congressional Record*, 80th Cong., 1st Sess., Pt 3, pp. 3786–7.
12. For examples of these statements and others, see *The Congressional Record, loc. sit.*, pp. 2994–5, 3732–3, 3773–8, 3760; Pt 4, pp. 4956–7, 4964–7, 4974; Pt 2, pp. 2213, 2342, 2584–5; also Fleming, *op cit.*, p. 456.
13. In the Senate, sixty-seven voted for the programme; twenty-three against. In the House of Representatives, the vote was 287 for; 107 against. (*Ibid.*, Pt 3, p. 3793; Pt 4, p. 4975.)
14. Among historians delivering this verdict on Taft are Eric Goldman, *The Crucial Decade and After*, New York, 1960; Selig Adler, *The Isolationist Impulse*, New York, 1957; and Norman Graebner, *The New Isolationism: A Study in Politics and Foreign Policy Since 1950*, New York, 1956.
15. *The New York Times*, March 13, 1947, p. 3.

16. *Vital Speeches*, XII, October 1, 1946, pp. 738–41. Wallace's views cost him his position in the Truman administration.

17. *The New York Times*, March 16, 1947, p. 1.

18. D. F. Fleming, *The Cold War and Its Origins*, 1917–1950, I, Garden City and New York, 1961, p. 456.

19. *The New York Times*, April 11, 1947, p. 13.

20. *Ibid.*

21. Robert A. Taft, *A Foreign Policy for Americans*, New York, 1951, p. 112.

22. *The New York Times*, April 11, 1947, p. 13.

23. Taft, 'The British Loan', *Vital Speeches*, XII, June 1, 1946, p. 506; 'Guaranty of Full-Time Employment at Standard Wages' (address to the National Industrial Conference at New York City, January 18, 1945); *The Congressional Record*, 79th Cong., 1st Sess., Vol. 91 Pt 10, p. A220.

24. Taft, speech before St Andrew's Society of Philadelphia, Pa., December 1, 1947, *The Congressional Record*, 80th Cong., 1st Sess., Vol. 93, Pt 13, p. A4735.

25. Taft, *A Foreign Policy for Americans*, p. 101.

26. Taft, 'The Republican Party', *Fortune Magazine*, 39, April 1949, p. 118.

27. Taft, 'The Hope for World Peace' (speech before the American Polish Association in the East at New York City, May 20, 1945), *The Congressional Record*, 79th Cong., 1st Sess., Vol. 91, Pt 11, p. A3413.

28. Taft, speech before the Ohio Society of New York, November 10, 1947, *The Congressional Record*, 80th Cong., 1st Sess., Vol. 93, Pt 13, pp. A4252–3.

29. Taft, 'Lincoln Day Address', St Paul, Minnesota, February 12, 1948, *The Congressional Record*, 80th Cong., 2nd Sess., Vol. 94, Pt 9, pp. A995–6.

30. *The Congressional Record*, 80th Cong., 2nd Sess., Vol. 94, Pt 2, March 12, 1948, p. 2641.

31. *The New York Times*, March 15, 1948, pp. 1, 17.

32. *The Congressional Record*, p. 2643.

33. *The New York Times, loc. cit.*

34. *The Congressional Record*, 81st Cong., 1st Sess., Vol. 95, Pt 7, July 11, 1949, p. 9210.

35. US Senate, Committee on Foreign Relations and Committee on Armed Services, 'Hearings: Assignment of Ground Forces of the United States to Duty in the European Area', 82nd Cong., 1st Sess., Microfilm Reel 50, 1951, p. 613.

36. Taft, 'The Washington Report, August 3, 1949' in Caroline Harnsberger, *A Man of Courage: Robert A. Taft*, Chicago, 1952, p. 330.

37. Taft, 'The Washington Report, November 2, 1949', pp. 237–8.

38. Taft, *A Foreign Policy for Americans*, p. 64.

39. *The Congressional Record*, 82nd Cong., 1st Sess., Vol. 97, Pt 1, January 5, 1951, p. 56.

40. Taft, address before the Economic Club of Detroit, Michigan, February 23, 1948, *The Congressional Record*, 80th Cong., 2nd Sess., Vol. 94, Pt 9, p. A1073.

41. *The New York Times*, January 3, 1950, p. 10.

42. Taft, *A Foreign Policy for Americans*, p. 108.

43. 'Quizzing Taft', *US News and World Report 32*, March 14, 1952, p. 52.

44. *The Congressional Record*, 82nd Cong., 1st Sess., Vol. 97, Pt 3,

March 29, 1951, p. 2990.

45. Taft, address before the National Council of Christians and Jews, Cincinnati, Ohio, May 26, 1953 in Peter V. Curl (ed.), *Documents on American Foreign Relations, 1953,* New York, 1954, p. 112.

46. Taft, 'The Korean War and the Dismissal of General MacArthur' (speech at the Yale Club, New York, April 12, 1951), *The Congressional Record,* 82nd Cong., 1st Sess., Vol. 97, Pt 12, p. A2031.

47. *The New York Times,* September 17, 1947, p. 19.

48. Fleming, *The Cold War,* esp. chapters 15–17; William A. Williams, *The Tragedy of American Diplomacy,* Cleveland, Ohio, 1959, esp. p. 165; Gar Alperovitz, *Atomic Diplomacy: Hiroshima and Potsdam,* New York, 1965, pp. 234–5; John Lukacs, *A History of the Cold War,* New York, 1962, pp. 75–7; David Horowitz, *The Free World Colossus,* New York, 1965, pp. 84–5.

49. James F. Byrnes, *Speaking Frankly,* New York, 1947, pp. 295–6.

50. See, for example, relevant quotations in Horowitz, *op. cit.,* p. 85.

51. The lectures, with an additional chapter, are reproduced in George F. Kennan, *Russia, the Atom and the West,* New York, 1957, p. 19.

52. In this connection, see especially Williams, *Tragedy;* Fleming, *The Cold War;* and Alperovitz, *Atomic Diplomacy.*

53. *Ibid.*

Counter-Insurgency: Myth and Reality in Greece

TODD GITLIN*

On Greek affairs in 1944–45 I seemed to find myself out of step. But today it seems I was pursuing the exact policy which, little more than two years later, the United States has adopted with strong conviction. This is to me a very intense satisfaction.

> WINSTON CHURCHILL, quoted in *The New York Times*, April 12, 1947

In Greece [in 1947] . . . it is true, the government did not have the support of the people. . . . The question that took first priority was the encroachment from the north of Communist forces across the border. We had to back not the good guys but the bad guys in Greece, to put it simply in the vernacular. We did not back the people. We backed the monarchy; we backed those who happened to be in the driver's seat at that moment. We took a chance of Greece raising its level of economy and in improving the quality of its own government. It was a case of putting first things first. . . .

> SENATOR GALE MCGEE (Democrat, Wyo.) in the Senate, February 17, 1965

What is to be said when 'outlaws' are more law-abiding than the government, and behave to us more decently?

> Old Greek shepherd, 1947, quoted in Smothers, McNeill and McNeill, *Report on the Greeks*, New York, 1948

Now it's Uncle Sam sitting on top of the world.
Not so long ago it was John Bull and, earlier yet, Napoleon and
    the eagles of France told the world where to get off at.
Spain, Rome, Greece, Persia, their blunderbuss guns, their spears,
    catapults, ships, took their turn at leading the civilisations of the
    earth—

* The author expresses his gratitude to the Anne Parsons Educational Trust for support in doing research for this essay.

140

One by one they were bumped off, moved over, left behind, taken
for a ride; they died or they lost the wallop they used to pack,
not so good, not so good.
One by one they no longer sat on top of the world—now the
Young Stranger is Uncle Sam, is America and the song goes,
'The stars and stripes forever!' even though 'forever' is a long
time.
Even though the oldest kings had their singers and clowns calling,
'Oh king, you shall live forever.'

CARL SANDBURG, *Good Morning,*
America (Verse 14), 1928

GREECE was the Vietnam of the 1940s in more than a rhetorical sense.
She was the first major battlefield of anti-communist containment.
In Greece as in Vietnam, the nature and history of a National Liberation Front were clouded by deceptive talk of 'aggression from the
North.' There too, the United States came to the aid of a set of
fragile and repressive governments whose ambit was the great cities,
while the countryside was in revolutionary turmoil. There too, terrorism was the common currency of the conflict, liberal politics were
discredited by inaction, and revolutionary violence was a choice imposed by western betrayal and the repressive violence of the right.
Then too, a western power occupying the country after the defeat
of the Axis turned to the repression of a popular left-wing movement
spawned by wartime resistance, the United States coming to the aid
of its drained ally, and the Soviet Union standing back. On Greek
soil some of the earliest notions of counter-insurgency, 'pacification'
and containment were tested, and American arrogance rewarded, with
the future desolation of Vietnam as its direct consequence.

Years afterwards, President Truman registered the historical consensus when he wrote that his 1947 speech asking Congress to vote
funds for Greece and Turkey (the 'Truman Doctrine') was 'the turning point in America's foreign policy.' (31, p. 128.*) At least since
that time there has been a definite continuity in the American
approach to popular insurgency in economically or geopolitically
strategic territory. While there may be momentary changes in emphasis or terminology, these are but technical differences within the
main thrust of policy. Vietnam is no more an aberration, a miscalculation, a function of one presidential personality, than Greece was.
Rather, both exemplify the cruel reality of American interven-
tionism; both reveal the shallowness of the mythology with which
American ideologues clothe their interventions in good intentions.
The more genteel anti-communists insist that American policy is
designed to promote economic development and democracy, changing

* See the numbered list of references at the end of this essay.

the *status quo* to defeat communism more efficiently and perhaps humanely; others, more crudely, defend the *status quo* as the best bulwark against 'the Red menace.' Indeed, high public officials prefer the first, glad-handed, missionary sort of myth, with Greece an important, fist-pounding case (we won, didn't we?) and Vietnam the current 'challenge'. For some decision-makers the mythology of counter-insurgency is an article of faith, for others just a convenient façade, but regardless of intention the mythology obscures the truth about events and needs to be exposed.

The central text in this mythology lies in Truman's declared intention 'to support free peoples who are resisting subjugation by armed minorities or by outside pressures.' (10, p. 272.) Just as Lyndon Johnson today blames Vietnamese guerrillas for having rudely disrupted Ngo Dinh Diem's 'economic miracle,' so did Harry Truman thunder in 1947 that at the time of liberation from the Germans 'a militant minority, exploiting human want and misery, was able to create political chaos which, until now, has made economic recovery impossible.' (10, pp. 269–70.) Since myths begin by falsifying history, the general mythology, an interwoven fabric of myths, will have to be broken down into sequential units, to be examined one at a time and chronologically.

I

The first myth is that the Greek guerrillas from 1941 to 1944 (like the South Vietnamese National Liberation Front) were inflexible, diehard terrorist revolutionaries and that the Greek resistance coalition was a communist front under Stalin's control, a fifth column for his expansionist aims.

Although he could not comprehend his own insight, Truman was correct in noting that 'the condition of Greece had its beginning in the World War II occupation of that nation.' (31, p. 120.) The Germans occupied Greece in April 1941, and ruled until October 1944 through a succession of quisling governments. The first sign of organised resistance was the founding in September 1941 of a National Liberation Front (EAM), organised by the Greek Communist Party (KKE). By the time of liberation, four parties besides the KKE had affiliated with the EAM: the (Socialist) union of Popular Democracy under Professor Svolos; the Socialist Party; the United Socialist Party; and the Agrarian Party. (24, p. 69.) The EAM excluded no one from membership because of party affiliation, not even Royalists. (26, p. 44n.) General Sarafis, wartime head of the National Liberation Army (ELAS), wrote that he had tried to

get various Liberal politicians interested in the resistance. 'Nowhere
did I find any inclination for real work but only talk.' (21, p. 9.)

Guerrilla bands were already fighting in the Greek mountains when
the EAM formally established ELAS in December 1942; the guerrilla army remained subservient to the parent political body throughout the war. There were other resistance groups operating in some
regions, notably General Zervas' conservative republican EDES, but
none approached ELAS in numbers, morale or national base. The
conservative Sweet-Escott, estimates that in 1944 ELAS had about
40,000 men under arms as against EDES' 10,000. (29, p. 29.) The
American reporter Leland Stowe gives ELAS credit for 'at least
60,000 guerrillas.' (28, p. 259.) But the fighting strength of ELAS
is but one index of the EAM's wartime popularity.

The weight of the evidence tends to confirm Professor Stavrianos'
assertion that 'to a very considerable degree the EAM became a
national liberation front in fact as well as in name.' (26, p. 45.) It
was never anti-clerical (no anti-clerical movement could hope for
success in highly Orthodox Greece); many priests and even a few
bishops were members. (17, p. 99.) Workers were organised into the
EEAM (Workers EAM), youth into the EPON (United All-Greece
Youth Organisation); these two branches, along with ELAS and the
EAM National Mutual Aid relief group, each had one representative
on the EAM Central Committee. City and regional EAMs likewise
had representatives, along with delegates from the five constituent
parties. According to the American historian W. H. McNeill, who was
in Greece at the time and was later an assistant military attaché in
Athens: 'By the time of liberation, the EAM numbered about two
million members, out of a total population of over seven million.
They were incomparably superior to all rivals in their organisation
and enthusiasm. . . .' (17, p. 132.) According to Stavrianos,* 'Estimates of the total membership in all EAM groups range from half
a million to two million. . . .' (24, p. 69.)

> It is this network, reaching into every village and town, into every
> group in the cities, and spreading out among all classes and occu-
> pations, that explains why the EAM was the only *national* resistance
> organisation. It was the only one which ever developed a wide-
> spread following and which offered effective resistance to the Ger-
> mans. The other resistance leaders wavered back and forth until
> their obvious weakness in comparison to the EAM drove them to

* In much of this essay I rely heavily on Stavrianos' book *Greece: American Dilemma and Opportunity*, Chicago, 1952. Of it, Dr Floyd Spencer,
a Library of Congress consultant and author of a thoroughly annotated
bibliography, has written: 'Stavrianos' book is the most complete we now
have in any language on the recent background and current problems of
Greece until the present day.' (23, p. 67.)

complete dependence on and subservience to the British, and in some cases even to secret collaboration with the Germans and Italians. The other resistance groups were regional, almost exclusively military, and dependent on the personality of one leader or another. The EAM, in contrast, was literally a state within a state. In fact, toward the end of the occupation period, it was a state in its own right, governing the two-thirds of Greece which it had freed. (24, p. 72.)

Was the EAM communist? To answer the question properly, it is necessary to break it down into constituent parts. First, what was the EAM programme? A September 1942 pamphlet *What Is EAM and What Are Its Aims?* listed the following purposes:

1. The protection of the people against hunger, illness and want.
2. Passive and active resistance against the occupying forces and those collaborating with them. The raising of the people's morale. Opposition to all forms of collaboration.
3. Daily paralysing of the occupying forces to ensure that their war arms are not served by Greek labour or Greek materials.
4. Active resistance to force, answering force by force, armed struggle and a final armed rising.
5. When the occupying forces have been expelled:
   a. The formation of a Government from the leaders of the National Liberation Struggle, from the parties and bands which will have guided the struggle during the fight and during the victory.
   b. The immediate re-establishment of all popular liberties, of press, of speech and of assembly. A general amnesty.
   c. The immediate calling of elections for a National Constituent Assembly, where the form of popular government of the country will be drawn up. (17, p. 92.)

If the EAM programme was not particularly 'communist' neither was its membership confined to the small, though growing, Greek Communist Party (KKE). Stowe, who was in Athens in early 1945, wrote that 'Out of 1,250,000 Greeks in the greater Athens area, probably 80 per cent or more were EAM supporters; mostly workers and the poor.' (28, p. 252.) Support was not limited to the lower classes; probably the class make-up of the organisation corresponded to that of the population at large: 'The EAM represented the people of Greece as much as any organisation could during the period of occupation.' (24, p. 85.) The Twentieth Century Fund team sent to Greece in 1947 reported that during the war, 'no Communist monopoly of EAM existed, and it won broad support among the peasants by inviting their participation in resistance activities.' (22, p. 24.)

What, then, was the actual shape of EAM rule in the areas which it controlled? Foreign observers of the left, centre and right agree to a surprising extent. One of the first things that impressed the Republican, non-Communist Sarafis about the ELAS troops was that they 'did not go into the peasants' houses.' (21, p. 33.) EAM-ELAS respected the sanctity of private property, except for that of collaborators. Village councils were elected, although in most cases the village EAM committee drew up a slate of candidates that was ratified because of the esteem in which the EAM was held. Indeed, according to the Twentieth Century Fund team, EAM slates, like the ruling committees themselves, 'were often broadly representative of the community, even including traditional royalists on occasion.' (22, pp. 24–5.) Women were allowed to vote for the first time. Trials were public and fair in an elaborate system of 'people's courts'. Since most land was held in small family plots, with the individualistic ethic well entrenched, collectivisation was an impossibility, even had some elements of EAM advocated it (as their programme and practice did not). (24, pp. 80f.) Ştavrianos summarises by saying that 'the administrative system in Free Greece stimulated mass participation in local government to an unprecedented degree. There is much difference of opinion concerning EAM policies and actions on the higher level, but there is little doubt that in the villages, 'self-government and people's justice' were a reality.' (26, p. 54.) The Royalist Col. C. M. Woodhouse, Chief of the British Military Mission to occupied Greece, grudgingly paints a similar picture:

> The initiative of EAM-ELAS justified their predominance.... Having acquired control of almost the whole country, except the principal communications used by the Germans, they had given it things that it had never known before. Communications in the mountains, by wireless, courier, and telephone, have never been so good before or since; even motor roads were mended and used by EAM-ELAS. Their communications, including wireless, extended as far as Crete and Samos, where guerrillas were already in the field. The benefits of civilisation and culture trickled into the mountains for the first time. Schools, local government, law-courts, and public utilities, which the war had ended, worked again. Theatres, factories, parliamentary assemblies began for the first time. Communal life was organised in place of the traditional individualism of the Greek peasant.... Followed at a distance by the minor organisations, EAM-ELAS set the pace in the creation of something that the governments of Greece had neglected: an organised state in the Greek mountains. All the virtues and vices of such an experiment could be seen; for when the people whom no one has ever helped start helping themselves, their methods are vigorous and not always nice.... (24, p. 9.)

If democracy has something to do with a spirit among common people of their common undertaking, the EAM injected more democratic potential into the liberated areas than has any movement before or since. In Free Greece, the word 'Mister' vanished as a relic of an oppressive past; instead, the common form of address was *synagonistes*—'fellow-fighter.' (24, p. 85; 18, *passim*.) The American correspondent Constantine Poulos, who travelled through several of the liberated provinces in 1944, reported that

> Hopeful expression for a bright future prevailed everywhere. The peasants talk of rural co-operatives and agricultural schools. 'We must have enough schools where our children can be taught modern farming methods,' one peasant told me. 'For fifty years I thought olive trees produced only every other year,' he said. 'Now I learn that with proper care they can produce every year.'
>
> Fishermen talk of co-operative canneries. Old people talk of public works programs to build roads, bridges, sewage and water systems and public utilities. The younger people talk of schools, libraries, and of exchange scholarships.
>
> Mothers talk of free hospitals, visiting nurses, public clinics and public dispensaries. 'It has to change,' an old grandmother said, 'Ever since I was a little girl whenever one was seriously sick, he either had to set out to Athens with its hospitals and doctors, or die.' (24, pp. 85–6.)

But democracy, while requiring a spirit and process of commonalty, requires more than that: it requires shared decision-making. Here there is more question about EAM practice, although the picture is by no means simple. The chief EAM official in each liberated village was the Ipefthinos, or Responsible One. The Ipefthinoi were appointed from above, and generally shared the political orientation of the leaders of the EAM. In one sense, then, the EAM was 'Communist-dominated': 'Communist control of the Ipefthinoi insured a Communist majority, in the national central committee, although only about a tenth of the total EAM membership were also members of the Communist party.' (26, p. 46.) Yet Communist domination nationally, insofar as it existed, had its limitations at the village level. Authoritarianism would not work in the villages. Self-government and people's justice had to be real if the EAM was to gain popular support. Even McNeill says:

> It is not at all clear how many of the subordinate officials of the EAM regime were Communists. Many of them were members of the party, but most of them probably were not, and took the democratic and disinterested slogans of the EAM more or less at face value, looking forward to a social and political regeneration of Greece under their own leadership after the war. (17, p. 97.)

Even at the top, 'Communist control' was flexible in both extent and timing. A present-day member of the KKE Politburo refers to his party as having been only the 'moving spirit' of the EAM. (33, p, 43.) According to McNeill, only the two Socialist parties in the EAM

> were truly independent of the Communists. The others were headed by Communists and followed the wishes of the Political Bureau of KKE in all things. Despite this fact, Communist control of EAM was inconspicuous during its early days. The movement succeeded in attracting great numbers of non-communists, and generated such enthusiasm among them that *for a while it seemed possible that the Communists would be submerged by the greater numbers of the others and lose control of the movement.* (17, p. 73. Italics—T.G.)

At the highest level of political leadership, Communist 'domination' was non-exclusive: 'genuine non-Communists of liberal tradition held high place. . . . Until the outbreak of hostilities with the British in December 1944, Svolos and other EAM leaders of liberal-democratic convictions were able to exert influence for national unity, moderation, and democratic methods.' (22, p. 20.)

If McNeill could grant even the possibility that the Communists might be swamped within the EAM's highest councils, a static analysis of the EAM's makeup and policy must give a highly limiting and distorting perspective. Why did the Communists only 'eventually' become 'dominant at the top'? (22, p. 20K.) How firm was their developing domination? Indeed, what breed of Communists were these?

The prewar head of the KKE, Nikos Zachariades, spent the occupation period in the concentration camp at Dachau. He was a cosmopolitan revolutionary, indeed 'Moscow-trained,' with close connections with the Comintern. His wartime replacement, George Siantos, was much more the shrewd, rough-hewn Greek peasant. 'If Zachariades represents the professional internationalist revolutionary, George Siantos may be taken as typical of a more distinctly national type of Communist.' (17, p. 69.) The overwhelming evidence is that he and the membership of the KKE were left to their own devices by Stalin's besieged Russia. Even the wartime British ambassador to Greece, Sir Reginald Leeper, concurs:

> I thought at that time and I still think that, while the war was still in progress, the Soviet Government occupied itself very little with Greece. For the moment Greece had been left as a British operational sphere and the Kremlin were not prepared to take active steps against us there, although naturally they would do nothing to facilitate our task. (13, p. xvi.)

General Sarafis on at least one occasion requested ammunition and arms from the Red Army, but the Russians never complied. (21, p. 225.)

For their part, the KKE, while celebrating the role of the Red Army in pushing back the Germans (as who did not?), tended to the affairs of Greece in a thoroughly nationalist way. Among Greek Rightists and collaborationists, however, both the KKE and EAM were being tarred with the brush of 'Slavism'. In particular, they were accused of harbouring hopes for a 'Greater Macedonia' carved out of the Macedonian territories of Greece, Yugoslavia and Bulgaria. Yet in August 1943 the EAM and EPON held a Congress to 'Keep the Bulgarians out of Macedonia.' (21, p. 107.) The wartime United Front policy strengthened the nationalist tendencies in the KKE, and governed its behaviour within the EAM. As Stavrianos writes,

> It appears that the Communists were genuinely interested in organising as effective a resistance movement as possible, but at the same time they were confident that their leadership in the resistance struggle would attract to them such a large proportion of the population that 'the will of the people' would mean a postwar regime in which they would have substantial or dominant influence. It should also be noted that the fifth plenum of the central committee of the Greek Communist party (January 30–31, 1949) adopted a resolution condemning 'right-wing opportunistic deviations' during the occupation period. Owing to these 'deviations,' according to the resolution, the EAM Army was organised as a purely resistance body rather than as a 'people's revolutionary army', with the result that it was successful against the Axis but succumbed to British intervention in December 1944. The same point was made in 1950 by the wartime Communist leader, D. Partsalides, and by the secretary-general of the Greek Communist party, N. Zachariades. (26, p. 43n.)

More recent corroboration of this retrospective diagnosis comes from Zografos:

> The leadership of the Communist Party correctly directed *all its efforts* at ensuring allied victory over Hitler Germany. But it failed to expose and rebuff the intrigues of the British imperialists and to prepare the people to resist British intervention; it did not harness the will of the people to the struggle for democracy. (33, p. 43. Italics—T.G.)

In this, the KKE was pursuing the Comintern line of international United Front; but, most likely, of its own accord. Siantos had no known contact with the Russians until July 26, 1944, when a Col. Popov visited the ELAS headquarters to convince resistance leaders to retract certain political demands and join the British-sponsored government.* (25, p. 816; 12, p. 193.)

In sum, the opportunist KKE was bending over backwards to satisfy non-Communist, even anti-Communist members of the EAM coalition—towards the end of the resistance, because of Soviet pressure *but mostly because it genuinely believed in national unity against the German occupation as the central objective.* Is it hard to accept the nationalist integrity of a Communist-dominated movement? Consider then that most postwar 'nationalist' Greek politicians spent the wartime period in inaction (as General Sarafis said) or in exile, hovering about the King and looking for British favours. Consider too this unusual rhapsody from the vehement anti-Communist D. G. Kousoulas: 'In the desperate hours of the occupation, the proclamations of EAM served as a brilliant beacon of hope piercing the darkness, bringing solace and courage to an enslaved nation.' (12, p. 151.)

Naturally the KKE continued to be Communist; but in the interests of resistance (and for fear of alienating British support) it was quite willing to bide its time, to consider a wide range of futures for the EAM. At his first meeting with an EAM representative, Sarafis was horrified to discover that they did not intend to condemn any collaborator *a priori* as potential participant in a post-occupation government. Moreover the very structure of the EAM strengthened this orientation, especially the prominence of non-Communists—including two major labour leaders as well as the Socialists—in its leadership until the end of 1944 at least. As for its programmatic malleability, this was tested again and again in the wartime negotiations with British-supported absentee prime ministers. Consistently the EAM did what the British asked of it, even before Stalin insisted. Certainly the KKE expected postwar political rewards; certainly it could not tolerate a reinstatement of the prewar dictatorship, or destruction of its resistance accomplishments; but both its programme and its operating code attested to its readiness to compromise.

Despite the incontestable evidence, the official image of the EAM-ELAS as an organisation of die-hard revolutionaries is often shored up by references to rebel terrorism. This reflects a confusion between terrorism and political militance or revolutionary intransigence. Some, perhaps many, atrocities were committed by EAM units in their zeal to clear the country of German influence. A merchant said he had seen 'a group of ELAS Communists pull a man's teeth out one by one and then, while he was still conscious, dig out both his eyes and shove them into his mouth.' But the same merchant also 'saw some Rightists of the [German-organised] Security Battalions

* See also p. 159 below.

form a circle round a prisoner and kick him from side to side till he was dead.' (1, pp. 194–5.) Terror during the occupation was no special property of either side; occupation and resistance inspired high, even horrible emotion in most of Europe, and atrocities were beyond politics in every occupied country.

Later, official British policy was to have it that the EAM thrived on terror; to admit otherwise was to grant the possibility that people adhere to a left-wing movement voluntarily, and, from the British point of view, the more dubious this proposition, the better. After the British opened fire in Athens on Bloody Sunday, December 3, 1944, it was particularly important for the British that they prove recent terrorism on the part of the Left. Thus Churchill, defending his strike at the EAM in December 1944, read before the House of Commons this cable from Leeper:

> Ever since the Germans left, a small but well-armed Communist Party has been practising a reign of terror all over the country. Nobody can estimate the number of people killed or arrested before the revolt in Athens actually began, but when the truth can be told there will be a terrible story to tell. (24, p. 124.)

No wonder that he had wired General Scobie, the British commander in Athens, to act as if he were 'in a conquered city, confronted by local rebellion.' (24, p. 134.) Were not all anti-imperial rebels terrorists at heart?

But Leland Stowe filed a dispatch with the *New York Post* (February 17, 1945) documenting precisely the opposite:

> In Athens I met half a dozen British and American correspondents whose integrity I can vouch for over a period of years. Since mid-October they had traveled from one end of Greece to the other. These experienced reporters had never encountered anything remotely resembling 'a reign of terror'—until the shooting began [by the British] in Athens—and then there was plenty of terror on both sides. . . .
>
> Frank Gervasi of *Collier's* and M. W. Fodor of the *Chicago Sun* journeyed from Athens north to Salonika. There the British Commander told them there had not been a single reprisal execution by ELAS since Salonika was liberated November 7. Gervasi and Fodor did not encounter any pillaging or 'massacres' in Thebes, Lamia, Larissa or other towns on their trip of several hundred miles. They went, trying to verify atrocity stories—and couldn't find any. . . .
>
> All the evidence I could dig up in the period between Oct. 15 (liberation day) and Dec. 3 (when the Athens fighting began) conforms with the verdict of M. W. Fodor, the most experienced correspondent in Greece through these weeks, and one of the greatest authorities on the Balkans among contemporary journalists. Fodor said: 'In 25 years I've seen almost every revolution in Europe.

This, right here, was the quietest, calmest and most civilised revolution I've ever seen—until the shooting began by the police and the British intervened.' (24, pp. 124–5.)

This McNeill verifies on the whole:

As the Germans withdrew, the guerrillas came down from the hills to the towns and enjoyed the sweets of a more civilised life than they had known in the remote villages of the back country. In some places there was a little bloodshed, notably at Kalamata in the southern Peloponnese where ELAS executed about 30 persons; but through most of Greece the guerrillas obeyed the order of General Scobie that there should be no wholesale punishment of collaborators. . . . Peace and order were on the whole remarkably well maintained. (17, p. 150.)

As for that part of the myth which claims that Soviet policy dictated an aggressive policy to the EAM, nothing could be further from the truth. Churchill and Stalin had concluded in October 1944 an agreement dividing the Balkans into spheres of influence. Britain was granted a free hand in Greece, Stalin a free hand in Bulgaria, Rumania and Hungary, with Yugoslavia split 50–50 between them. By Churchill's own account, 'Stalin . . . adhered strictly and faithfully to our agreement of October (1944), and during all the long weeks of fighting the Communists in the streets of Athens, not one word of reproach came from *Pravda* or *Izvestia.*'* His general conservatism, amply documented in studies of Soviet foreign policy during this period, found in Greece no exception. Far from being interested in other countries' revolutions, he scorned them; he was more concerned with stabilising Russian borders. For most of the war, Stalin might as well not have existed, so far as the EAM was concerned. When he intervened at all, it was only to temper and discourage the demands of the Left.

For their part, independently of the Russians, the EAM had every good reason to suspect the motives of the British, first for their preoccupation with returning the King to Greece and then for their support of the Rightist refusal to disband Royalist armed forces throughout the period between liberation and the December fighting. In the event, however, the EAM failed to anticipate the magnitude of the British threat. Years later, the returned Zachariades was to accuse Siantos of actually having favoured the British against the revolutionary interests of the KKE. Indeed the policy of the KKE in the crucial month of October 1944, as British troops arrived to dampen the Left, was to 'keep order' and welcome 'the brave children of Great Britain, our freedom-loving Ally.' (12, p. 197.) And even as unarmed women and children of the EAM were fired on in the

* Churchill, *Triumph and Tragedy*, Boston, 1953, p. 293.

Athens massacre of December 3, 1944, the correspondent of the *Chicago Sun* heard them shouting, 'Long Live Churchill! Long Live Roosevelt! Down with Papandreou [the right-of-centre Prime Minister]! No King!' (18, p. 41.) Kousoulas says that 'favorable references to the US were not unusual among Greek Communists' even as late as the end of 1945. (12, p. 227.)

There is good reason to believe that this partly naïve, partly sub-servient (to Stalin), partly calculating openness to the west applied even at the highest levels of the EAM. They had consistently nego-tiated in good faith with the Government-in-Exile in Cairo, and later at the Lebanon and Caserta Conferences in 1943 and 1944; not even Ambassador Leeper faults their accommodating attitudes on these occasions. The compromising line of the KKE drew no rigid boundaries for post-war policy—not even excluding collaborationists *a priori,* as we have seen—although the point of greatest contention was the British attitude towards the King. In pursuit of consensus on a post-war Republic, representatives of the EAM and two other resistance groups journeyed to Cairo in 1943 to bargain with the British Mission and the Greek politicians who clustered around it. According to Stavrianos,

> The mission to Cairo was a turning point in Greek affairs. With all Greek parties in rare agreement on the dynasty question, the other differences might have been settled peacefully. But Churchill backed the King and the King sat tight. The EAM's suspicions were confirmed and they became increasingly intolerant of rival organisations. The latter, in turn, were encouraged by British policy to take a provocative line against the EAM. The failure of the Cairo mission led to civil war within Greece. . . . (24, p. 102.)

Agreement with this view comes from a surprising source. Field Marshal Lord Wilson, the British Commander-in-Chief for the Middle East, thought that the EAM might have been kept in the 'middle of the road' by a more accommodating British attitude on the question of the monarchy. (29, p. 25n.) But he was overruled by the British political chain of command running from Leeper to Churchill, which made its decision on the basis of crude anti-com-munism, the fear of popular government, and spheres of interest. The Labour MP Francis Noel-Baker also noted the facility of the British for making self-fulfilling prophecies that the guerrillas could not be worked with:

> One of the tragedies of the situation was that the British Govern-ment was helping to bring about just that situation which it sought so desperately to avoid. Instead of making Greek resistance more moderate, more democratic, more truly representative of the mass of Greek opinion, we drove it to extremes. Instead of helping to

strengthen EAM by encouraging non-communist elements to join, we tried to weaken its influence, to prevent it from 'monopolising' the liberation movement, by aiding its political opponents. The 'nationalists' we tried to use were just those people with whom German propaganda against the 'red menace' was most effective. And Göbbels was working day and night to prove that all resistance to the Germans was communist-inspired. Little wonder that so many of our 'nationalist' friends turned frankly quisling. (19, p. 43.)

But neither Wilson nor Noel-Baker could guess that Churchill might prefer to have his dire prophecies fulfil themselves, the better to justify a course of action decided well in advance of the presumed provocations without interest in moderation, or democracy, or representation.

British hostility towards the EAM finally took its toll. The British, and later the Americans, were predisposed to thinking that the EAM was monolithic and diabolical, in the face of overwhelming evidence that the movement was open-ended, nationalist, and disposed—by virtue of geographic and economic necessity and the Stalin-Churchill pact—to an accommodation with the west. That a communist party was a powerful, perhaps predominant, influence in the movement, was sufficient reason to vilify it, terrorise it, exclude it, and ultimately to crush it. In very large part, thinking made it so.

Even had Churchill not been so wedded to the Greek monarchy,* it would have been argued that the EAM would serve only communist purposes (whatever they were). The KKE was thus vested with a power and a cunning that would presumably brook no internal challenge, no fraternal checking within the community of 'fellow-fighters.' A knowledge of the Greeks, though, would have prohibited any easy conclusion that the EAM would or could have made Greece into a dictatorship. Even discounting their 1941–44 United Front policy as tactical, one must take into full account the expectations that were aroused among the population during EAM rule, which no dictatorship could have satisfied. Even Ambassador Leeper later admitted that 'the Greeks are most unlikely to tolerate that form of government [dictatorship] for long. It is not at all their way of life.' (13, p. xxi.) Not even flamboyant KKE rhetoric could avert this reality, or their experience in the EAM.

Edmund Wilson, who visited Greece in the summer of 1945, wrote that the EAM was 'neither a chess play directed from Moscow nor a foray of bandits from the hills—but a genuine popular movement which had recruited almost all that was generous, courageous and

* See 29, pp. 27n., 49; 17, p. 123; 7, p. 186 for samples of Churchill's attitude.

enlightened in Greece; the most spirited among the young, the most clear-sighted among the mature.' (7, p. 185.) This was the same movement that Leeper called 'a silly little band of Communists.'† (24, p. 133.)

The British believed Leeper because they wanted to. They did not test what he said because they feared the possible outcome: popular government. They never defined what they wanted from the EAM because they had written them off. The direct result was the civil war they claimed they did not want. Counter-insurgency is the weapon of those who have discounted, *a priori,* the legitimacy of a popular or revolutionary force; who have stopped asking questions and making distinctions. It is a sophisticated abandonment of that reason that creates justice, and it presages the most vulgar violations of democratic possibilities.

In Greece late in 1944, the handwriting was on the wall.

II

Here the second myth overlaps: that once outright fighting broke out between guerrillas and government, the insurgents would not accept any government they did not entirely control; that they had their minds set on civil war and military victory. In Vietnam the same myth takes the form of American insistence that Hanoi keeps 'hanging up the phone' and will accept nothing less than total authority.

After the December 1944 Athens massacre, ELAS remobilised to fight the British, the cooperating Greek governments, and the terroristic monarchist 'X' bands. The ELAS and EAM leaders had strained consistently—cravenly, some Communists later said—to avert open warfare, but the Rightist governments, their backbones steeled by promises of British support, did not yield.

General Scobie had come to the Caserta conference of September 1944 with a draft proposal containing this paragraph:

> The Commander-in-Chief of the forces in Greece explained that his aim was to restore law and order in Greece, so that the reconstruction of the land would be undertaken under the guidance of the Greek Government during the time when relief material would be distributed to the people.

But at the insistence of the EAM representatives, the reference to 'law and order' was struck out because, as Sarafis argued, these 'were

† In 1945 Molotov is supposed to have called the Chinese communists 'a bunch of frustrated old ladies hiding in the hills.' Sneering makes odd bedfellows.

purely internal matters coming under the exclusive jurisdiction of the Greek Government.' (18, p. 9.) But the British did not long take this excision to heart.* They still construed their mission, as Sweet-Escott puts it, 'as being how to accustom to the rule of law a people which had for three years known no Government which they could respect or indeed which they did not feel it their moral duty to flout.' (29, p. 33.) The British military writer B. H. Liddell-Hart wrote later that armed resistance to the Germans throughout Europe 'left a disrespect for "law and order" that inevitably continued after the invaders had gone.' (14, p. 65.)

But men never fight for 'law and order'; they fight for causes, good or bad. 'Law and order' is an abstract principle that people accept when it suits their interests and reject when it does not. It happens, as we have seen, that most Greeks had already accepted the EAM version of 'law and order,' but this the British could not, or did not want to, understand. They preferred, instead, the 'law and order' of the Right, just as the United States today tries to 'pacify' an unwilling countryside into the arms of the tragicomic-opera Ky regime, and American big-city mayors uphold the 'law and order' that keeps black people locked in ghettoes. This the Left could not accept; in this sense Liddell-Hart was right: those who had shown disrespect for the Germans' *Recht* were equally unlikely to yield to inequitable demands and defenceless surrender to the British and a murderous Right.† Thus, in an important way, the uprising of 1944–5 (and the guerrilla movement of 1946–9) were only extensions of the wartime resistance.

As in the earlier period of its existence, the EAM-ELAS leadership made concession after concession during the period of fighting between December 1944 and February 1945. Indeed, within the EAM itself there was great pressure to take up arms again. Sarafis tells of the struggles of the EAM-affiliated party leaders, before demobilisation, to convince their men to give up their arms while civil liberties were still not in force. (21, p. 296.) Even after the December 3 atrocity, EAM leaders, including the Communists, hoped for a rapid

---

* Scobie himself might have been willing, for a while at least, to accept the excision. According to the United Press, in a speech to ELAS at Corinth on October 25, he said, '. . . your internal questions do not interest me . . .' (18, p. 12); or perhaps the British had simply decided to try to allay left-wing fears of a betrayal, which by then were justifiably great.

† For details of these demands and counter-demands, see (24, pp. 126ff.). The main issue was whether the ELAS demobilisation would be the only one, or rather whether EDES, the other guerrilla bands and the Royalist brigades would be disbanded as well. The EAM showed good faith throughout.

end to hostilities. Several formal protests were sent to Scobie. (18, pp. 41f.)

> Until about the 12 or 13 December EAM leaders still hoped for a diplomatic settlement. Terms of agreement were discussed between Siantos and Scobie on one of these two days. The Communist leader was relatively conciliatory but General Scobie insisted on the full measure of his original demands: evacuation of Athens and the disarmament of ELAS throughout the country [while the Royalist, British-organised Mountain Brigade and the Rightist, even collaborationist guerrillas were to be maintained] as had been ordered. Such terms were not acceptable to Siantos and the interview broke off without accomplishing anything. (17, p. 179.)

Even on December 15, the ELAS Central Committee declared 'that it does not wish to seize power. . . . It does not wish a one-sided Government of the Left.' (18, p. 59.) On December 4, Premier Papandreou had approached the Liberal Sofoulis and asked him to form a government. The EAM was agreeable. But the next day Leeper informed Sofoulis that Churchill opposed a change of government, and Sofoulis, an old man, yielded back to Papandreou.*

On the morning of December 6 Scobie ordered British aircraft to strafe an EAM stronghold on Ardettos Hill in Athens, one of the major poor neighbourhoods in the city. Numerous civilians (mainly EAM supporters, of course, since they predominated in the city and especially in the poorer quarters) were killed. McNeill writes that 'it is probable that the deaths from British aeroplanes did much to harden the feelings of the moderate elements in EAM and make them willing to accept the Communist revolutionary lead.' (17, p. 178.) Again it was the British who were narrowing the Left's room for manoeuvre. But even this 'Communist revolutionary lead' was dubious. For one thing, fully a week later the Communist Siantos was 'relatively conciliatory,' by McNeill's own account. And we have it from Zografos that the KKE 'failed to expose and rebuff the intrigues of the British imperialists and to prepare the people to resist British

---

* McNeill writes that, before December 3, 'With serious doubts of the King and even deeper distrust of a republic, the British policy in practice was little more than one of wait and see, meanwhile keeping the Left from exclusive power'; and '. . . the whole policy of the British Government was directed towards preventing EAM from taking over control of the Government of Greece.' (17, pp. 162, 173.) The British assumption was that any EAM presence in the government would end up swallowing it; therefore the 'deep distrust of a republic' (aside from Churchill's monarchist sympathies) except one it could control. Not a shred of evidence has been offered for this distrust, although the EAM could easily have seized total power, unilaterally, right after liberation (if it had wanted to). Only an abstract anti-communist demonology has been put forward as a reason.

intervention.'* (33, p. 43.) Indeed, when Churchill visited Athens at Christmas 1944, EAM-ELAS asked him for an appointment; he refused, insisting that he did not want to 'meddle' in the internal affairs of Greece. (18, p. 73.)

The fighting dragged on. Towards the end of December ELAS controlled 'all of Greece, save for a patch of land in the centre of Athens, another stretch along the Bay of Phaleron, and two small zones in Salonika and Patras. Success in Athens would have sealed their victory.' (17, p. 177.) It was then that two more British divisions were brought into Greece (in American troop transports flown by American pilots). (24, p. 141.) On the night of January 4–5, ELAS slipped out of Athens, leaving behind an armed populace (its reserve) and many snipers. Both sides then slipped into the mutual horror that marks civil war:

> The British arrested large numbers of people on suspicion of sniping and transported many of them to North Africa. When it was reported that 14,500 people had been seized for this purpose, ELAS took 15,000 supposed Rightist sympathisers and marched them out of Athens toward the north. The brutality of their guards and the rigors of the march killed about 4,000 of these people, an event which did much to cause EAM swiftly to lose its majority support in the nation. (7, p. 181.)

There were other factors as well that brought this fighting to a close. Vast numbers of people in ELAS-held territory depended for their food on British supplies; they were reluctant to see the British pushed too far to the wall. (24, p. 144.) The British were running into world censure for their part in the strife: Churchill was later to write that 'The *London Times,* the *Manchester Guardian,* joined with a very large proportion of American newspapers in their censure of "British Imperialist aggression in Greece." I was astonished to see what a bad press I got in America.'† (24, p. 144.)

Perhaps the greatest influence on EAM-ELAS by this time was the Soviet attitude. At Yalta in February, according to US Secretary of State Stettinius, Stalin asked Churchill 'what was going on in Greece,' quickly adding that 'he was not criticising the British in Greece but merely seeking information.' (27, p. 217.) An armistice had finally been signed on January 11, and a final agreement slated for February 12. Siantos got the message, and phrased his accommodation most

---

* This after-the-fact accusation has not been the sole property of any particular KKE faction. Zachariades, who was purged in 1956 by Zografos' group, wrote in 1952: 'The KKE leadership failed to realise that as a result of EAM's movement . . . a clash with British imperialism, then the main foreign oppressor in Greece, was inevitable.' (12, p. 159.)

† For data on subsequent American opinion on the events in Greece, see below, p. 169n.

boldly at a press conference on the eve of the signing: 'Since the allies have decided that it is useful for the British army to be in Greece, then it is beneficial.'* (12, p. 217.)

The Varkiza Agreement was signed on schedule, providing that:

1. ELAS should surrender its arms within two weeks.
2. The Communist Party and EAM should be recognised as legal political organisations, although they were not to be represented in the Plastiras government.
3. Elections and a plebiscite on the constitutional question should be held within the year.
4. Legal prosecution of those implicated in the uprising should be confined to those who violated criminal laws and should not extend to political offences.
5. The purging of the public services, the security battalions, the gendarmerie, and the city police should begin at once. (24, p. 143.)

Even at this point, ELAS still controlled about three-fourths of Greece, according to the United Press. Yet they relinquished most arms and accepted Varkiza by returning to civilian life once again, although their leaders rightly suspected that, in the words of Professor Forster, Varkiza would be 'in a sense a victory of the Right over the Left.' (8, p. 226.) With considerable naïveté (but also great weariness) the EAM rank-and-file hoped the Yalta agreement would protect them, just as Vietnamese resistance fighters (not just Communists) accepted the guarantees of the 1954 Geneva Agreements, at the urging of Communist leaders, against the reality of partition and resettlement. The EAM leadership tried to justify their 'revisionism' and to keep faith with their movement in their proclamation demobilising ELAS:

> The agreement of February 12th terminates our armed struggle. The hour has now come to lay down in honour your glorious arms. But, your task has not been completed.
>
> The second great aim of our struggle, the safeguarding of the popular sovereignty and the creation of the necessary prerequisites for the unhindered democratic development of the country, is awaiting its realisation.
>
> We are certain that you will now devote yourselves to the accomplishment of this great aim with the same faith, with the same enthusiasm, and the same discipline which you showed as soldiers of the ELAS.

* On the Communists' expectations of American anti-colonialism, see above, p. 152. Note that in line with those expectations, the wartime resistance experience and Soviet conservatism, Ho Chi Minh's September 1945 declaration of independence from the French was modelled directly on the American Declaration of Independence.

We believe that the lofty ideal of the ELAS which made it possible for you to bring to an end your glorious armed struggle, will also be maintained by you in the political struggle in which you will be the pioneers. With such a spirit, we will surely win in the political battle too.

United and indivisible in the organisations of the EAM, fellow-fighters in the political arena as in the military, let us close and broaden our lines so that we shall definitely ensure the people's sovereignty, democracy, the progress and the well-being of the land. (24, pp. 144–5.)

But this moderate and face-saving spirit had to reckon with a British-supported Rightist counter-revolution that turned its peaceful hopes to dust, though even after Varkiza the Left acted with startling restraint. Yet in the interlude, some of the hardening of the EAM that the British had portrayed as accomplished fact did come to pass.

In April, the two most prominent Socialist leaders, Tsirimokos and Professor Svolos, announced their departure from the EAM, founding a new United Socialist Party. 'In breaking off they spoke harsh words against the Communists,' writes McNeill, 'accusing them of having dominated and perverted the whole EAM movement. How many of the EAM rank and file followed the Socialist leaders, it is impossible to say. . . .' (17, p. 200.) What in particular Svolos and Tsirimokos had objected to in KKE dominance is not clear. After the Lebanon Conference, Communists had revoked some concessions made by Svolos in the name of the EAM. On the other hand, McNeill reports that in August 1944, three EAM representatives, including Svolos, had entered the Papandreou cabinet only, said Svolos, after 'his two Communist colleagues went to the Russian Legation in Cairo and were there advised to join the Cabinet without further bargaining.' (17, p. 144.) Zografos refers genteelly to 'under-estimation of our allies in the EAM' during this period, but does not elaborate.* (33, p. 45.) Whatever the causes, no doubt the loss was a serious blow to the EAM, though not a crippling one. At the time of the March 1946 elections, EAM still incorporated the Communist, Socialist, Agrarian, Radical Republican and Democratic Union parties. (24, p. 168.)

Most commentators agree that the short-lived governments that ruled Greece throughout 1945 and 1946 were 'weak and corrupt,' honeycombed with collaborators, tolerant of—if not actively engaged

---

* Smothers, McNeill and McNeill, as well as Kousoulas, say that Svolos and the others resigned because 'they opposed civil war and least of all wanted a conflict with the British'. (22, p. 28; 12, pp. 201f.) But in this case it is not clear why they waited until after Varkiza, what assured them that ELAS planned violence, or why Svolos was confiding in Papandreou. (12, p. 203.)

in—Right-wing terrorism directed against all non-Royalists. They were incapable of feeding the people, halting a disastrous inflation, or taking any steps whatever to reconstruct the war-torn nation or put its people back to work. (22, pp. 33f.) Only two months after Varkiza, the *London Times* correspondent in Greece wrote that

> EAM and its followers are being penalised in a variety of ways. Former ELAS men are beaten up, arrested, and tried on trumped-up charges. Hundreds of employees of public utility companies in Athens are being discharged for what is described as 'anti-national' activities, which simply means membership in EAM.... Thus the Varikiza Pact, which looked at the time of its signature as if it might be the means of ending civil strife, has become a dead letter. Fresh strife is brewing.... (24, p. 148.)

Svolos himself was deprived of an appointment in what can truly be described as a reign of terror: arbitrary arrests, state-sponsored massacres, the smashing of newspaper presses, torture, and the rest of it. (29, pp. 53–4.) The British stood by and watched. 'In brief,' Stavrianos summarises, 'the smashing of leftist military power in December put extreme rightists in control of the essential state organs, and the refusal of the British to correct the balance made the Varkiza Pact a dead letter from the beginning.' (24, p. 150.)

Yet still the KKE refused to challenge British pre-eminence more than a whit. The farthest the just-returned Zachariades could go— even in private—in questioning the Stalin-Churchill protocol was a mild revision made in late June:

> Greece is located in one of the strategic, most sensitive and significant points on one of the most vital communication arteries of the British Empire. As long as there is a British Empire, this artery will remain, and England will do everything in her power to preserve it. A realistic foreign policy cannot ignore this fact.... a correct [Greek] foreign policy must move between two poles, that of the European-Balkans with its centre in Soviet Russia, and that of the Mediterranean with England as its centre. (12, p. 223.)

While the *de facto* collapse of Varkiza was forcing the KKE to reconsider its peaceful plans (12, pp. 219f.), even a victorious Party would still adopt an independent foreign policy. But just as the United States sneers at the Vietnamese NLF programme of neutrality, so would the British refuse to settle for anything less than the full measure of the Stalin-Churchill arrangement.

As the economy made no recovery and 'inflation swiftly wiped out the modest gains that were made,' fresh strife was indeed brewing. (12, p. 220.) A succession of right-wing governments refused to postpone the elections planned for March 1946, although 'strong support for postponement came not only from the left and *most of the centre,* but also from the *London Times,* the conservative *Observer,* and the

News Chronicle.' (24, p. 168.) Royalist terrorists ran rampant; election registers dated back before the war; Royalists controlled most of the electoral apparatus. The supporters of the King were able to argue that the west would abandon Greece unless a Royalist parliament was elected; there was, indeed, no evidence to the contrary. (24, p. 170.) In January 1946, Foreign Minister John Sofianopoulos resigned, charging that free elections were impossible unless 'a wide amnesty is granted . . . terrorism by state organs ceases . . . and the State machine . . . [is] purged of all Fascists and reactionary elements.' On March 9, Vice-Premier Kafandares resigned, calling the forthcoming elections a 'comedy.'

The Left had vacillated and the cautious Russian hand was still in evidence. In mid-January the EAM and KKE leaderships had endorsed the elections, but, as Kousoulas says, 'as the time grew nearer even the rank and file began to lose confidence in the outcome,' and the EAM Central Committee reversed itself less than a month later, deciding on abstinence unless the government resigned and a more representative one (not necessarily EAM-dominated) was formed. Two weeks later, though, the Russians suggested participation in the elections, pointing out that they were committed to honouring the results. But the EAM and KKE, in a new show of independence, stuck with the decision to abstain, an indication perhaps of how strong was the popular belief in the elections' fraudulence. (12, p. 233.) At the same time, Kousoulas admits that 'the excesses of the extreme Right were forcing many vacillators into the Communist fold.' (12, p. 237.)

But the Labour government in Britain insisted that elections be held on schedule (Greek politics mattering less than British imperial interests), and so they were, although the Svolos Socialists and three other non-Communist parties in addition to the EAM bloc boycotted the polls. Not unexpectedly, the Royalists won overwhelmingly, and the Rightist terror mounted correspondingly. Even the weak Liberal ex-Premier Sofoulis was moved to protest. A plebiscite on the return of the King was then held in September in conditions described by the BBC as 'anything but quiet. . . . Everybody feels that conditions indispensable for a free expression of the will of the people do not exist.'* (24, pp. 163–9, 174–5.) This conclusion too was foregone.

---

* In comparable circumstances the United States supported a farcical 'referendum' between Ngo Dinh Diem and the playboy Prince Bao Dai in 1955. Diem won with an incredible percentage in a patent fraud. (Cf B. S. N. Murti, *Vietnam Divided*, London, 1964, pp. 140ff. Murti was the Deputy Secretary-General of the International Control Commission in Vietnam.) The west makes a practice of ratifying its power with fraudulent elections; it makes no difference whether the victor is royalist or republican, as long as he suits western strategy at the time. (See also the jailkeeper's remarks, p. 171 below.)

Now Stalin's restraining hand had to be thrown off, for the sake of the political survival of the Left if nothing more.

During the spring and summer of 1946, several thousand armed men drifted to the hills. According to government estimates, there were about 10,000 guerrillas in action by the end of the year. (24, p. 178.) The Twentieth Century Fund team sums up the proceeds of this sordid period thus: 'Government repression had played into the hands of the most violent element in Leftist leadership.' (22, p. 41.) Thus was civil war thrust upon an unwilling and unready Left—and a population that desperately wanted peace and reconstruction.

III

But the myth number three—and a classic—is that the Communists and/or the EAM fomented civil war in 1946 and perpetuated it thereafter. In the case of Vietnam the same kind of assertion is made. In all such situations the myth is useful and necessary in isolating communists as purveyors of violence while denying any initiative to large numbers of the self-motivating oppressed.

We have Zografos' testimony that the Central Committee of the KKE did not endorse 'armed struggle' until February of 1946, when the farcical nature of the coming elections was already abundantly plain. Even then, 'the national conference [of the KKE] held on April 16–17, 1946 . . . posed before the membership tasks that had nothing to do with' guerrilla warfare.

> The decision of the Seventh Congress (October 1945) dissolving the rural organisations of the Party and instructing their members to join the Agrarian Party was now being implemented. This disorganised the Party in the rural areas at a time when all its branches should have been strengthened in every way, and when, according to the instructions issued by the leadership, the armed struggle was to be started—and indeed had started—in the countryside. . . . The decision on armed struggle ran counter to the sentiment of the masses: *Even many Party functionaries and members did not agree with it*. . . . Armed struggle, if only in the form of guerrilla action in the countryside, is sooner or later bound to lead to the banning of the Party and all other democratic organisations. Consequently it is essential to take steps in advance to ensure underground Party activity. . . . But these things were not done. . . . It should also be borne in mind that the Party leadership paid little attention to preserving the military cadres of ELAS, in particular the former regular army officers, whose training and skills were essential for building up the Democratic Army and especially for staff work. (33. Italics—T.G.)

'The policy of the Party leadership at this time,' says Zografos, 'was clearly contradictory and vacillating.' (33, pp. 45–6.) Not until August 1946 did the KKE send General Markos Vafiades to co-ordinate guerrilla activities in the mountains. (12, p. 240.)

This vacillation and half-hearted implementation make sense given the fact that the earliest armed bands sprang up before the Communists made their decision to opt for armed resistance. The existence of these bands posed the KKE with an urgent need for decision, to which their easiest response would be to hedge all bets: to endorse the guerrillas, in order not to lose face, but not to send more; to continue, rather, legal organisation in the hope that the appearance of the guerrillas could provoke a governmental crisis that would bring themselves and the EAM closer to power. Stavrianos says that 'the Communists took over the leadership of the armed bands as they had done during the occupation.' (24, pp. 178–9.) The implication is that there had been something to take over. The Twentieth Century Fund team supports this outlook. Only 'some' Communists went into the hills in 1946, they discovered. Most of the guerrillas had left their villages for one or a combination of three reasons: because of poverty; because of political repression; or because others had gone ahead of them. Only a minority of the guerrillas had fought with ELAS during the occupation. (22, pp. 154f.)

In any case, certainly the Communists (and other Leftists and Republicans) had been sufficiently provoked by the summer of 1946; the violent course of events from liberation on makes that clear. Although Zografos says (perhaps over-defensively) that the outbreak of guerrilla violence 'ran counter to the sentiment of the masses,' Stavrianos insists that 'when the Communists resorted to open rebellion, they received much support throughout the country.' (24, p. 176.) This despite the power of the Right and its monopoly and misuse of the legal and military apparatus of the state; despite the fraudulence of the elections; despite the universal longing for a return to peacetime pursuits.* Even the 9–15 per cent allegiance attributed to the KKE by an unfriendly Allied Mission at the time of the elections was considerable in the terror-ridden context. (2, pp. 149–50.)

In any event, according to Zografos

* There is a very clear parallel between the Greek situation and the Vietnamese. In Vietnam 'the insurrection existed before the Communists decided to take part, and . . . they were simply forced to join in. And even among the Communists, the initiative did not originate in Hanoi but from the grass roots, where the people were literally driven by Diem to take up arms in self-defence.' (Philippe Devillers, 'The Struggle for the unification of Vietnam,' *North Vietnam Today*, ed. P. J. Honey, New York, 1962, p. 42.)

one of the basic mistakes of the Party leadership at the time was that, having turned the Party towards an armed struggle, *it allowed 18 months to go by* before any efforts were made to prepare for the struggle. (33, p. 45, Italics—T.G.)

Meanwhile, against all odds, the Communists and the EAM sought to function as counterweights to the Rightist surge. In August 1946 a British parliamentary delegation including Labour, Liberal and Conservative members visited Greece. Its report excoriated the 'armed Right-wing bands,' the 'tax-free rich,' the 'active pro-Monarchist gendarmerie,' and the lack of 'detailed plans for reconstruction,' and recommended a general amnesty or, at least, a 'generous policy of clemency towards political offenders'; 'the restoration of constitutional liberties'; the cancellation of the 'special security decrees' and the return of political exiles; 'new elections, on an up-to-date register'; the restoration of union executives to their positions; and the formation of 'an All-Party Government . . . with the support of Great Britain, to include all sections with the possible exception of the Extreme Left.' The EAM Central Committee told the delegation that it would support such a government *although EAM itself were not represented.* Stavrianos points out that the delegation's programme was almost completely identical with the programmes of the Greek Left *and Centre.* (24, pp. 180–2.) But the British never acted on it, nor did the Americans after them; oddly, the Report was not even made public until January 1947.

Still, the Communists and the EAM sought to bring the struggle down out of the mountains. Throughout late 1946 and early 1947, they sought coalition with the Liberal Sofoulis, who was trying to convince other Centrist politicians 'that a policy of conciliation and political moderation would bring the guerrilla bands from the hills. . . .' But either wily old Sofoulis was too insistent on his terms of alliance, or the Communists were by that time sufficiently fed up with his manoeuvres, for early in July 1947, as McNeill recounts it,

negotiations between Sofoulis and the Communists were broken off, and Sofoulis came out publicly with a denunciation of both the Greek Communist party and the government. Upon meeting this check, Communist policy hardened for war. Previously, the guerrillas had been held more or less in reserve, as a counter in the game of high politics. The Communists had used them to discredit and demoralise the government, and as a lever for bargaining with Sofoulis. *It was only after the first week of July 1947,* when the Communist high command was compelled [by Sofoulis in one sense—T.G.] to abandon hope of coming to power legally, *that the guerrillas became an instrument of out-and-out civil war.* (16, pp. 36–37. Italics—T.G.)

This account matches quite squarely with Zografos', and with the Twentieth Century Fund team's impression during its three months in Greece in 1947, that the guerrillas in the mountains indulged in little more than some sporadic raids.

Far from fomenting civil war, the Communists were on the receiving end—and still they hemmed and hawed as long as they possibly could. And the die was not even then entirely cast until sometime in 1947—sometime after President Truman had committed America to spell the flagging British in Greece.

Even after the Truman Doctrine speech there were cracks in the neat conventional western wisdom that the Left was bent on destruction. Even after Sofoulis had abandoned negotiations with the Communists, General Markos Vafiades, the guerrilla chieftain, went to the extraordinary length of addressing a peace offering to the London *Times*. According to Sweet-Escott, his letter, published September 10, 1947,

> stated that the Greek democratic army had only democratic aims and that it was ready to cease fire if a Government was formed of the parties including EAM and a general amnesty was proclaimed. It is significant that the letter stated also that Greece's frontiers were regarded as 'inviolable'. (29, p. 65n.)

At a time when the wartime alliance was breaking up at an alarming rate, the guerrillas retained their nationalism. About this time also the Twentieth Century Fund team found that the EAM was willing to negotiate on the basis of the following programme:

—Socialisation of industry;
—peasant proprietorship of the land;
—the harnessing of water power, the development of industry, modern agriculture and education (along the lines of the programme of the UN Food and Agricultural Organisation);
—foreign aid from all nations if without strings;
—a US-USSR-UK guarantee pact;
—a broad coalition government (even if the EAM were outnumbered in it);
—cessation of hostilities;
—a general amnesty;
—reform of the armed forces;
—new elections. (22, pp. 206–7.)

How seriously these proposals were offered is impossible to determine, though according to Stavrianos other non-Royalist, non-EAM groups were ready to accept them. (24, p. 189.) All that is certain is that neither the United States nor the governments it sponsored and maintained were at all interested in anything but the destruction of the guerrillas and the dismantling of the Left. Their continued intransigence took its toll. The guerrillas extended no further offers to negotiate, and their tactics hardened.

IV

Such intransigence is often employed to justify a fourth myth: that the United States is interested in supporting centrist, even mildly 'socialist' governments which 'reform away' the reasons for the insurgency. In this model, the guerrillas fruitlessly pursue their opposition because they cannot stand to see their own program taken over by the government. 'Diem's economic miracle' is a variation on the same theme.

This is the shibboleth of the new theoreticians of counterinsurgency. Often, as in Greece, it is a device of public relations: with a great flourish the American government ostensibly orders reactionary regimes to Reform or Perish. At other times it serves as a rationale for programs like the Alliance for Progress, which seek to bolster old middle classes or to create new ones as buffers between old, landholding classes and the impoverished majority. The assertion lends comfort to liberals who seize on the purportedly unique 'pacifying' powers of reformist governments as the clinching argument for supporting such regimes. Yet the argument goes mostly unexamined. The fact of the matter is that in Greece it was an unreconstructed Rightist regime that was able to triumph over the guerrillas —aided by acts of the United States, of the guerrillas themselves, the flabbiness of the Greek moderates and of Stalin and Tito. In the process, the Right, and the United States by its fraternal support, as in Vietnam, undercut the Centre and the moderate Left as well as the EAM and Communist Left—with consequences that continue to this day.

The Truman administration was apparently aware of the character of the governments it was supporting. Truman himself complained that 'the Greek government . . . continued to show itself mostly concerned with military matters . . . even as we undertook to bolster the economy of Greece to help her combat Communist agitation, we were faced with her desire to use our aid to further partisan political, rather than national, aims.' (31, p. 132.)

One of those 'partisan political' aims was to discredit not only the EAM but much of the Centre and moderate Left as well. Smothers, McNeill and McNeill cite quotation after quotation from Rightist newspapers in 1947 to illustrate the point: 'Announcement of the program for aid to Greece and Turkey by the United States was interpreted by the Rightists as an endorsement of their attitude' of monopolising the state apparatus, sanctioning and organising terror, and refusing to widen the government, let alone negotiate with the guerrillas. (22, pp. 32f.) Most of the Centre and the moderate Left opposed unilateral western intervention, seeking instead some security through linkage between east and west; they well foresaw their fate given an American commitment that could only be viewed as an endorsement of the ruling Royalists. (22, p. 47.) Even Sofoulis, who came to titular power in a Royalist-Centre coalition in September 1947, was disappointed that so much of the American aid was military. 'Communism cannot be defeated by force, or Red-baiting,' he complained. 'Economic reconstruction and reform are the ways to fight Communism—not the spending of money for killing Greeks.' (22, pp. 196, 197.) Thus do the Vietnamese Buddhists rightly complain that US support for Marshal Ky, intentionally or not, undercuts their position and makes both peace and reform impossible.

Between March 1947 and June 1949, the United States spent $400 million in military aid to the Greek government, and $300 million in economic assistance. Like AID expenditures in Vietnam, much of the latter was dissipated in futile 'show' projects and common graft, although a US public health team did succeed in wiping out malaria, and some reconstruction was undertaken. Inflation ran rampant again, in part because of the war but also because the rich, in their time-honoured manner, refused to pay taxes. What taxes were collected were regressive. No wonder that throughout the war, fully one-third of the population was on relief. As long as the war continued, the best US economic aid could do would be to prevent mass starvation. Early in 1949 the hapless Sofoulis admitted that his coalition government had been unable 'to take the proper measures against the economic and political oligarchy of the country.' (24, pp. 192–4, 198.)

The fault was not principally Sofoulis'; his were but the trappings of power. When the United States backs a moderate at all it prefers a powerless one, in the interests of a more generous image emanating from an unchanged reality. While cabinets rose and fell between 1947 and 1949, 'the political situation was basically the same as in the period of British predominance in 1945 and 1946.' Besides the Royalists and the Centrist Liberals, they included a variety of minor parties that had, according to Stavrianos, 'essentially the same principles and policies as the major parties. The only difference lay in the individual twist of each leader's political ambitions.' The

juggling of formal power took place only on the tip of the iceberg.*
The United States, by intervening in September 1947 to establish
Sofoulis as Premier, changed nothing but the appearance of that tip,
as

> The extreme Right kept its tight grip on the state machinery. In
> 1949, as in 1945, the rightists monopolised the top offices in the
> bureaucracy and the armed services. The terroristic bands of Anton-
> Tsaous in the north, the notorious 'X' group in the south, and all
> the rest still had a free hand in the provinces and were equipped,
> directly or indirectly, by the regular Greek army and ultimately
> by the United States. (24, pp. 197–8.)

Even Socialists like Professor Svolos, who no longer carried any
brief for the EAM, despaired at the effects of American intervention.
'Like all men of the Left and many of the Centre, Svolos was deeply
disillusioned by the Truman Doctrine. As Sofoulis had done, he
pointed to its effect of increasing Rightist violence in Greece. *He
was much less inclined to believe than Sofoulis seemed to be that this
resulted from royalist misunderstanding of America's purposes.*' (22,
p. 203. Italics—T.G.) As American aid mounted, the situation grew
worse. Men like Svolos and even Sofoulis were effectively undermined
by the American insistence that the Rightist regimes, sufficiently
shined and polished, could 'do the job.' Between March 12, 1947
and the end of the fighting in 1949, 'Rightist newspapers often cited
Mr Truman's speech as clinching evidence that the government was
correct in blaming the Slavs and the Greek Communists for all the
strife raging in Greece.' (22, p. 210.) In America, this was denied by
Under-Secretary of State Acheson in testimony before the Senate
Foreign Relations Committee in the Spring of 1947:

> It is not claimed that all persons involved in the present armed
> challenge to the Greek Government are Communists. There are
> among them many persons who honestly, but in our opinion
> mistakenly, support the Communist-led forces because they do not
> like the present Greek Government.† (32, p. 852.)

But such ambiguous denials, like Secretary Rusk's admissions at the
present time, were strictly for home consumption; they were not, they
could not be trumpeted in Greece with the tangible intensity of US

---

* Could the analogy with Vietnam be any clearer?

† The *Herter Report on Greece* to the Select Committee on Foreign Aid
in 1948 corroborated this: 'Perhaps only 10 per cent of the guerrilla forces
are professional Communists who have had training and indoctrination in
Communist schools. . . .' But the *Report* went on to maintain that all the
other guerrillas were coerced into fighting. (29, p. 74.) Indeed America
finds it very hard to admit that guerrillas anywhere may fight freely for
legitimate reasons.

arms and advice. The dynamic of the American intervention there-fore crippled men like Svolos and gave others, indeed, no other way to express their contempt for the government than the taking up of arms.

Throughout the month following the surprise promulgation of the Truman Doctrine, Walter Lippmann complained that by his un-equivocal support of the Right Truman had surrendered all bargain-ing strength with the 'obviously unrepresentative' government of Greece. He predicted that by such a course the United States would 'separate ourselves from the masses of the people almost everywhere.' It was 'an intolerable commitment' to take sides in the Greek civil war, he wrote, when the American purpose should have been 'not to support the civil war but to settle it,' and to align itself with the 'middle' parties.* (7, pp. 450–51.)

Yet the effect of American policy was and is to *neutralise* the 'middle' parties, to disembowel them, and to pose the nation with an either-or: the insurgency of the left or the heavy hand of the right (varnished as it may be by the appearance of reform). Thus did the US intervene to overthrow the moderate South Vietnamese Premier Quat early in 1965, after Quat decided that the countryside needed peace with the guerrillas above all. Anti-communism cannot even tolerate moderate regimes. Despite the sophisticated rhetoric, 'self-determination' in the official American version disenfranchises not only communists but others who do not think that communism is the devil itself. The world abounds in popular moderates and reformers —Arevalo, Arbenz, Bosch, Quat, Svolos, Goulart, and the rest—who have been deprived of legitimate power because their modest hopes challenged American power or the American definition of com-munism.†

* Little did it matter to Truman that his policy was unpopular, not only in the American press but with the American public; the sanction of the big myth and the established fact would absorb opposition, in time. In the very month of his intervention speech the National Opinion Research Centre asked a sample, 'Do you think we should or should not provide military supplies to help the Greek government put down armed attacks led by Greek Communists?' 37.2 per cent supported Truman, 48.3 per cent opposed him, 14.5 per cent were undecided. Nine months later the question was posed on the basis of the *fait accompli*: '(As a matter of fact, some military supplies are being sent to Greece.) Do you favour or oppose this policy?' This time, predictably, the answers were almost exactly reversed: 45.1 per cent in favour, 37.2 per cent opposed, the rest uncertain. (Data in possession of the author, courtesy of the Roper Public Opinion Research Center in Williamstown, Mass.) So awesome is an American president's power of the deed.

† See also pp. 178f. below.

V

Once American policy overcomes even the best American impulse towards reform and succeeds in undercutting the claims of the moderates, it continues to appeal to public opinion by investing the rightist government with the presumed trappings of good faith. Specifically, there is myth number five: that the counter-insurgent government offers amnesty and peace, so that if the guerrillas do not lay down their arms and accept the offer, they are to blame for perpetuating civil war. Again, Vietnam has its well-publicised 'Operation Open Arms,' for which Greece provides an intriguing precedent.

On September 7, 1947, Sofoulis, at the urging of the American Mission, formed a coalition government composed of thirteen Royalists and eleven Liberals. He seemed a more convincing reformist than the Royalist Tsaldaris, although the latter continued as Vice-Premier and Foreign Minister and the Royalist Stratos stayed in his post as Minister of War. Sofoulis' first official act was to issue, on the next day, an offer of amnesty. 'The Government,' it read, 'makes a final appeal for peace and to this end proclaims with all faith and sincerity that it will grant an unconditional amnesty to all those who ... lay down arms forthwith and return to a peaceful life.' (13, p. 232.) If the rebellion would end, the government would 'cast full and absolute oblivion on the past,' and extend the amnesty to those imprisoned or deported for political crimes. But—continued Sofoulis—if the guerrillas continued to fight the government would, 'with deep sorrow, rally the whole nation and crush the rebellion, as well as those adhering to it or supporting it, in the most relentless way.' (24, p. 188.)

But the deck contained four jokers.

First, the Sofoulis offer stopped with amnesty. It promised no political changes. The EAM 'maintained that the substitution of Sofoulis for Tsaldaris did not loosen the rightist grip on the state machinery.... Sofoulis in effect acknowledged the validity of this position when he openly and repeatedly admitted that he was "a political decoration" and "a captive liberal."' (24, p. 189.)

Second, the guerrillas knew that 'so long as the army and gendarmerie were rightist-controlled, there could be no guarantee that the amnesty provisions would be respected.' (24, p. 189.) Leftists thought they had been forgiven at Varkiza too, only to encounter murderous repression afterwards. While some guerrillas this time accepted Sofoulis' offer, and his pledge, many of them—and those others who had been tempted—learned their lesson. One graphic illustration of their treatment occurs in a young American's report of his conversation in 1949 with a hard-boiled Greek who had recently been a jailkeeper in one of the provinces;

'This was a prison till last summer,' he said, drawing back his shoulders as if in the pleasure of reminiscence. 'We had them packed inside those cells down there, fifteen or twenty in each; they had to lie on top of one another.'

I asked, 'Who were they?'

'Communists,' he said. 'But there was a time when we had prisoners of every sort, from ELAS, from EDES, from the *Khi* [the 'X' bands] . . .'

'You had Rightist prisoners too! But how so?' I asked.

'Eh, you know that in 1946 we had the plebiscite for the return of the King; *anyone who didn't vote the right way*—' He paused. '*There were killings,*' he went on casually. '*That sort of thing happens.* . . . A few were given sentences, but they didn't stay in prison long. They were our brothers, after all; we had served together in the Security Battalions during the Occupation when the condition of the country forced us to take sides with the Germans. After that we had been together in the *Khi;* so a couple of years ago when there was the amnesty we let them out. "Back to your villages, quick!" we said, and we made as if we didn't see them.'

'And your other prisoners?' I asked.

He gave me his gold and silver grin. '*That amnesty,*' he said, '*was for the benefit of what newspapers call "world opinion"— for the Americans chiefly.* But it was for us to enforce it—or not. In '44 EAM and ELAS took over this town; in one day they had a public trial of all the educated people—lawyers, merchants, doctors—and they sentenced them to death and killed them in the square. Two years they ruled here; no one's life was safe. But our turn came after the plebiscite. As you can understand, we had no wish then to let the amnesty apply to the Communists. We kept them here another year or two, then sent them to the camps on the islands where foreigners don't interfere with us.' (1, pp. 106–7. Italics—T.G.)

The Greek government claimed that 3,419 guerrillas accepted the offer between September 14 and November 14, 1947.* (29, p. 74.) But even this figure seems high. Perhaps the government statisticians counted prisoners and refugees from rebel-held territory in their total—and then some. Stavrianos states that 'only a handful of guerrillas surrendered.' (24, p. 189.)

* The British journalist Thomas Anthem states that more would have done if their commanders had not prohibited them from reading Sofoulis' message (2, p. 147); but he cites no evidence for his claim. Anthem also cites the surrender figure as 9066 (2, p. 147), but clearly he includes the 5,647 Rightists who, according to Sweet-Escott, surrendered to the authorities during the same period. If Kevin Andrews' interview is at all typical, little wonder that so many Rightists who had committed terrorist acts were willing to accept the Sofoulis offer. (29, p. 74.)

Third, the amnesty offer came at a time when the EAM had promulgated a moderate political programme—including cease-fire—that had won the support of much of the Centre and moderate Left. General Markos' letter in the London *Times* had appeared only two days after Sofoulis' pronunciamento, so it must have been written before it. But having been rejected in their demands for a Centre-Left coalition through the summer and after, the KKE and EAM had plenty of reason to doubt the importance of the offer. While Sofoulis may have intended it sincerely, in the face of their *political* demands it seemed not only a trap but insulting as well.

Fourth, the offer apparently did not extend to members of the Communist Party. This at least seems to be what Sweet-Escott implies:

> The policy of attempting to reconcile the rebels by the granting of amnesties continued throughout the war [though not uninterruptedly; Sofoulis' offer lasted only two months; it was picked up again only in September 1949, with the war virtually over].... But the policy was doomed to failure from the start. For though such a programme of clemency and reconciliation sounded promising to Western ears, and this was possibly why it was never abandoned, no amnesty could stop the war unless it was wide enough to include members of the KKE; and to do this would merely have been once more to admit a Trojan Horse into the Greek state. (29, p. 74.)

No doubt this was very close to the thinking of the government and its American advisers at that point. In other words, the offer was less one of amnesty than one of surrender.

One other factor may bear on the cold reception given by the guerrillas to Sofoulis' late, half-hearted and jokered offer: the optimism of the guerrillas, at least throughout the year 1947 and on into 1948. On December 24, 1947, the 'Free Greece Radio' announced the establishment of the 'first Provisional Government of Free Greece,' with General Markos as Premier and Minister of War. (24, pp. 189–90.) The establishment of a rival government is almost always the mark of insurgent optimism. Aid was flowing from the countries to the north (see below, p. 37); the Greek army was beset by low morale, desertion, dissension and purges (24, pp. 179, 192); it was bogged down in orthodox and unsuccessful field-army tactics. (23, p. 102.) American arms and ammunition were not to arrive in quantity until late in 1948. (24, p. 190.) Most standard commentators have noted that one important factor in all guerrilla movements is their ability to convince people that they will win. When this ability is lost, the 'water' in which the 'fish' swim tends to evaporate. Much of the guerrillas' ability to transmit this hope depends on their own mood. Thus, not only was the amnesty offer compromised and offered in a vacuum and probably hypocritical, it also came at the wrong time. As James E. Cross writes,

> Massive efforts to buy off the guerrillas while the rebellion is in full swing are likely to be unsuccessful and, worse still, may smack of the ancient British custom of paying the Danegeld, the tribute which the Saxon kings of England periodically paid to buy off the Danish raiders who threatened to ravage the eastern coasts of Britain. (4, p. 115.)

Cross suggests that the guiding motif of amnesty must be its attempt to divide the 'ordinary' from the 'hard-core' guerrillas. Ramon Magsaysay's amnesty, often taken as a model, did indeed draw almost all of the Huk guerrillas out of the Philippine jungles in the early 1950s. But Magsaysay offered them free land, food and tools as well, and rigorously enforced his promises. The elections he enforced were far more free than those the peasants had been accustomed to. The landlords were deprived of their large holdings, and what did it matter for the moment that they were well compensated in the process? (30, pp. 42–50.)

While Magsaysay fiercely repressed the die-hard guerrillas, the carrot was generally waiting to soothe the sting of the stick.* The trapped Sofoulis could not do the same, but he did enough to satisfy an American government more interested in the appearance of forgiveness than in its reality; hungrier for a sham justice than an equitable peace.

VI

When all other arguments fail, the American position finds a predictable resting-place. It labels the guerrilla movement as an 'aggressor' by citing aid from communist countries. As Acheson later put it, 'The existence of the state itself was threatened by large forces supplied, organised, and led by neighbouring Communist movements' (London *Daily Telegraph,* January 16, 1966). The sixth myth, then, is that whatever success the guerrillas have stems from external support (from Russia, China, Cuba, North Vietnam, according to the circumstances). That American decimation of North Vietnam has far from ended the present war is an inconvenient objection. In the Greek

---

* Even then it is important to note that the Huks have recently reappeared in force (see, for example, *Chicago Sun-Times,* July 24, 1966). The ascendance of Magsaysay may be taken to mark the high-water point of the more sophisticated and reformist counter-insurgents.

case the myth still stands in the form that the guerrillas finally failed only when, and solely because, they were deprived of assistance 'from the North.'

The first and most important fact is that the first foreign assistance was not Russian or Yugoslav or Albanian or Bulgarian—but British. Moreover, it was not merely 'assistance' but open military intervention which decisively transformed the internal balance of forces in Greece and determined the course of everything that followed. This is not to deny that throughout 1947, 1948 and part of 1949, the guerrillas benefited from several levels of support from the countries bordering Greece to the north, Yugoslavia, Albania, and Bulgaria: the shipment of some arms; the use of their territory for attack, re-grouping, and training; hospitalisation for wounded guerrillas.* However, most of the guerrillas' arms (Italian, German, British) dated from the resistance, just as the NLF has relied heavily on French and American weapons. Truman's intervention speech of March 12, 1947 itself did not even go so far as to attribute the guerrillas' success to foreign assistance.

The exact extent of material aid from the north could not be determined by the UN Special Committee, perhaps largely because its teams were denied access to the offending countries. Certainly it was to be expected that communist regimes would aid their comrades to the south, partly for the sake of fraternity but as well for reasons of state. (According to McNeill, government 'maps of the new "Greater Greece" showed a generous slice of Yugoslav territory included in the new Greek boundaries.') (17, p. 251.)

The Russians, for their part, offered no assistance whatsoever; whatever influence they had was, characteristically, a dampening one. Stalin as early as February 10, 1948 told the Yugoslavs that the Greek revolt 'should fold up immediately.' He was still committed to the spheres-of-influence agreement reached with Churchill in 1944. 'The uprising in Greece must be stopped, and as quickly as possible,' he said. The revolt had 'no prospect of success at all.' He asked Djilas, 'What do you think? That Great Britain and the United States —the United States, the most powerful state in the world—will permit you to break their line of communications in the Mediterranean Sea? Nonsense. And we have no navy.' (6, pp. 181–2.) Firmly entrenched in that policy, Stalin did not even recognise the rebel government. (12, p. 249.)

What in fact has given rise to the exaggerated *ex post* claims for the *decisiveness* of foreign support is the series of events launched by the expulsion of the Yugoslav party from the Comintern in June

---

* The documentation is in the various reports of the UN Special Committee on the Balkans. (9, pp. 14ff.)

1948. The KKE supported the Comintern, resorting to the crude and ungrateful accusation that Tito was harbouring Greek government troops. Tito thereupon decided to sever the cord binding him to the guerrillas, announcing in a speech of July 10, 1949 that the Yugoslav-Greek border would henceforth be shut. In fact, he had cut off virtually all aid to the guerrillas as early as November 1948. (24, p. 201.) In some cases during the spring of 1949, Yugoslav troops even detained guerrillas who had taken refuge over the frontier. (29, p. 63.)

But the military consequences of Tito's defection were indeed rapid and far-reaching. The closing of the Yugoslav border not only deprived the guerrillas of often-needed sanctuary but left their forces adjacent to the Albanian border isolated from those operating near Bulgaria. The guerrillas felt pressed to consolidate their northern bases and made the mistake of hurrying too quickly into the stage of large-scale military movements. A series of crushing defeats administered by a revitalised Greek army brought the civil war to a close during the summer of 1949.

But note: the guerrillas in 1948 were active not only in the northern mountains but also in the Peloponnesus and on several of the Greek islands, where assistance from the north could not have played a significant role.* And the Greek army in 1940–1 had defeated a fully equipped Italian army in the northern regions where they had such difficulty in combating a much smaller number of guerrillas in 1947 and 1948. Thus it would be far too simple to pin the guerrillas' successes on their northern alliances: just as simple as it would be to attribute their collapse to the Titoist heresy alone. (24, pp. 7–8.) Moreover, the Viet Minh General Giap made, in 1950–1, the same mistake of leaping prematurely to the conventional-assault stage of guerrilla war; but in that case the error, while costly, turned out not to be fatal. The search for the causes of failure must be as discriminating as that for the roots of the guerrillas' earlier successes.

One place to look is at the non-military ramifications of the Stalin-Tito dispute. After Tito left the Comintern, its leadership resurrected the old Greek bugaboo of Macedonian independence as a means of challenging its affiliates to support an autonomous Macedonia composed of the relevant parts of Greece, Yugoslavia and Bulgaria. (29, p. 63.) Also in February, the KKE leadership passed formally from the nationalist Markos to the more subservient Zachariades, who endorsed Macedonian independence as enthusiastically as the EAM had always shunned it. (12, p. 263.) Although Markos 'resigned' for the time-honoured 'reasons of health,' the suddenness of his departure

---

* Similarly, one of the main areas of guerrilla control in South Vietnam is the Mekong Delta, farthest from North Vietnam.

left little doubt that he had been squeezed from his post. But Markos was not only a nationalist; he was extraordinarily popular with his men and gifted as a tactician. The ideologue Zachariades was no match for him. (29, p. 63.) There was also a military dimension to this transfer of power. Markos had favoured the continued use of small, mobile guerrilla bands. But in November 1948 the Democratic Army high command reorganised the guerrillas into conventional-sized units: a sign that Markos was already slipping and Zachariades on the rise. (20, p. 225.) Until then, says Lt.-Col. Edward R. Wain-house, writing in *Military Review*, the guerrillas' tactics had been 'sound.' (20, p. 224.)

At the same time, it was announced that the Central Committee of the KKE had met January 30-31 to denounce 'right-wing opportunism' as 'the basic enemy within the Communist party.' (24, p. 201.) Perhaps thinking wishfully or defending the continuity of his leadership, Zachariades later wrote that the guerrillas 'fought from the very beginning for the social revolution' and that 'wherever it [the Democratic Army] was victorious it established the dictatorship of the proletariat.' (33, p. 45.) Whether he was defending only the 'adventurism' of his own period of leadership, or accurately reflecting the guerrillas' mood under Markos as well, or getting back at Siantos for his moderation in 1944 and 1945, is hard to know. But it seems clear that, even in the last year of Markos' formal pre-eminence, the guerrillas resorted to tactics that were bound to cost them dearly in popular support.

The most severe and famous was the abduction of several (perhaps 25) thousand Greek children from their villages beginning early in 1948. (29, p. 71.) The rebel radio announced in March of that year that the 'evacuation'—to Albania, Bulgaria, Czechoslovakia, Hungary, Poland, Rumania and Yugoslavia—was designed to 'protect' the children 'from the effects of the war' (29, p. 71) and subsequent events do not entirely disallow this explanation, although most likely many of the children were taken as hostages to guarantee the 'good behaviour' not only of enemies but of fellow-fighters as well. Floyd Spencer speculates that the increasingly powerful Zachariades feared for the loyalty of the veterans of ELAS, Markos' following in partic-ular, and 'sanctioned more and more atrocities . . . to keep the people in line and prevent the veteran Eamites and Elasites from deserting.' (23, pp. 116f.) Possibly the removal of the children became more and more a method of guaranteeing the fealty of war-weary guerrillas and peace-hungry civilians. 'Terrorism,' as Brian Crozier notes, 'is a weapon of the weak.' (5, p. 159.) Desperation and internal fault-finding are, likewise, traps for the weak. They make it easier for moderates to gravitate towards the government as the either-or becomes sharper. This has been an underestimated factor in the success or failure of guerrilla insurgency. In this case, both the Left and the Centre were at fault.

The guerrillas also suffered from the revitalisation of the Greek army. General Papagos, the hero of the 1940–1 Albanian campaign, was appointed commander-in-chief in January 1949. Interestingly, he was later to write that at the end of 1948 communism looked like an 'unconquerable hydra'—although Tito had already at least begun to phase out his support. At any rate, Papagos succeeded in unifying the Greek army command and persuading his soldiers to pursue the attacking guerrillas. American 'advisers' were distributed down to division level, and the energetic Lt.-Gen. Van Fleet had become military head of the American Mission in February 1948. (29, p. 64.) American supplies—as in Vietnam, far more in both quantity and quality than the guerrillas had ever received from the north—actually *doubled* the size of the Greek army, making it far more mobile and attractive. (12, p. 258.) The United States supplied the newly invented napalm bomb and recoilless rifle, and employed the technique of forcibly regrouping villagers to deprive the guerrilla 'fish' of 'water,' as later it did so self-defeatingly in Vietnam.* (12, p. 259.) At the time of its last, successful offensive in the summer of 1949, the Greek army numbered some 197,000, against the guerrillas' 17,000. (24, p. 203.)

Perhaps even all these gains would have come to nought had the guerrillas maintained their momentum. Possibly the rebels could have survived the loss of their principal foreign provider. But their own factionalism and desperation did not afford them the chance, for they were thereby accelerating the erosion of the popular base on which they had stood so long. In the end the massive American aid proved decisive. It had taken five long and bloody years and hundreds of millions of American dollars and British pounds, but Leeper's bitter accusation—'silly little band of Communists'—had finally fulfilled itself as prophecy.

CONCLUSION: THE DYNAMICS OF BLACK, WHITE AND GREY

What, in the end, did the American intervention accomplish? According to Acheson, 'the opportunity to develop toward democratic government by consent' (London *Daily Telegraph*, January 16, 1966). 'A release of forces for large-scale development,' implies

---

* Athens, though, showed more tactical acumen than Saigon. The Greek government resettled villagers tactically and for short periods, whereas Saigon made the tactic the keystone of its entire repressive strategy.

Containment and Revolution

US News and World Report (August 8, 1966):

> Vietnam is viewed [by President Johnson] as the 'Greece' of Southeast Asia. Just as Europe was unable to relax and forge ahead after World War II until after Red aggression had been stopped in Greece, so it is felt that Vietnam holds the key to a release of forces for large-scale development and progress in Asia. If Communists are stopped, regional development will show a burst of activity.

This is the final deadly myth.

For Greece has gone nowhere since the civil war. On December 12, 1958, more than nine years after the remaining guerrillas had either been captured or had taken refuge to the north, the conservative Athens newspaper *Kathimerini* wrote: 'In the nearly 15 years since the Second World War we have been unable, despite Truman doctrines, Marshall plans, American aid and so on, to make Greece capable of maintaining and feeding her own population.' (33, pp. 48–9.) Not much has changed for Greece since then. Power is still in the hands of the western-sponsored irresponsible rich who resist those reforms that would enable the country to stand on her own feet. The countryside is still overpopulated, urban workers unemployed or desperately underpaid. Taxes still fall 'heavily on the shoulders of the lower income groups.' (12, p. 282.) The economy is still dependent on the whims of a world market which is itself an instrument of the rich world against the poor. There has been some economic growth, but only enough to make negligible progress in meeting the needs of a booming population.

This makes nonsense of official American claims that underdeveloped countries will advance naturally as soon as guerrilla insurgencies are squashed. In the classic exposition of this argument, Kennedy- and Johnson-adviser Walt W. Rostow told a graduating class of the Army's Special Warfare Centre at Ft Bragg in 1960 that 'Communists know that their time to seize power in the underdeveloped area is limited. They know that, as momentum takes hold in an undeveloped area—and the fundamental social problems inherited from the traditional society are solved—their chances to seize power decline. . . . They are the scavengers of the modernisation process.' (20, p. 465.) We are supposed to infer that guerrillas, communists in particular, are bad sports, intervening violently solely for the sake of power just when society is on its way to solving ancient problems. Poor nations unmarked by guerrilla uprisings are supposed to be making good progress. Never mind that countries, say, like Portugal, which have avoided guerrilla war, are still as backward as ever. Never mind that in Greece the end of the civil war left little to mark itself but many dead, many refugees, and much pain. The Right was able to enlist the United States and to use guerrilla missteps to maintain and consolidate its power. Rostow told the new generation of counter-revolutionaries that 'Communism is best understood as a disease of the transition to modernisation.' (20, p. 465.) But whatever 'modernisation' there has been in Greece since the civil war has benefited mostly the worldly rich who were in the best position to take advantage of it. Who, indeed, are the 'scavengers of the modernisation process'?

In earlier stages of the cold war, American apologists seem to have felt less than a total compulsion to whitewash the recipients of US largess. As we have seen, Truman was sensitive to the diversion of US aid. Acheson on March 24, 1947 said that 'our primary purpose is to help people who are struggling to maintain their independence and their right to democratic development' (31, p. 871); he referred, disingenuously, to their *'right'*, not to any accomplished fact. Joseph Jones, a State Department speech-writer who wrote the first draft of Truman's March 12 address, was somewhat more blunt about what was being defended: 'It was not a choice between black and white, but between black and a rather dirty grey.' (10, p. 186.) The black, of course, were the guerrillas; the 'rather dirty grey' was the government, which might, 'with US aid and pressure . . . become a respectable white.' (10, p. 186.)

This odd colour scheme guided both the British and the Americans in their dealings with Greece—when they recognised the 'rather dirty grey' at all. In fact they didn't have to. On the assumption of the guerrillas' blackness, anything else became preferable. Not only that, but by choosing to back the much deeper government shade the intervenor would tragically darken the other. Neither Britain nor America chose to apply aid and pressure to the continually flexible insurgents; both embraced the intransigent Right, prodding it only as much as necessary to successfully disembowel the Left, or to keep hands clean. Both Britain and America accomplished only the hardening of the *real* black and the darkening of the long-promising grey. Whatever good intentions there might have been simply paved the road. Only the Greeks were the losers.

The reason, at bottom, had little if anything to do with the 'right to democratic development,' or 'freedom,' or the 'liberties of the individual citizen.' (10, p. 146.) Some Americans might have cared, but 'reforms' and 'pacifications', real and imagined, only served, as they serve today, to lend a respectable name to stagnation, repression and the thwarting of self-determination. As former Secretary of State James Byrnes said, 'We did not have to decide that the Turkish government and the Greek monarchy were outstanding examples of free and democratic governments.' (3, p. 302.) All that was necessary was that the west decide that communism had to be contained (as if it were a jelly that flows from jars) and that therefore the guerrillas must be entirely isolated from power. Only in that context could the interventions be finally justified, even to Congressional leaders in 1947. (10, p. 142.) Truman thought that the alternative to intervention 'was the loss of Greece and the extension of the iron curtain across the eastern Mediterranean.' (31, p. 123.) His speech talked about 'assisting free peoples to work out their destiny in their own way,' but everyone knew what he meant by 'free', which 'own ways' were permissible and which were not.

But to believe that 'the loss of Greece' would come if the guerrillas were not written off, it was not necessary to believe that they were foreign agents living on Stalin's gold. The liberal Jones, foreshadowing Hubert Humphrey, insisted that as long as there were Communists in the coalition, the EAM was an 'instrument' of Soviet 'expansionism'! (10, p. 72.) Thus could the intervenors justify shooting first and asking questions later, if at all.

For containment and anti-communism were rationales sufficient unto themselves. British and then American policy were, under the surface, as crude as the strategy that governed them: not to contain foreign aggression but domestic revolution; not to bring democracy but to maintain its absence; not to avoid violence but to thwart radical change by violence if necessary; not to bring freedom, but bases. That policy weakened and finally obliterated the possibility of reconciliation by never making the attempt. It closed doors in the name of opening them, because it preferred the doors closed. The sophisticated vocabulary of counter-insurgency amounted, then and now, to little more than the sophisticated default of the open mind; the twisting of compassion in defence of a not-so-sophisticated *status quo;* the clever words that promise paradise and burn villages, but do not always keep suffering men from standing up and shouting: Enough!

REFERENCES

1. Kevin Andrews, *The Flight of Icaros,* Boston, 1959.
2. Thomas Anthem, 'The Challenge of Greece', *Contemporary Review,* Vol. CLXXIII, March 1948, pp. 146–50.
3. James Byrnes, *Speaking Frankly,* New York, 1947.
4. James Eliot Cross, *Conflict in the Shadows: The Nature and Politics of Guerrilla War,* Garden City, 1963.
5. Brian Crozier, *The Rebels,* London, 1960.
6. Milovan Djilas, *Conversations With Stalin,* New York, 1962.
7. D. F. Fleming, *The Cold War and Its Origins,* I (*1917–1950*), Garden City, 1961.
8. Edward S. Forster, *A Short History of Modern Greece, 1821–1956* (3rd ed. revised and enlarged by Douglas Dakin), London, 1958.
9. Harry N. Howard, *Greece and the United Nations, 1946–49: A Summary Record* (bound with the Report of the UN Special Committee on the

Balkans), US Department of State Publication 3645, Washington. 1949.
10. Joseph M. Jones, *The Fifteen Weeks*, New York, 1955.
11. Dimitrios G. Kousoulas, *The Price of Freedom: Greece in World Affairs, 1939–1953*, Syracuse, 1953.
12. — *Revolution and Defeat: The Story of the Greek Communist Party*, London, 1965.
13. Sir Reginald Leeper, *When Greek Meets Greek*, London, 1950.
14. B. H. Liddell Hart, *Defence of the West*, New York, 1950.
15. John Lukacs, *A History of the Cold War*, Garden City, 1962.
16. W. H. McNeill, *Greece: American Aid in Action, 1947–1956*, New York, 1957.
17. — *The Greek Dilemma: War and Aftermath*, Philadelphia, 1947.
18. National Liberation Front (EAM), *White Book, May 1944–March 1945*, New York, Greek American Council, 1945.
19. Francis Noel-Baker, *Greece: The Whole Story*, London, 1946.
20. Franklin Mark Osanka (ed.), *Modern Guerrilla Warfare: Fighting Communist Guerrilla Movements, 1941–1961*, New York, 1962.
21. Stefanos Sarafis, *Greek Resistance Army: The Story of ELAS* (translated and abridged by Marion Pascoe), London, 1951.
22. Frank Smothers, William Hardy McNeill, Elizabeth Darbishire McNeill, *Report on the Greeks*, New York, 1948.
23. Floyd Spencer, *War and Postwar Greece: An Analysis Based on Greek Writings*, Washington, 1952.
24. L. S. Stavrianos, *Greece: American Dilemma and Opportunity*, Chicago, 1952.
25. — *The Balkans Since 1453*, New York, 1958.
26. — 'The Greek National Liberation Front (EAM): A Study in Resistance Organisation and Administration', *Journal of Modern History*, XXIV, 1, March 1952, pp. 42–55.
27. Edward R. Stettinius, Jr, *Roosevelt and the Russians: The Yalta Conference*, New York, 1949.
28. Leland Stowe, *While Time Remains*, New York, 1946.
29. Bickham Sweet-Escott, *Greece: A Political and Economic Survey, 1939–1953*, London, 1954.
30. Charles Thayer, *Guerrilla*, New York, 1965.
31. Harry S. Truman, *Years of Trial and Hope, 1946–1952*, New York, 1965.
32. US Department of State, *Aid to Greece and Turkey. A Collection of State Papers* (Bulletin Supplement), Washington, 1947.
33. Zizis Zografos, 'Some Lessons of the Civil War in Greece', *World Marxist Review*, VII, 11, November 1964, pp. 43–50.

The Origins of China's Foreign Policy

JOHN GITTINGS

IT is conceded by China's friends and enemies alike that the new People's Republic will one day become the world's third greatest power. However important other areas of the world may be, the tripartite relationship between the United States, China and the Soviet Union will clearly be of paramount importance in the foreseeable future. The rise of China has complicated the relatively simple bilateral relationship between the United States and the Soviet Union of the immediate post-war years. The complication would be solved if China identified itself with either one or the other, but this path has been rejected.

This paper attempts to examine some of the historical reasons for China's rejection of US-Soviet bipolarity in international affairs. In particular, it tries to explain the background to the first major foreign policy decision of the new Chinese government in 1949–50, to 'lean to one side', the side of the Soviet Union (temporarily, as it turned out), and to cast the United States in the role of major enemy. This decision is often regarded as an 'inevitable' expression of Chinese ideological dogma. It is also presented in such a way as to justify western policy towards China since then, on the grounds that whatever else might have been done by the west, it would have made no difference to China. There are two basic objections to the 'inevitable' argument. First, it assumes that the formation of communist foreign policy, unlike that of any other system, is a wholly unilateral process, which is unaffected by the past or present policies of other countries. Second, it is for the most part not based upon serious research, but upon generalisations which were first coined during the acutest period of cold war. This paper will discuss, of necessity in a very sketchy fashion, three major historical themes which lie behind post-1949 Chinese foreign policy. These are: US policy towards China, Soviet relations with the Chinese Communist Party (CCP), and the influence of Chinese nationalism.

* * *

I

UNITED STATES POLICY TOWARDS CHINA

The introduction to a standard work on Chinese foreign relations asks the following question: 'One of the great puzzles of recent international politics is the problem: Why, in the course of a few years, did the relations of China and the United States change from friendship to hostility?'[1] The use of the word 'puzzle' betrays in itself an inability to come to terms with the fact that China has rejected the west, and especially the United States, as a model. In the last analysis this act of rejection is still widely regarded as some sort of aberration, whose principal cause was the implacable anti-western dogma of the Chinese Communist leadership. Among Americans in particular, Communist China's rejection is felt almost as a personal affront to their good intentions, and as a betrayal of the wishes of the ordinary Chinese to enjoy the benefits of the Decent Society. Much of America's China psychosis since the Communist Liberation can be explained by this fatal tendency to sentimentalise the previous relationship between the two countries, and by a total failure to grasp that the Chinese Communists' anti-imperialism gave expression to a deep-rooted vein of popular anti-western resentment which the United States itself had helped to create.

The Open Door policy

The United States has always been prone to regard its treatment of China as in an altogether different category from that of the other imperialist powers. This view can be found in classic form in Dean Acheson's letter transmitting the 1949 White Paper on United States relations with China.

> The interest of the people and the Government of the United States in China goes far back into our history. Despite the distance and broad differences in background which separate China and the United States, our friendship for that country has always been intensified by the religious, philanthropic and cultural ties which have united the two peoples, and have been attested by many acts of goodwill over a period of many years, including the use of the Boxer indemnity for the education of Chinese students, the abolition of extra-territoriality during the second World War, and our extensive aid to China during and since the close of the war. The record shows that the United States has consistently maintained and still maintains those fundamental principles of our foreign policy toward China which include the doctrine of the Open Door, respect for the administrative and territorial integrity of China, and opposition to any foreign domination of China.[2]

The main objection to this posture of benevolent imperialism is simply that the great majority of Chinese were and are unable to see it the same way. True, no American soldiers had fought with the British in the Opium War of 1840, or with the British and French in the war of 1858–60. But American diplomats lost no time in securing by treaty the privileges which their allies had already won for them by force. The Treaty of Wanghia, signed by the American envoy Caleb Cushing on July 3, 1844, was 'merely a gross copy of Sino-British treaties that had been signed previously',³ i.e. of the Treaty of Nanking and the supplementary agreements with which the Opium War was concluded. It was by these treaties that the western powers secured the privileges of extra-territoriality and of 'most-favoured-nation' which provided the legal sanction for their encroachment upon China's territorial integrity in later years.

It was, ironically, a clause in the Treaty of Wanghia providing for treaty revision after twelve years which furnished the western powers with a legal pretext for their next major assault upon China—the second Anglo-Chinese War. Whereas the Chinese interpreted this clause as providing merely for some modification of the treaty, the powers saw it as an opportunity to secure greater freedom of trade, of access to the court in Peking, and further rights for their citizens in China. The American envoy Parker was instructed by Secretary of State Marcy in 1856, when the treaty became due for revision, that the revised treaty should ensure

> ... the residence of the diplomatic representative of the United States at Peking, the seat of the Imperial Court, the unlimited extension of our trade, wherever, within the dominions of China, commerce may be found, and restrictions to the personal liberty of our citizens should be removed.

Marcy did not approve of the use of force against China, believing instead in the efficacy of *'friendly, firm* and *judicious* diplomacy'; especially if backed up by united action on the part of the three powers. He wrote that 'if the three Powers should concur in any line of conduct, it would be much less likely to meet with opposition or resistance from the authorities in China.'⁴ In October 1856, the 'lorcha *Arrow*' incident provided Britain with the necessary pretext for a demonstration of force against the Chinese. Negotiations and the war continued intermittently until the capture of Peking and the burning of the summer palace by British and French forces in 1860. The United States took no military part in this war, but its envoys Reed and Ward accompanied the allies and negotiated parallel treaties. Indeed, it mattered little what treaties they signed, since the 'most-favoured-nation' clause ensured that they would secure whatever privileges Britain and France had won. On June 18, 1858, Reed concluded the Sino-American Treaty of Tientsin, on the 26th the Sino-British treaty was signed, on the 27th the Sino-French treaty. Thus, as one scholar describes it, 'the Celestial Empire at last was completely opened up for free trade to all Western nations'.[5]

The right of free trade was the key-note of American policy towards China in the 19th century, and the Open Door policy, with whose formulation the century ended, merely gave formal expression to it. The Open Door was not a demonstration of disinterested concern for Chinese territorial integrity. It was conceived of in 1898–9, the years of the great battle for concessions and of the extortion of spheres of influence by Russia, Germany, France and Britain, when the United States feared that the resultant carve-up would leave its own business interests out in the cold. Hippisley, an English member of the Imperial Maritime Customs and one of the architects of the Open Door policy, described it as a means of protecting '... the rights possessed under the existing treaties of Tientsin... the equality of opportunity which all nations have hitherto enjoyed under those treaties for (a) commerce, (b) navigation and (c) exploitation of mines and railroads.' Rockhill, director of US diplomatic affairs for the far east, and the prime mover behind the Open Door, wrote that '... spheres [of influence] have now been recognised by GB as well as by France, Germany and Russia, and they must be accepted as existing facts.' There was no question of challenging the concept of spheres, but simply of securing the best possible commercial entry into them. Rockhill went on to write that '... we should insist on equality of treatment in the various zones, for equality of opportunity with the citizens of the favoured powers we cannot hope to have'.

The first Open Door proposal, from Secretary of State Hay, of September 6, 1899, acknowledged the existence of 'so-called "sphere(s) of influence"', only seeking to avoid interference by the occupier of the sphere of influence 'with any treaty port or vested interest'. Indeed, later in 1900 Hay himself sought a naval base in Fukien, and was thwarted in his designs by Japan. The US Minister in Peking also suggested that in the event of partition of China, the United States might choose the province of Chihli as its own sphere. Spheres of influence were only to be deplored in so far as they impeded America's freedom of commercial opportunity. In 1901, after the Alexeiev-Tseng Agreement which entrenched Russian special interests in south Manchuria, the other four powers formally protested the agreement. But Hay in private fully recognised Russia's rights to take action. 'We would even have understood if she had gone further along this path... if we have the assurance that our trade would not suffer and that the door would remain open.' Any theoretical opposition to the carve-up of China took second place to the interests of great-power diplomacy. While protesting the agreement, the United States made it clear that 'we are not at present prepared to attempt singly, or in concert with other powers, to enforce [our views on Chinese integrity] by any demonstration which could present a character of hostility to any other power.' A year later, Hay confirmed that 'We are not in any attitude of hostility towards Russia in Manchuria. On the contrary, we recognise her exceptional position in Northern China.' American policy, according to Hay, merely asked that Russia should grant the United States full trading rights in Manchuria, in which event no objection would be raised to Russian domination in that area.

The basic attitude behind the Open Door is epitomised in the person of Willard Straight, Consul-General in Mukden from 1906 to 1908 and an enthusiastic supporter of the policy, who once described himself as 'a believer in peaceful penetration through the medium of money'. China's territorial integrity—or at least an avoidance of too blatant infringements upon it—was desirable because it would fulfil a primary aim of US policy, to 'safeguard for the world the principle of equal and impartial trade with all parts of the Chinese empire', as the 1900 Hay note described it. The Open Door was the diplomatic prerequisite for dollar diplomacy, according to Taft's definition of American foreign policy as including 'active intervention to secure for our merchandise and our capitalists opportunity for profitable investment'. The best pronouncement on the Open Door remains that of President Wilson, who described it as 'not the open door to the rights of China but the open door to the goods of America'.[6]

This is not to say that the Open Door was merely a cynical deception, solely designed to provide an apologia for American economic imperialism, in total disregard for China's own interests. On the contrary, Americans saw no contradiction at all between the opening up of China to American capital and the best interests of the Chinese nation. Indeed, they were seen as complementary to each other. American investment in China would help to counter-balance the predatory designs of the foreign powers. At the same time, it would assist the development of the industrialisation of China on liberal democratic lines, which the Chinese people themselves were believed to desire as passionately as their American friends.

As Ambassador Reinsch wrote in 1914 at the time of Sarajevo,

> It is certainly true that the Chinese people are anxious to follow in the footsteps of the United States if they may only be permitted to do so.
>
> Any development of enterprise which increases American com-

mercial interest in China is incidentally favourable to Chinese independence; because, through the enlistment of neutral [i.e. American] interests, the desire of outsiders for political control can be counterbalanced.[7]

This bland assumption, which was widely shared among American statesmen who dealt with the China problem, and which lay at the root of the Open Door policy, was probably much more dangerous in the long run, both for China and America, than the simple pragmatic self-interest of the other imperialist powers. It involved a large measure of self-deception which has helped to bring about America's China psychosis in recent years. For if it was inconceivable that China could reject the benevolent patronage of the United States of its own free choice, then such a rejection could only be satisfactorily explained by some evil and perverse influence. What was more, it followed that any Chinese government which did turn its back upon the United States would pose a hostile threat to American interests and security. It also followed that in the course of time, the Chinese people themselves could be expected to return to the true path of Sino-American friendship, and to throw out their false prophets.

Reinsch wrote again in 1919 that 'The Chinese people ask for no better fate than to be allowed freedom to follow in the footsteps of America; every device of intrigue and corruption as well as coercion is being employed to force them in a different direction, including constant misrepresentation of American policies and aims . . .' If, he continued, America was unable to maintain Chinese confidence in its ability to counteract the efforts of those who corrupted and intrigued against the Chinese state, '. . . the consequences of such disillusionment on her moral and political development would be disastrous, and we instead of looking across the Pacific toward a peaceable industrial nation, sympathetic to our ideals, would be confronted with a vast, materialistic military organisation under ruthless control.'[8]

What Ambassador Reinsch in 1919 feared might happen, Secretary of State Acheson thirty years later regarded as an accomplished fact. The Chinese Communists, he said, were attempting to establish a totalitarian domination over the Chinese people in the interests of a foreign power. They had already succeeded to such an extent that the United States was powerless to prevent them. But they were doing so 'on the basis of unproved assumptions as to the extent of their own strength and the nature of the reactions which they are bound to provoke in China and elsewhere'. The evil genius in this case was 'Soviet imperialism', and the silver lining was Acheson's confidence that the Chinese people would ultimately 'throw off the foreign yoke'. After all, said Acheson, were not the goals of the Asian peoples and of the United States the same?

...The basic objective of American foreign policy is to make possible a world in which all peoples, including the peoples of Asia, can work, in their own way, towards a better life...

The American people—and we believe the Asian peoples, when they have an opportunity fairly to appraise their interests—oppose Soviet Communism for the same reason that they opposed Nazism, Japanese imperialism, or any other form of aggression—that is, because it denies to the people whom it engulfs the right to work toward a better life in their own way.[9]

The examples cited by Acheson as proof of America's benevolent intention towards China betray the same wishful thinking which characterised the Open Door policy. The surrender of extra-territorial rights in 1943 was supposed to count for more than their possession for almost a century. It is worth recalling that the United States showed only a marginally greater degree of sympathy towards the movements for tariff reform and treaty revision which stemmed from the 1922 Washington Conference than did the other powers. As one writer has commented,

...Before the Washington Conference the United States Government never, so far as I am aware, showed any greater disposition to dissociate itself from the maintenance of the treaty-port system as a whole than Great Britain had shown. Moreover, it was after the Washington Conference, when the ink of the resolution regarding extra-territoriality was barely dry, that the United States ...evinced a firm determination to lose none of the advantages of the extra-territorial system.[10]

Again, the use of the Boxer indemnity—or rather of that portion of it which was remitted to China after 1908—for educational and cultural purposes was somehow supposed to cancel out the imposition of the indemnity in the first place. Britain too remitted part of the Boxer indemnity for the financing of public works in China and for cultural and philanthropic purposes, although admittedly not until 1922. No British politician, to the knowledge of the present writer, has ever regarded this belated act of generosity as grounds for special consideration by the Chinese people.

It is, in any case, almost a truism in international affairs that charity, even if it *is* entirely disinterested, does not necessarily endear the donor to the recipient. This is particularly true in the case of American aid to China against Japan, where American motives were the reverse of disinterested. Throughout the 1930s, as Japanese aggression against China increased in scale and intensity, the United States remained neutral for all practical purposes. Any theoretical desire which some American officials felt to help maintain China's territorial integrity took second place to the policy of preventing a clash with Japan. In 1937, after the outbreak of open war in China,

Roosevelt adopted a position of moral condemnation of the Japanese, but his government continued to refrain from any positive action which might embroil it either singly or with its allies in the conflict. The prevailing course of American policy was, as one authority has written, that 'within the foreseeable future the primary aim of our Far Eastern policy should be to avert trouble with Japan and that the best means of achieving this objective was for the most part to adhere to a strategy of inaction.' And the same writer concludes that 'the degree of passivity which the United States government maintained is the feature of our record in the Far East in the mid-1930s that is most likely to seem astonishing in retrospect.'[11]

At the most charitable interpretation, therefore, the respect for China's territorial integrity professed in the Open Door policy was a pious expectation which the United States hoped to urge upon other powers by moral suasion alone. When the chips were down, America's own interests and desire to remain uninvolved took precedence. This was true for the 1930s, when Japanese aggression against China became fully-fledged. It was also true from the very start in 1914, when the process of aggression got under way with Japan's annexation of Kiao-chow, and Acting Secretary of State Lansing told his ambassador in Peking that

> The United States desires China to feel that American friendship is sincere and to be assured that this government will be glad to exert any influence which it possesses, to further, by peaceful methods, the welfare of the Chinese people, but the Department realises that it would be quixotic in the extreme to allow the question of China's territorial integrity to entangle the United States in international difficulties.[12]

Logically enough, it was not until Pearl Harbor forced war with Japan upon the United States that aid began to flow to China in appreciable quantities. 'Now is the time', said Stanley Hornbeck, political adviser to the State Department, 'for us to tie China into our war (which is still her war) as tight as possible'.[13] Some American aid had been given since 1937, but in the period 1937–41, American credits which were actually utilised totalled only US$121 million. This compared with Soviet aid utilised over the same period to an estimated total of US$170 million. (From 1941 onwards, Soviet aid dwindled in volume as western aid increased.) According to Arthur N. Young, financial adviser to the Chinese government over this period, 'it was Russia that provided to China the only prompt credits and military aid'. Until 1941, he writes, external aid to China was 'too often too little, late, and not the kind best suited to strengthen China's resistance and add to her chance of survival as a free nation'.[14]

To conclude this brief sketch of American policy towards China over the century leading up to Pearl Harbor, and of the vast discrepancy between it and the official myths embodied in Acheson's remarks. Until 1941 there was no reason why the United States should enjoy any special gratitude from any section of the Chinese people except perhaps for that small westernised section which had come under American religious and/or educational influence. America's intentions, if not its actions, were perhaps more favourably disposed towards China than those of the other powers. But under the aegis of the Open Door, American economic penetration of China was as corrosive and destructive of China's national sovereignty and as harmful to China's emergence on the world scene as the more blatant forms of British, French, Russian and Japanese imperialism. Whether the United States could have been expected to pursue a different policy, and whether this would have materially altered China's status in the 20th century for the better, is not a very fruitful question to ask. Nor are the idealistic intentions of some (though not by any means all) Americans engaged in the formulation of China policy relevant to the argument. The fact is that the fine differences between American policy and that of the other powers were not readily apparent to the great majority of Chinese. What was apparent was the essential *similarity* between the United States and the other powers, and their common aim in seeking to force China into close contact with them by the scruff of China's neck and to their own economic advantage. The illusion that a special historical bond of confidence existed between the United States and the Chinese people in general is peculiar to Americans, not to Chinese. Thus John K. Fairbank, generally regarded as a distinguished scholar of modern Chinese history, maintains the thesis that

> We have a record there [in China] of 50 years or so of real sacrifice on our part in some cases to preserve a Chinese nation, to prevent it being taken over by the various imperialist powers and finally, of course, by the Japanese, and this is something that we have to our credit in the annals of history which we don't try, perhaps, as we should, to capitalise on.[15]

This is a gross over-simplification, to say the least, of the blend of ineffective idealism and commercial self-interest which characterised American policy towards China for an entire century.

The United States and the Chinese Communists in the war against Japan

The Chinese Communists first came into meaningful contact with the United States during the second half of the anti-Japanese war.

Little significance is usually attached to the effect of this period upon subsequent Communist policy towards the United States. The expressions of goodwill and requests for aid made by the Communist leadership in their capital of Yenan are seen as obvious tactical moves which they would have been foolish not to make. This may be so, but the psychological effect of these contacts and of their eventual failure may well be more significant than is often thought.

The question of American aid to Yenan had been raised from time to time in informal contacts between the US embassy in Chungking and Communist representatives from 1942 onwards. As early as August 1942, Chou En-lai had said that Yenan would welcome a visit by American officers. Chiang Kai-shek's consent to this was finally secured in June 1944, and an Allied Observers' Group (AOG) was sent forthwith to Yenan. At the same time, a party of foreign and Chinese correspondents was permitted to visit the Communist areas—the first to do so since Edgar Snow's visit of 1937. Both the AOG and the foreign correspondents sent back generally sympathetic reports, and it was through those of the latter group that Yenan's conciliatory attitude became widely known.[16]

Repeated requests were made by Yenan for American military aid. The Communists were prepared to submit to an Allied High Command, if this command controlled all forces in China including those of the Nationalists. The Communist leaders shared the widespread belief at that time that US forces would have to make a landing on the north China coast, and were willing to cooperate by guerrilla activities behind the Japanese lines. As Commander-in-Chief Chu Teh pointed out,

> We can facilitate Allied landings in various parts of China. We control considerable stretches of coast line, especially in Hopeh and Shantung provinces in North China and in Kiangsu and Chekiang provinces in Central China. . . . What is even more important, we can assist Allied expeditionary forces everywhere in their progress through Chinese territory. We can effectively protect the flanks of Allied troops and are especially well prepared for all those tasks.[17]

It was clearly in Yenan's interest to win American support at the expense of the nationalists, but this does not necessarily invalidate the sincerity of their willingness to cooperate. The noble aims of Rooseveltian rhetoric struck a vein of sympathy in China, perhaps to greater effect among the opposition to the nationalists than within their own ranks. The professed democratic and anti-totalitarian aims of the allies seemed very much in keeping with those of the anti-KMT opposition. Besides, it was widely believed in Yenan as elsewhere that the war against Japan would last for several years, that there would be a China landing, and that the war would end with the United

States in a position of dominant influence. As Mao Tse-tung observed, 'There is no such thing as America not intervening in China'. He argued that this was no bad thing, as long as the United States pursued a 'constructive and democratic policy' in China, and expressed the view that the United States was 'the only country fully able to participate' in China's post-war economic development.[18]

Many American officials within China felt that Yenan's offers should be taken seriously. One foreign service official with the AOG even suggested diplomatic negotiations between the United States and Yenan in order to put pressure upon Chiang Kai-shek to accept political reform.[19] Both General Stilwell and his successor General Wedemeyer put forward plans to use the communist troops. Roosevelt himself was anxious to use them.[20] One enterprising agent of the US Office of Strategic Services (the same agency which engineered Ho Chi Minh's return to Vietnam at about the same time) even negotiated an independent agreement with Yenan, which would have provided for the placement of special American units alongside Communist guerrillas in north China, and the supply of arms and ammunition, in return for the 'complete cooperation' of the Communist forces. At this point Yenan, presumably under the impression that this agreement had been approved by General Wedemeyer, took a remarkable step, asking him to secure secret passage for Mao Tse-tung and Chou En-lai to Washington in order to confer with Roosevelt.[21] But the agreement was repudiated by Wedemeyer, and neither it nor any other plans for military aid were ever implemented.

At the political level, General Hurley, Roosevelt's special representative to China, made a good beginning with his attempt to bring the Kuomintang and the Communists together. In November 1944 he signed with Mao Tse-tung in Yenan a five-point draft agreement. This agreement would have provided for the establishment of a coalition government with Communist participation, and—as an implicit *quid pro quo*—the submission of the Communist forces to Nationalist control. But the draft was firmly rejected by the Nationalists, and Hurley had to explain that he had only signed the draft 'as a witness'.

Yenan's overtures to win American aid failed for a number of reasons. One reason was that allied strategy in the war against Japan underwent a radical shift in the winter of 1944. The choice was whether to invade Japan via Formosa, in which case a China landing would be necessary, or via the Philippines, which would mean that China could be bypassed. With the decision to land on Leyte in October, the Formosan alternative was eliminated. Ironically, the attack on Leyte, which swung allied policy away from the Chinese mainland, encouraged Mao Tse-tung in the opposite direction. Mao wrote in December that 'we must cooperate with the allied offensive.

192

America has already attacked Leyte island; and it is probable that she will land in China'.[22]

Secondly, those American officials with whom Yenan had on-the-spot dealings were more sympathetic towards Communist aspirations than official US policy warranted. The United States was not prepared to act without the approval of its Nationalist ally, which of course was not forthcoming for any measure which would strengthen the Communist position. It was the established policy of the United States 'to maintain Chiang Kai-shek as Generalissimo of the Armies and as President of the Government and to prevent the collapse of the Nationalist Government.'[23] Leaving aside the question of whether this was the right policy, it meant that Yenan could expect nothing from American mediation. In retrospect, the Communists may be thought to have shown some naïveté in supposing that it could ever be otherwise. One first-hand observer of the scene has even suggested that Mao Tse-tung risked his own party position by accepting American mediation at all. Michael Lindsay, who was in Yenan at the time, has written that '. . . Mao Tse-tung and Chou En-lai . . . seriously risked their positions and influence in accepting American mediation, and in hoping that civil war could be avoided by compromise.' Lindsay reports that even in 1945 many people in Yenan 'were critical of this policy and openly said that American imperialist power could never serve as an honest mediator.'[24] If true this would help to explain Mao's subsequent bitterness when mediation broke down and his critics were proved correct.

A third possible factor behind the failure of these tentative relations between the Chinese Communists and Yenan still awaits closer investigation. As far as European policy is concerned, it is common knowledge that Roosevelt's death and his replacement by Truman led to the adoption of a much tougher policy towards the Soviet Union. The concept of close cooperation between the United States and the Soviet Union, and the spirit of optimism as to the future of such cooperation, were peculiar to Roosevelt. It is at least possible that if Roosevelt had lived, he would have insisted upon more effective sanctions against the KMT in China to bring about a coalition government including the Communists, which he regarded as a 'perfectly reasonable' proposition. It is also possible that the United States would have refrained from aid to the KMT after the war. There was certainly a noticeable toughening up of the State Department's attitude towards the Chinese Communists in 1945 after Roosevelt's death. As late as February 1945, the State Department had endorsed the desirability of arming the Chinese Communists, although only in the case of operations being undertaken along the China coast.[25] The hypothesis that Roosevelt's death materially affected US policy towards the Communists has been put forward by Edgar Snow among others, who writes that

> Roosevelt died the next month [April 1945]. Soon afterward all talk of a North China landing or any serious military collaboration with Yenan abruptly ended, as all our support was thrown behind Chiang Kai-shek and the big gamble on the survival of one-man rule. That closed the chapter on our chance to find out how the Chinese Communists would behave toward us—and toward Russia—if treated as our ally in the common war against Japan, as happened in the case of the Yugoslavian Communists in the joint war against Hitler.[26]

United States policy in the Civil War

Hurley's efforts to bring about a political settlement between the Nationalists and Communists were continued by General Marshall, from his appointment as Truman's special representative in December 1945 until January 1947. These efforts were in any case probably doomed to failure, since Chiang Kai-shek was determined to crush the Communists by force and they were well aware that he would attempt to do so. The only hope for effective American mediation would have been to withdraw all economic and military aid from the Nationalist government until it reached a settlement. In theory this was not illogical. Such aid had only been provided in the first place when the United States became at war with Japan. Once its rationale had disappeared and the war had come to an end, it could have been withdrawn. In practice this was not on the cards. The United States could not afford to be seen to desert its wartime ally, nor could it run the risk of letting the Soviet Union take its place.

Much has been made of the inadequacies of American support for Chiang Kai-shek during the civil war. The United States is said to have effectively 'abandoned' or 'withdrawn from' China. This requires a good deal of qualification. American policy towards China excluded two clear-cut alternatives, and operated within the very large area which they encompassed. The first alternative, already mentioned, was to withdraw all support from the Nationalist government until it reformed itself. A few gestures were made in this direction, but it was never tried systematically over a period of time. The second alternative was to become physically involved in China, underwriting the Nationalist government to the very limit in terms of aid, material and even of direct military commitment. This second alternative was wholly unrealistic, though not because the United States had any inhibitions about interfering in a civil war, or because it was prepared to acquiesce in its outcome. But a full-scale military commitment to

China would have involved the United States in the situation which had hitherto been shunned of fighting a land war in Asia. It would have been electorally unacceptable at home, in the postwar mood of 'bring the boys home'. It would have conflicted with what seemed to be a much more immediate commitment to the cold war in Europe. As Secretary Marshall pointed out in February 1948,

> We cannot afford, economically or militarily, to take over the continued failures of the present Chinese government to the dissipation of our strength in more vital regions where we now have a reasonable opportunity of successfully meeting or thwarting the Communist threat, that is, in the vital industrial areas of Western Europe with its traditions of free institutions.[26a]

As the civil war progressed, it became even clearer that nothing short of whole-scale intervention in China would save Chiang Kai-shek. In the words of Acheson's verdict,

> A realistic appraisal of conditions in China, past and present, leads to the conclusion that the only alternative open to the United States was full-scale intervention in behalf of a Government which had lost the confidence of its own troops and its own people.[27]

This realisation came only in the last year of the civil war, however. Until then, the United States still hoped that a judicious combination of giving aid to the Nationalists and at times of withholding it would produce the right blend of strength and reform by which Chiang Kai-shek could avert defeat. This calculation was mistaken; the aid was taken, but the reforms were not made. When the aid was withheld, domestic pressure in the United States combined with pressure from Chiang Kai-shek (who at one stage threatened to turn to the Soviet Union for help) to start it flowing again. And contrary to general belief, the sum total of American aid to Chiang Kai-shek during the civil war was very considerable. There is a tendency to minimise the importance of this aid as a factor in contributing to the hostility of subsequent Communist policy towards the United States. Without access to the deliberations of the Chinese Communist Party leadership, it is impossible to determine exactly what weight should be attached to this factor. But it is contrary to common-sense to suppose that American active intervention in the shape of aid to KMT did not have an appreciable effect upon the Communists against whom the aid was used.

American economic and military aid to China from 1937 up to V-J day totalled US$1515.7 million. American economic and military aid to China from V-J day up to March 21, 1949, i.e. during almost all of the civil war, totalled $3087 million. Thus during the three years of civil war, the United States gave roughly twice as much aid to China as during the eight years of war against Japan. The increase was most noticeable in economic aid: $1986.3 million after V-J day as against $799 million before V-J day. But there was also a very significant increase in military aid alone, especially if the shorter time span is taken into account. Military aid before V-J day amounted to $845.7 million. Military aid after V-J day totalled $1100.7 million. The latter figure includes $694.7 million in lend-lease supplies, $17.7 million under the wartime SACO agreement, $141.3 million for the transfer of US navy vessels, $102.0 million of surplus military equipment and $125.0 million under the China Aid Act of 1948. Two items are not included in the official statistics and are therefore additional to the total. These are: (1) The sale of a 'broad assortment of military supplies in west China' on the departure of US troops in 1946. These were transferred to China at a nominal price of $20 million, but the procurement value, i.e. their real value, was not calculated. (2) The transfer between April and September 1947 by the US Marines in north China of approximately 6,500 tons of ammunition *gratis*. Once again no estimate of their procurement value is available.

'Aid' is often a misnomer for what should properly be regarded as straightforward business transactions. This is not so in the case under discussion. Just over 25 per cent of the post-V-J day military lend-lease was subject to repayment and the remainder ($513.7 million) took the form of a grant. Almost every item of military material which *was* paid for was purchased by the Nationalist government at a wholly nominal price. Thus the item described as 'surplus military equipment' to a procurement value of $102.0 million changed hands at a price of $6.7 million. 130 million rounds of rifle ammunition were purchased by China at 10 per cent of the procurement cost; 150 C-46 transport planes valued at $232,000 each were purchased at $5,000 each. The China Aid Act provided an outright grant of $125 million, and this money too was used in some cases to purchase materials at a fraction of their procurement cost.[28]

American aid to China after V-J day was not in any sense a follow-through or residual commitment left over from the war against Japan. As far as military aid was concerned, only the $17.7 million expended to complete the SACO agreement, and a small amount of lend-lease supplies (for completing the reequipment of 39 divisions, which was 50 per cent accomplished at V-J day) were needed to fulfil residual commitments. The bulk of military aid was committed under fresh agreements which were concluded at intervals throughout 1946–8.

It is necessary to describe American military aid to China in some detail, because it is so often alleged that it was of inconsiderable dimensions. Far from being so, it was a most formidable array of weapons, materials and transports. It was not the fault of the United States that so much of it found its way so quickly into the hands of the Chinese Communists. The nuances of American support for Chiang Kai-shek were easy enough to detect in Washington. But as far as many Chinese were concerned, the tangible evidence of that support was part of their daily life. American bullets were fired from American rifles against Chinese Communists, and many who were not Communists. Whether or not American aid was sufficient, too little or too much, to 'save' China from the Communists was irrelevant. The fact was that in the eyes of many Chinese, the United States was siding with a reactionary, unpopular and moribund government. The historian Tang Tsou, who is on the whole very kind towards the United States, writes in his study of this period of

> ... the commonly held belief that Chiang was leading the country to ruin and that he could not do so without American support. The China Aid Act was condemned by a large segment of Chinese opinion as a factor in prolonging the civil war and strengthening a detested regime.[29]

American trade followed aid in a predictable pattern. During the pre-Pearl Harbor years from 1937 onwards, American exports to China formed only 15–21 per cent of China's total annual import bill. In 1946–8 the American share, excluding aid, ranged between 57.2 per cent (1946) and 48.4 per cent (1948). Chinese exports to the United States were less than 25 per cent of imports from the United States in any year.[30]

American policy on recognition and containment, 1949-50

It can hardly be denied that the United States has failed to recognise China, and has pursued a policy of containment against that country. But whereas what the United States did or did not do in 1949–50 is commonly believed to have had very little influence on the 'dogmatic' Communist Chinese, what China did do is presented as significantly affecting American policy decisions. Thus the decision not to recognise is held to be largely a result of Communist Chinese provocation—the imprisonment of the US Consul-General in Mukden and his staff in October 1949, the sequestration of the American consular compound in Peking in January 1950, and other incidents. The containment policy is shown as a result of the Korean War, for which 'the Communists', if not China itself, are held responsible.

First on the question of recognition: this was under consideration during 1949, and was urged by leading American sinologues. But it was never *favourably* considered by the administration. At the end of April 1949, a Communist official in Nanking had broached the subject of recognition with Ambassador Stuart, and received a discouraging answer. On May 6, the State Department made the first of several moves to persuade its allies to delay recognition until a 'common front' had been adopted. When the People's Republic was set up, America did not reply to the official notification sent to the foreign powers. According to Acheson,

> We did not answer that [the notification]. The British, I think, sent a communication which said that they would be glad to consider it and hoped that all their relations would continue to be pleasant and one thing or another. I think the other nations made some noncommittal reply.[31]

US policy on recognition was consistently unfavourable, without ever categorically saying 'no'. Recognition was said to depend upon whether the new government could be deemed to have the support of the Chinese people, and the ability to maintain relations with other nations according to international standards. In theory, this formulation was not an unfair test of the right to recognition. But as interpreted by Acheson, recognition was clearly ruled out for the indefinite future. As early as August 1949, in his statement on the release of the White Paper, Acheson had concluded that the Chinese Communists were working 'in the interests of a foreign power', although they had 'for the present' been able to win popular support. His conclusion, developed further in later statements, was that the *apparent* popularity of the Chinese Communists would disappear when the Chinese people came to realise that they were being sold out to the Soviet Union. Despite appearances, therefore, the People's Republic did not have popular support. As for China's maintaining foreign relations according to international standards, Acheson made it clear that the acid test would be how the new government treated 'foreign property interests'. It was a foregone conclusion that they would not be treated kindly. As long before as February 1947, the CCP's Central Committee had declared that it considered invalid all treaties, agreements and loans concluded by the Nationalist government with foreign powers during the civil war.

Thus the United States adopted a policy which was clearly not going to lead to recognition of a Chinese government which was both communist and opposed to foreign capitalism. The imprisonment of the Mukden Consul-General and other such 'provocations' postdated the formulation of this policy. This does not necessarily mean that they would not have occurred if a different policy had been adopted by the United States, but simply that they were used by the United States as *post facto* justification for a policy which had already been adopted. Nor were such provocations confined to the Chinese side. In Hong Kong, for instance, US officials went to great lengths to secure the transfer of planes belonging to two Chinese airlines to an American corporation. This was done in order to thwart their legal reversion to the new regime. As the US Consul-General in Hong Kong wrote to a State Department official, 'You are familiar with the rearguard action we have been fighting to keep them from getting the planes and aviation equipment of the two former Nationalist airlines'. The action was successful, and 'our major objective of denying them to the communists . . . had been achieved'.[32]

On July 18, 1949, Mr Acheson instructed Ambassador-at-Large Philip Jessup to draw up possible programmes of action in order to contain 'the spread of totalitarian communism' in Asia. China by now was regarded as a tool of Soviet imperialism. It mattered little that the result of the civil war was admitted to be 'the product of internal Chinese forces', as Acheson's letter of transmittal to the White Paper conceded. From the American point of view, a communist government, regardless of its antecedents, was objectively speaking an instrument of Soviet imperialism. Logically, therefore, Mr Acheson expressed his hope in the same letter that 'the profound civilisation and the democratic individualism of China will reassert themselves and she will throw off the foreign yoke'. To the Peking Communists, this could only be interpreted as a sign of implacable American enmity to their government, and of a desire to see its overthrow.[33]

It is true that Acheson conceded that it was no longer possible for the United States itself to interfere with the course of events inside China. It is also true that the line of containment was apparently drawn at first so as to exclude South Korea and Taiwan. These were both tactical decisions of great importance. But the strategy of containment, with all the hostility towards the People's Republic which it implied, was an integral part of American policy long before the Korean War. The outbreak of the war extended the line of containment, and intensified the degree of hostility; it did not lead to any qualitative change in policy.

Whether a different course of action by the United States would have produced a different response from the People's Republic on a given issue is impossible to say. By 1949 the United States was committed to prevent the 'spread' of communism in any shape or form, and the cold war was at its height. It was logical that the United States should be hostile to a communist China and that the Chinese Communists should expect it to be so. It would have required an unparalleled act of faith in the good intentions of the United States for Mao Tse-tung to have leant to the American side or even to have remained neutral between the United States and the Soviet Union.

It does not follow from this that Mao Tse-tung's decision to lean to the Soviet side was taken blindly or wholeheartedly without reservation. Ideological considerations no doubt played their part, both in accepting the Soviet Union as an ally, and also in rejecting the United States. But just as the practical experience which the Chinese Communists had over the years of the United States had influenced the act of rejection, so it is reasonable to assume that their acceptance of the Soviet Union as an ally was modified by their not altogether happy relations with Stalin in the past. The decision to 'lean to one side', far from being an ideological inevitability, was in all likelihood only reached after considerable heart-searching.

II

STALIN AND THE CHINESE REVOLUTION

According to the official Maoist interpretation of the Chinese revolutionary period, the CCP leadership suffered from a succession of incorrect 'lines' before evolving a 'correct line' under the direction of Mao Tse-tung himself. These were respectively: the 'capitulationist' line of Ch'en Tu-hsiu, who is held responsible for the failure in 1927 of the United Front strategy with the KMT; the first 'left' line under Ch'u Ch'iu-pai in the winter of 1927, which led to the Canton uprising in December 1927, and other abortive or 'putschist' attempts to stage urban insurrections; the second 'left' line of 1929–30 under Li Li-san, which again led to such adventurist attempts at armed insurrection as the attacks on Nanchang and Changsha in August-September 1930; and finally the third 'left' line under Wang Ming and Ch'in Pang-hsien, which was blamed for the failure to withstand KMT encirclement of the Kiangsi Soviet, and for the consequent need to abandon Kiangsi and to embark upon the Long March. It was not until the Tsunyi Conference of the CC Politburo, held in January 1935 during the Long March, at which Mao was elected chairman of the Politburo, that this succession of 'left' lines was ended, and a correct political line adopted. From that time until the successful end of the revolution in 1949, the CCP leadership under Mao is held to have avoided all incorrect lines, whether of the right or the left variety. Deviations did however persist among some Party members and cadres, and in 1942–4 the Rectification (*cheng-feng*) movement was carried out within the Party under Mao's personal supervision in order to eliminate them. It was at the conclusion of this movement that the official version of the Party's history—which has been summarised above—was written by Mao Tse-tung, approved by the Central Committee, and endorsed by its seventh plenary session of April 1945.[34] In the first half of 1948, a further rectification movement was carried out. This had a number of purposes connected with the need to prepare the Party for taking power, but it was also concerned to eliminate a 'right' tendency towards capitulationism and 'pessimism' which had appeared within the Party during the second year of the civil war.

There has always been an implicit connection between the various deviations listed above and the events to which they led, and the policies of the Soviet Union, operating both through Soviet advisers in China, through the Comintern and later personally through Stalin, towards the CCP. Ch'en Tu-hsiu's capitulationism was largely the result of Stalin's insistence upon a united front tactic towards the KMT, even when it was clear that Chiang Kai-shek intended to purge his organisation of CCP members. Ch'u Ch'iu-pai acted in accordance with Stalin's conviction that 'a new revolutionary up-surge' was taking place in China. Li Li-san's doctrine of 'prepared insurrection' was formulated at the CCP's Sixth Congress, held in Moscow in July 1928 under manifest Soviet influence and guidance. The third 'left' line was conducted by Wang Ming and other members of the 'returned student' faction from the Sun Yat-sen University in Moscow. A major purpose of the Rectification movement was to sinify Marxism-Leninism and to purge it of foreign formalism. According to Po I-po, a member of the Central Committee, 'the *Cheng-feng* taught us that the CCP must have its own principles. It was not necessary that we travel the same road as the Soviet Union.'[35] Once again, Wang Ming and the returned students were a primary target of the movement. The Rectification movement of 1948, in its attack upon —among other things—'pessimism' within the CCP, was combating an attitude which had a close affinity with Stalin's own pessimism towards the CCP's chances of victory in the civil war.

This connection, between Soviet policies and deviations in the CCP, is made explicit in the following extract from the recent Chinese polemic *On the question of Stalin*.

> ... While defending Stalin, we do not defend his mistakes. Long ago the Chinese Communists had first-hand experience of some of his mistakes. Of the erroneous 'Left' and 'Right' opportunist lines which emerged in the Chinese Communist Party at one time or another, some arose under the influence of certain mistakes of Stalin's, in so far as their international sources were concerned. In the late 'Twenties, the 'Thirties and the early and middle 'Forties, the Chinese Marxist-Leninists represented by Comrades Mao Tse-tung and Liu Shao-ch'i resisted the influence of Stalin's mistakes; they gradually overcame the erroneous lines of 'Left' and 'Right' opportunism and finally led the Chinese revolution to victory.[36]

Mao's election as chairman of the Politburo at the Tsunyi Conference took place at a time when the CCP was isolated from contact with the outside world, and was almost certainly not endorsed beforehand by Stalin or the Comintern. In earlier years Mao had himself been criticised by exponents of the various 'left' lines for his excessive emphasis upon the role of the peasantry in the revolution. He was even dismissed in November 1927 from his position as alternate member of the Politburo for having committed 'deviations' in organising the peasant movement. Conversely, the 'left' leaders were later criticised by Mao for their failure to understand that '. . . the Chinese bourgeois-democratic revolution is in essence a peasant revolution and that the basic task of the Chinese proletariat in the bourgeois-democratic revolution is therefore to lead the peasants' struggle.'[37] Throughout the revolution, however, the Maoist leadership avoided all overt criticism of Stalin on the same score. Stalin was formally acknowledged as 'leader of the world revolution', the direct successor to Marx, Engels and Lenin, and the source of doctrinal inspiration.

If there were no Stalin, who would there be to give directions? It is really fortunate that there is a Soviet Union in the world; a Communist Party and furthermore, that there is a Stalin. Thus, the affairs of the world can be dealt with all right.[38]

Stalin and Mao Tse-tung were scrupulously represented as being in agreement upon every issue. It was however made quite clear in an important article by the Communist theoretician Ch'en Po-ta, published shortly after the Communist victory of 1949, that Mao had not simply followed the Stalinist line. Mao was said to have '. . . developed Stalin's theory regarding the Chinese revolution in the course of the concrete practice of this revolution.' He was a 'creative Marxist' who combined Marxist-Leninist theory with Chinese practice. Furthermore, Ch'en explained that for various reasons Mao was one of '. . . many comrades in our Party who were actually leading the Chinese Revolution but who did not have an opportunity to make a systematic study of Stalin's works about China. . . . But despite this situation, Comrade Mao Tse-tung has been able to reach the same conclusions as Stalin on many fundamental problems through his independent thinking based on the fundamental revolutionary science of Marx, Engels, Lenin and Stalin.'[39] In this way, formal deference to Stalin was neatly combined with an insistence upon Mao's originality of thought.

The Soviet Union declared war upon Japan on August 8, 1945, and entered Manchuria on the next day. On August 11, General Chu Teh ordered his men to move into the north-eastern provinces. Over 100,000 troops were launched in a well-prepared operation, joining the popular guerilla forces already there, and by the end of the year pro-Communist forces in Manchuria numbered 300,000. The presence of the Soviet army in Manchuria undoubtedly helped the Chinese Communists under General Lin Piao to strengthen their position. One can however distinguish between specific acts of Soviet policy which gave a certain amount of material and moral aid to the Chinese Communists, and an overall strategy which sought to avoid civil war in China and to intensify Soviet relations with the existing Nationalist government. In Manchuria the Soviet occupying forces turned over large quantities of Japanese arms and equipment to Lin Piao's forces. The Soviet decision to retain their troops in Manchuria beyond the original deadline, and their obstruction of the entry of Nationalist forces, also helped the Communists to establish themselves in force and to interdict the movement by land or sea of Nationalist troops into Manchuria. At the same time, however, the Soviet forces began to remove large quantities of industrial plant and machinery which they regarded as legitimate 'war-booty'. They also attempted, without success, to negotiate joint Sino-Soviet management of key Manchurian industries with the Nationalist government.[40] Even the pro-Soviet Chinese Communist Li Li-san admitted to a western reporter that 'there were instances of faulty Soviet behaviour in Manchuria', although he insisted that these were 'small matters compared with Russia's sacrifices in the war with Japan and with her helping the liberation of Manchuria.'[41]

It is not therefore surprising that a Soviet document in the Sino-Soviet polemics should complain of anti-Soviet behaviour by two senior Communist officials in Manchuria. P'eng Chen was chairman of the Politburo of the Central Committee's North-east Bureau, set up when Lin Piao's forces moved into Manchuria. Lin Feng was chairman of the North-east Administrative Committee set up in early 1946. Both continued to hold authority in the region until August 1949, when P'eng became secretary of the Peking Party Committee. Lin remained in the north-east as a deputy-chairman of the North-east People's Government. According to the Soviet accusation, P'eng and Lin, together with the associates, had 'maliciously distorted the role of the Soviet army, and spread slander about the USSR.' Their 'mistakes' were condemned in July 1946 by the CCP Central Committee, but they remained in office, and in 1949 were once again merely criticised for 'nationalistic, anti-Soviet tendencies'.[42]

On the diplomatic front, the Soviet Union cooperated with the United States and Britain in efforts to bring about the negotiations which took place between Mao and Chiang Kai-shek at the end of August 1945. The three powers agreed that the Nationalist government alone should receive the surrender of Japanese troops in China, although Yenan claimed the right to participate.[43] The three powers were also reported to have made a joint démarche to Mao Tse-tung urging him to take part in the Chungking negotiations.[44] The signing of the Sino-Soviet Treaty on August 14, 1945, which restored Soviet rights in Manchuria and reaffirmed the independence of Outer Mongolia, was also thought to have helped to persuade Mao to negotiate. The Soviet Union itself credited the treaty with playing 'an important part in helping to unify the nation.'[45] Similarly, Soviet participation in the joint declaration on China by the Foreign Ministers' Meeting in Moscow in December 1945, which called for 'a unified and democratic China under the National Government', was believed to have helped bring about the Kuomintang-Communist truce agreement of January 10, 1946.

In *On the Question of Stalin,* already quoted above, the Chinese have confirmed that Stalin 'had given some bad counsel with regard to the Chinese revolution.' This probably refers specifically to the immediate post-Japanese war period, when a delegation from Yenan visited Moscow for consultations with Stalin.[46] According to Stalin's own admission, he invited the Chinese comrades to agree on a means of reaching a *modus vivendi* with Chiang Kai-shek. 'They agreed with us in word, but in deed they did it their own way when they got home: they mustered their forces and struck.'[47] According to another account, Stalin said he had advised the Chinese Communists to 'join the Chiang Kai-shek government and dissolve their army.'[48]

The course of Soviet policy towards the Chinese Communists during the civil war remains shrouded in mystery, but in broad outline it was distinctly luke-warm. Communist successes were not prominently reported in the Soviet press until the final year of the war. The Soviet Union maintained correct diplomatic relations with the Nationalist government almost until the very end. When Peking and Tientsin were captured by the People's Liberation Army in January 1949, the Soviet consulates were closed. When Nanking fell at the end of April, the Soviet ambassador Roschin followed the Nationalist government to Canton while all other foreign ambassadors remained in Nanking. In the first months of 1949, the Soviet Union attempted to conclude new agreements with Nanking on Soviet trade and mining rights in Sinkiang. On May 11, the Sino-Soviet agreement on joint rights in Sinkiang was extended for another five years.[49]

Some Nationalist leaders hoped to play off the Soviet Union against the Chinese Communists, and thereby to prevent their further advance south of the Yangtze. There were a number of rumours that the Soviet Union favoured a compromise solution to the war, possibly involving partition. There had been reports in December 1947 of a Soviet offer to mediate between the two warring factions.[50] In the same month, at a meeting of the CCP's Central Committee in Shensi province, Mao criticised those within the ranks of the party who 'overestimate the strength of the enemy' and who indulged in 'impotent thinking'. A resolution of the Central Committee that 'every effort should be made to carry the Chinese people's revolutionary war forward uninterruptedly to complete victory' carried the implication that there were those who favoured a more cautious policy.[51] There is no proven connection between the 'pessimism' among some CCP members which Mao criticised during the second half of 1947, and the apparently luke-warm attitude of the Soviet Union. But it was rumoured that as late as July 1948 at another meeting of the Central Committee, 'Stalin urged through Liu Shao-ch'i that the Chinese Communists continue guerrilla war and refrain from pushing their victory to a decisive conclusion'.[52] Rumours about Soviet reluctance to see the whole of China reunified under Communist rule continued to circulate during the KMT-CCP peace negotiations of January-April 1949.

Reports of Stalin's opposition to a total Communist victory in China as late as 1949, when it was already in sight may be exaggerated. In any case, from July 1948 onwards, Chinese Communist statements indicated quite clearly that the decision to 'lean to one side'—the Soviet side—had been taken in principle. Nevertheless, there is little doubt that the Soviet attitude towards the Chinese Communists was in general unenthusiastic, and that this has not been forgotten by the leaders of the People's Republic.

The decision to 'lean to one side'

The decision to 'lean to one side' is often ascribed to Mao's speech *On the People's Democratic Dictatorship* of June 1949. In fact, the policy had already been formulated half a year earlier, with the publication in November 1948 of articles by Mao and Lin Shao-ch'i which emphasised the need for China's adherence to the anti-imperialist camp headed by the Soviet Union.

As the prospects for final victory in the civil war grew dramatically nearer towards the end of 1948, so the problem of relations between a future New China and the Soviet Union had become more acute. Relations between fraternal parties could perhaps afford to be as ill-defined and loose as they undoubtedly were during the previous years; but it was quite another matter for relations between sovereign and neighbouring states. It was also necessary to put an end to controversy within the Party, and to combat the neutralist arguments of the non-Communist democratic and progressive groups in China.[53]

Liu Shao-ch'i in his article *On Nationalism and Internationalism* made a spirited defence of the Soviet Union against charges of 'red imperialism', expounded the principle of proletarian internationalism, and endorsed the 'two camps' thesis of world politics. Mao wrote in the official Comintern organ that the Soviet had built

> ... a new revolutionary front from the proletariat of the West through the Russian revolution to the oppressed nations of the East. ... Apart from such a revolutionary front there can be no other. *Has not the history of 31 years showed the utter bankruptcy of 'middle roads' or 'third roads'?*[54]

However, the implications of a 'lean to one side' policy had still to be spelt out. In itself, it amounted to no more than a formal commitment to the Soviet Union, and it is hard to imagine that in the circumstances of US single-minded support for Chiang Kai-shek and of international cold war such a commitment would not have been made. However hard done by Stalin the CCP might have felt itself to be, this did not invalidate the fact that the Soviet Union was for better or for worse the leader of the world communist bloc, and the only realistic major ally for a communist China. The decision to 'lean to one side' was a decision in principle. Its implications in terms of inter-state relations, diplomatic and economic, were still open to negotiation. The form that the new Sino-Soviet relationship was to take may be assumed to have emerged in the light of considerable debate both within China and between the two countries.

During his two months of negotiations in Moscow (December 1949–February 1950), which led to the Sino-Soviet Treaty of February 1950, Mao Tse-tung granted a brief interview to a Tass reporter. The length of his stay, he said, 'depends on the period in which it will be possible to settle questions of interest to the CPR.' He described his shopping list as:

> ... first of all the existing Treaty of Friendship and Alliance between China and the USSR, the question of Soviet credits for the CPR, the question of trade and a trade agreement between our two countries, and other matters.[55]

On none of these points, so vital for Chinese nationalist sentiment at home, did Mao obtain anything like complete satisfaction. The most significant concession was the fixing of a time limit (within three years or the signing of a peace treaty with Japan) for the surrender of Soviet rights in Manchuria. Otherwise the new treaty basically followed the pattern of the old one—and also of those between the Soviet Union and the east European people's democracies. The Soviet credit of US$300 million over five years could hardly be described as generous: Outer Mongolia was formally recognised as independent of China; Soviet interest in Sinkiang was extended in the form of joint-stock companies. Mao's visit could only be judged successful on the grounds that the terms of the Treaty and agreements might have been even *less* favourable to China.

There are some indications that the Chinese Communists expected more economic aid from the Soviet Union than they were to obtain under the Treaty and Agreements of 1950. During the second half of 1949 there was a noticeable tendency to justify the lean-to-one-side policy to a large extent in terms of the economic benefits which would accrue. Much was made of the 200 or more Soviet technicians who had been sent to serve in Manchuria and the north. These had helped to restore the north-east railways, to fight bubonic plague, to help with town planning in Peking and Tientsin, etc. They epitomised the friendly and sincere help of the Soviet people which was 'unconditional and asks for nothing in return'.[56] Trade between the two countries had been resumed, and the conditions proposed by the Soviet Union were 'friendly and self-denying'.[57] The Soviet-Manchurian trade agreement of July 1949 produced forecasts that the Soviet Union would supply complete equipment for factories and power stations in exchange for agricultural produce. China, it was said, had much to learn from Soviet experience in the production of industrial equipment and in the control of people's enterprises.[58] Kao Kang spoke of China's need for the 'many-sided help of the Soviet Union,'[59] and Liu Shao-ch'i spoke of the Soviet Union's advanced scientific and technical knowledge which China could learn and absorb. 'The Chinese people,' he said, 'should particularly prize their friendship and cooperation with the Soviet people for this reason.'[60]

By contrast the subject of Soviet economic aid to China was not accorded much attention after the Moscow negotiations. Thus an NCNA editorial, commenting on the Treaty, emphasised that it was for China to set its own house in order.

> The Chinese people are brave and industrious, China is a country of vast territory, plentiful resources and huge population. Through hard struggle under the leadership of the CCP, in addition to the favourable condition of assistance from the Soviet Union, the great CPR is certain to be swiftly transformed into a strong, prosperous and industrialised country.[61]

Did the CCP expect a better deal at the hands of Stalin, and was this expectation related to the decision to 'lean to one side'? Given their long experience of Stalin, as well as the precedent of satellisation in eastern Europe, it seems very unlikely that they cherished many illusions, apart from their possible expectations of greater economic aid. Why then did they enter upon negotiations which were to produce such unsatisfactory results? Simply because there was no alternative; regardless of its political colour, any Chinese government in the post-war world had to recognise the fact of Soviet influence in the far east and negotiate accordingly. A communist Chinese government, faced with a hostile United States, had even less freedom of manoeuvre. The lean-to-one-side policy can only be satisfactorily explained upon the assumption that the CCP leadership did *not* regard economic and territorial questions as determining factors in their relationship with the Soviet Union; that they were prepared to accept disadvantageous positions in these fields—at least for the time being —in the interests of an overall political alliance.

The real value of the Treaty and the alliance which it embodied to the Chinese Communists appears to have been a political one. It is necessary to remember that the danger of 'imperialist aggression' against China still seemed very real to the Chinese, both in the context of the past hundred years of western encroachments and in the more immediate context of the cold war. As Mao had emphasised to the People's Political Consultative Conference, '... the reactionaries and their running dogs, the Chinese reactionaries, will not resign themselves to defeat in this land of China. They will continue to gang up against the Chinese people in every possible way.'[62]

The treaty of 1950 provided China above all with an *ally*, both in the political and military sense. Article 1 stated: 'In the event of one of the High Contracting Parties being attacked by Japan or states allied with it, and thus being involved in a state of war, the other High Contracting Party will immediately render military and other assistance with all the means at its disposal.' It was this aspect which was underlined by the Chinese whenever the Treaty was justified in public. It was a political alliance between the 'two countries that play the decisive role in the East,'[63] according to which the Soviet and Chinese armies stood 'hand in hand in the front line in defence of peace in the far east and in the world.'[64] Alliance with the Soviet Union gave China the necessary military backing and political prestige to allow it to relax its efforts in the military field and to embark upon national reconstruction. It was this which made it possible for Liu Shao-ch'i to say that 'the international conditions for carrying out our construction are also very good' and to look forward to a 'peaceful environment' for the new China.[65] In the words of Mao Tsetung, the Soviet Union was a 'valuable ally', whose acquisition made it possible to 'fulfil domestic construction, jointly oppose aggression of our enemies and build the foundation for establishing world peace.'[66]

Internal policy was predicated upon the assumption that by and large a 'peaceful environment' for China was assured, with the Soviet Union as a guarantor. The liberation of Taiwan and Tibet still fell within the category of unfinished business, but these were expected to be completed by the end of 1950. Partial demobilisation of the PLA, cuts in the military budget, the land reform program, preparations for an economic plan, these and other measures indicated both the willingness and the need for China to return to a peace-time footing.

III

NATIONALISM AND LIBERATION

While acknowledging the moral help and inspiration of the Soviet Union, the Chinese Communists made it very clear that their success was due solely to the correct leadership of the CCP and Mao Tse-tung. There was a marked discrepancy between the Soviet and Chinese versions on this score. On the signing of the Sino-Soviet Treaty in February 1950, for instance, *Pravda* editorialised that 'the decisive victory of the Chinese people became possible in consequence of the defeat of German Fascism and Japanese imperialism, a defeat in which the Soviet Union, led by the great Stalin, played a decisive role,'[67] while Vyshinsky claimed that 'the Soviet people have in-variably demonstrated their sympathy with the cause of the libera-tion of the Chinese people.'[68]

Chou En-lai put the record straight in his reply:

> The great friendship between our two Powers has grown strong since the October Socialist Revolution. However, imperialism and the counter-revolutionary government of China hampered further cooperation between us. The victory of the Chinese people has brought about radical changes in the situation. The Chinese people, under the leadership of Chairman Mao Tse-tung, have set up the CPR and have made possible sincere cooperation between our two great States.[69]

The Chinese also made claims for the significance of their revolution which might seem somewhat extravagant in Moscow. It was, accord-ing to Mao, 'the third great victory of mankind after the October Revolution and the democratic victory of the Second World War.'[70]

In November 1949, the first Trade Union Conference of Asian and Australian countries, sponsored by the World Federation of Trade Unions, had been held in Peking. The final resolution of this con-ference called in effect for the WFTU to do more for Asia, and to strengthen the work of its liaison bureau with the trade unions of Asia and Australasia. The opening address of Li Shao-ch'i to the Conference is typical of the full-blooded approach of the CCP at this time to revolutionary movements elsewhere in the underdeveloped

world. 'The path which led the Chinese people to victory'—a united
front led by the working class, a militant communist party which
relies on 'armed struggles as the main form of struggle'—was seen
to be of universal validity.

> The path taken by the Chinese people in defeating imperialism and
> its lackeys and in founding the CPR is the path that should be taken
> by the peoples of the various colonial and semi-colonial countries
> in their fight for national independence and people's democracy.
> .. This is the way of Mao Tse-tung.[71]

The so-called 'bourgeois nationalist' leaders of Asia came in for
unrestrained criticism. Nehru was a lackey of US and British imperialism, and bracketed together with Sukarno, Quirino and Rhee
as the 'feeble-minded bourgeoisie of the East.' Independent Burma
was listed among the oppressed countries where the people's struggle
should be supported (in spite of its prompt recognition of China in
December 1949).[72] Thus in the first flush of enthusiasm after their
successful revolution, the Chinese saw themselves as the self-appointed
model for their Asian neighbours.

The Liberation of China heralded a new page in world history.
The people's line, as exemplified by the Chinese Revolution, would
hasten the total collapse of American imperialism. 'The face of China
and of the world will be vastly different in from three to five years.
There will be a new China and a new world.'[73] This kind of sentiment reflected a strong spirit of chauvinism and nationalist rejoicing
which runs through so many Communist statements at this time, the
feeling which led Mao to declare: 'Our nation will never again be
insulted. We have already stood up. . . . We have friends all over the
world'[74] and Liu in the same vein: 'The brightness [of the Chinese
people] will illuminate the whole world.'[74]

This mood of national pride and ebullience was by no means confined to those who held Party cards. It was widespread, particularly
among the students and intellectuals who had been alienated by the
moral and physical corruption of the Kuomintang regime. One eulogy
of the new government by the prominent (non-Communist) social
anthropologist Fei Hsiao-t'ung is worth quoting at some length, since
it so vividly conveys the feeling which many shared in the first days
of Liberation of looking upon a new China through new eyes:

> We have been familiar with the term 'democracy' for more than
> thirty years. What I found (in 1947) in America and England was
> something that looked like the real thing but was not. What I
> learned at the recent conference of people's representatives in
> Peking in six days exceeded all the knowledge that I had acquired on
> the subject in the previous six years. As soon as I set foot in the
> assembly hall I found a multitude of people in uniform, in working

garb, in short dresses, in long gowns, in foreign-style clothes, in skull caps. This was the first time in my life I saw such a cosmopolitan crowd assembled together. . . . These people did not come together as a result of elections held among the populace and formally they did not satisfy the conditions of democracy I had previously known. But could any body like this be produced in Britain or the United States? . . .

This was dictatorship, it is true. But only because of such a dictatorship were we able to have democracy in our conference hall. Understanding dawned on me. I realised now how democracy and dictatorship could be blended together.[75]

By mid-1950, the first steps had been taken to put China on its feet again. Part of the army was about to be demobilised; law and order had been restored throughout most of the country; strenuous efforts were being made to stabilise the currency; land and water communications were beginning to return to normal operations. On May 26, 1950, one year after Shanghai's liberation by the People's Liberation Army, Madame Sun Yat-sen, widow of the founder of the Kuomintang and China's national hero, wrote an article to the people of Shanghai which, allowing for hyperbole, also conveys something of the excitement and tempo of the new China:

This has been a year of learning. We have learned about ourselves. We have learned about our city. We have learned about our future.

What have we learned about ourselves? We have discovered that the Chinese people have a mountain of strength, bursting vitality and a genius that can competently meet any problem and overcome any difficulty. . . .

What have we learned of our city? We have found that the eyes of the nation are upon Shanghai. We have become the symbol of the struggle against the deadweight of imperialism and the cynicism of bureaucratic speculation. . . .

What have we learned of our future? We have found that the People's Republic of China is like an unusually strong and healthy new-born babe. While we are experiencing many of the illnesses of childhood, we have the resilience of youth; there is no question that we are going to grow up and be vigorous with the power to pay our own way in the world and with plenty to spare. . . .[76]

CONCLUSIONS

Alliance with the Soviet Union and rejection of the United States by the Chinese Communists in 1949 was only 'inevitable' in the context of the actual situation, both in China and on the world scene, and its historical antecedents. The Chinese Communists were in any case ideologically inclined towards the Soviet Union, and some form of closer relationship was therefore to be expected once they came to power. But the degree of inclination, the precise form which the relationship took, and its subsequent course, were bound to be affected by external factors. Since Nationalist China itself had been allied to the Soviet Union, a fresh alliance could hardly fail to have been concluded in 1950, whatever the circumstances. It was also to be expected that the Chinese Communists, in the first flush of victory, would go out of their way to demonstrate and dramatise their rejection of the west. This is a common phenomenon among the majority of new nationalist governments, and is by no means confined to those of communist origin. On the other hand, this did not necessarily preclude the eventual development of less strained relations with the west, and even America, if some willingness had been demonstrated on the other side.

It is difficult to judge just how far a consistent American policy of neutrality during the Chinese civil war might have materially affected the outcome. But the possibility that China would have adopted, either formally or tacitly, a 'Titoist' position towards the Soviet Union cannot altogether be ruled out. Nor was it 'inevitable' that the subsequent Sino-Soviet relationship should have lasted as long as it did. In view of the uneasy history of relations between the CCP and the Soviet Union in the past, and of the unequal nature of the alliance which was entered into in 1950, it may even be thought surprising that Sino-Soviet relations should have remained on a relatively even keel for as long as they actually did.

Even at the time, Sino-Soviet relations continued to be strained beneath the surface. The Soviet Union has recently admitted that 'elements of inequality in the relations between our countries [were] imposed during the Stalin personality cult'.[77] These were not corrected until after Stalin's death, when the new Soviet leadership '... withdrew our troops from countries where they had previously been stationed, including the troops from Port Arthur. We liquidated the economic joint companies in China and in other countries and took a number of other measures.'[78] An unofficial report of some remarks which Khrushchev is alleged to have made in 1956, although it must be treated with caution, may well convey the essence of the situation. According to this report, Khrushchev revealed that

> Stalin jeopardised China's alliance with the Soviet Union and thus endangered the solidarity of the Soviet camp by demanding too much in return for aid. Stalin faced Mao Tse-tung ... with a series of economic demands smacking of colonialism. He insisted that he, Stalin, must have the final word on the development of Communism within China as he had in other countries of the Soviet bloc. Mao was extremely embittered by Stalin's insistence on jointly controlled companies and mining and industrial concessions. He

refused to submit to Stalin's authority over Chinese affairs.

Had it not been for the hardness of US policy towards Communist China the Peking government might well have decided to break openly with Moscow as Marshal Tito did in 1948. The situation was said to have been eased by Mao's visit to Russia in 1949–50. But tenseness in relations continued right up to the time of Stalin's death in 1953.[79]

The outbreak of the Korean War served for the time being to intensify China's dependence upon the Soviet Union, both in a political and economic sense. The American decision to interdict the return of Taiwan to China also confirmed the United States's status in Chinese eyes, if confirmation were needed, as public enemy number one. Yet the Korean War itself contributed indirectly to the eventual break-up between China and the Soviet Union. Chinese resentment over Soviet delay in supplying aid, and over the price exacted for such aid when it did arrive, was never forgotten, and was a cause for recrimination when Sino-Soviet polemics later broke out. The immediate effect of the war was to create a mood in China of wholesale reliance upon the Soviet Union, in which the Soviet economic model was copied uncritically, and the entire country was exhorted by Mao himself to 'learn from the Soviet Union.' But this excessive reliance in turn produced its own reaction in the mid-'fifties, when the Soviet model proved totally inadequate, and China moved from wholesale acceptance to wholesale rejection.

There is no intention here to suggest that different circumstances in 1949 or previously would have led to an entirely different pattern of Chinese foreign relations under a communist government, but simply that those circumstances and their antecedents encouraged rigid and extreme positions from which it has become very difficult to retreat. The essential basis of Chinese foreign policy, as it has emerged in recent years, could already be discerned in 1949, although it was not until China at last returned to peacetime conditions and shed its dependence on the Soviet Union, in the mid-'fifties, that it could be given practical effect. This basis can be summarised under the following three headings:

1. Antipathy to the great powers—especially the United States—who had dominated China's foreign affairs for the previous century. In the case of the Soviet Union, this antipathy was temporarily modified by common ideological bonds. In the case of the United States, American hostility to China was already clearly visible in 1949, and the United States was regarded as a dangerous enemy to the new Chinese government.

2. Resurgent nationalism and vigorous assertion of national identity.

3. Determination to rid China of the vestiges of inequality, and to raise her to the status of a great power.

Unless China's entire experience of imperialist and semi-colonial aggression could have been abolished at a stroke of the pen, this was the only logical position which a successful revolution could be expected to adopt. But the modality of this position could still have been affected by different policies, especially by the United States, during the civil war and since 1949–50. This is true even today, although the passage of time has only served to make the task of rapprochement infinitely more difficult.

There is no simple lesson to be drawn from this examination of the origins of China's foreign policy, except one. China's foreign policy was not evolved in a vacuum. It emerged in the light of China's experience in both the immediate and more distant past. It was not inevitable; it was brought about by specific actions and policies operating from outside China. The lesson is very relevant today; for it would equally be a mistake to regard the future working out of Chinese foreign policy as a unilateral and inevitable process, to be left to the passage of time without external assistance. On the contrary, the western attitude towards China today may be as decisive in the long run as it was in the past.

REFERENCES

1. Henry Wei, *China and Soviet Russia*, Princeton, 1956, introduction by Professor Quincy Wright, p.v.
2. Letter transmitting *United States Relations with China*, in US Department of State, *Strengthening the Forces of Freedom*, Washington, DC, 1950, p. 155.
3. Tong Te-kong, *United States Diplomacy in China, 1844–60*, Seattle, 1964, p. 3.
4. Quotations from Marcy in Tong Te-kong, *op. cit.*, pp. 174–5.
5. *Ibid.*, p. 233.
6. The preceding discussion of the Open Door is based upon P. H. Clyde, *International Rivalries in Manchuria 1689–1922*, Ohio, 1926, and E. H. Zabriskie, *US/Russian Rivalry in the Far East*, Philadelphia, 1946. See also F. V. Field, *American Participation in the China Consortiums*, Chicago, 1931; Li Tien-yi, *Woodrow Wilson's China Policy, 1913–17*, New York, 1952.
7. Paul S. Reinsch, *An American Diplomat in China*, London, 1922, p. 106.
8. *Ibid.*, p. 338.
9. Address before Commonwealth Club of California, March 15, 1950, in *Strengthening the Forces of Freedom*, p. 154.
10. E. M. Gull, *British Economic Interests in the Far East*, London, 1943, p. 239.
11. Dorothy Borg, *The United States and the Far Eastern Crisis of 1933–38*, Cambridge, Mass., 1964, pp. 524, 544.
12. Lansing to Reinsch, November 4, 1914, Dept. of State, *Foreign*

Relations of the United States, 1914, Supplement, Washington, DC, 1928, p. 190.

13. Arthur N. Young, China and the Helping Hand, Cambridge, Mass., 1963, p. 206.

14. Ibid., p. 206.

15. John King Fairbank, 'Legacies of Past Associations' in Urban G. Whitaker (ed.), The Foundations of US China Policy, Berkeley, 1959, p. 84.

16. See for instance Israel Epstein, The Unfinished Revolution in China, Boston, 1947; Harrison Forman, Report from Red China, London 1946; Gunther Stein, The Challenge of Red China, London, 1945.

17. See interview with Chu Teh in Stein, Challenge of Red China, pp. 242–51.

18. US Relations with China, pp. 2378–80. Mao discounted the possibility of Soviet intervention. He said that it depended on 'the circumstances of the Soviet Union', and that the Chinese did not expect Soviet help.

19. Stilwell's Command Problems, pp. 432, 467.

20. See further Edgar Snow, Random Notes on Red China, Cambridge, Mass., 1957, pp. 125–30.

21. Yalta Papers, pp. 346–51, Hurley to Roosevelt, January 14, 1945.

22. Chieh-fang Jih-pao, Yenan, December 16, 1944.

23. C. F. Romanus and R. Sutherland, United States Army in World War II. China–Burma–India Theatre, III (Time Runs out in CBI), p. 252.

24. Michael Lindsay, 'China: Report of a Visit', International Affairs, January, 1950.

25. Time Runs Out in CBI, p. 337, n.11.

26. Random Notes on Red China, p. 130.

26a. US Relations with China, pp. 382–3.

27. Letter of transmittal, Strengthening the Forces of Freedom, p. 166.

28. Figures from US Relations with China, pp. 969–75, 1043–4. The total figures for economic and military aid post-VJ day include the procurement value of material supplied, where known, not the nominal sale price, which was much less.

29. Tang Tsou, America's Failure in China, Chicago, 1963, p. 478.

30. Yu-kwei Cheng, Foreign Trade and Industrial Development of China, Washington, DC, 1956, pp. 180–2.

31. US Senate, Committee on Foreign Relations, Nomination of Philip C. Jessup, Washington, 1951, p. 793.

32. Karl Rankin, China Assignment, Seattle, 1964, pp. 20, 41.

33. For exactly this interpretation, see the five commentaries written between August 14 and September 16, 1949 by Mao Tse-tung on the White Paper, in Mao Tse-tung, Selected Works, iv, Peking, 1961, pp. 425–59.

34. Mao Tse-tung, Selected Works, III, Peking, 1965, Appendix: 'Resolution on certain questions in the history of our party,' pp. 177–225.

35. Jack Belden, China Shakes the World, London, 1949, p. 67.

36. Editorial Departments of People's Daily and Red Flag, September 12, 1963; 'On the Question of Stalin', in Peking Review, September 20, 1963.

37. 'Resolution on certain questions in the history of our party', Mao, Selected Works, III, p. 195.

38. Mao Tse-tung, December 21, 1939, speech to celebrate Stalin's 60th birthday, NCNA (Peking), December 1949.

39. Ch'en Po-ta, 'Stalin and the Chinese Revolution', NCNA (Peking), December 19, 1949, in NCNA (London) Special Supplement, No. 39.

40. See further Charles B. McLane, *Soviet Policy and the Chinese Communists, 1931–1946*, New York, 1958, chapter 5.

41. Report from Harbin by A. T. Steele in *New York Herald Tribune*, September 8, 1946.

42. *Kommunist* leading article, 'Proletarian Internationalism the Banner of the Working People of the World', *Pravda*, May 6–7, 1964, extract trans. in *China Quarterly*, London, No. 19, July-September, 1964.

43. Herbert Feis, *The China Tangle*, Princeton, 1953, p. 359.

44. *New York Times*, August 24, 1945.

45. Moscow radio, September 28, 1945; *New York Times*, September 29, 1945.

46. The delegation may have included Mao himself: see McLane, *Soviet Policy and the Chinese Communists*, p. 254, n.165.

47. Milovan Djilas, *Conversations with Stalin*, London, 1963, p. 141.

48. Vladimer Dedijer, *Tito*, New York, 1953, p. 322.

49. Henry Wei, *China and Soviet Russia*, Princeton, 1956, pp. 230–4.

50. *US Relations with China*, pp. 265–6; *Survey of International Affairs, 1946–48*, London, pp. 295–6.

51. Mao, *Selected Works*, IV, pp. 158–9, 173.

52. C. P. Fitzgerald, *Revolution in China*, London, 1952, p. 164.

53. The NCNA foreword to Liu Shao-chi's *On Nationalism and Internationalism* states that 'This article is published in order to clear up certain of the misunderstandings and confused notions which exist at present both inside and outside the Communist Party concerning the question of proletarian internationalism and bourgeois nationalism and also to expose the extremely reactionary propaganda put out by fascist quarters regarding this question.' (NCNA, Special Supplement No. 12, London, December 28, 1948.)

54. Mao Tse-tung, 'Revolutionary Forces of the World Unite', *For a Lasting Peace, for a People's Democracy*, No. 21, 1948. The italicised sentence is omitted from the version in Mao's *Selected Works*. For full text see NCNA (London), Special Supplement No. 11, November 23, 1948.

55. *Soviet News*, January 3, 1950.

56. Liu Shao-ch'i, speech of October 5, 1949, NCNA (London), Special Supplement No. 30.

57. *Ibid.*

58. *Tung-pei Jih-pao* ed., August 8, 1949, in BBC *Summary of World Broadcasts. The Far East*, Nos. 17, 18.

59. Speech of August 14, 1949, *ibid.*, No. 18.

60. See note 56 above.

61. NCNA, February 15, 1950.

62. Mao, *Selected Works*, IV, p. 407.

63. NCNA ed., February 15, 1950.

64. Chu Teh, speech of February 23, 1950, on the 32nd anniversary of the Soviet Army.

65. Liu Shao-ch'i, May Day Address for 1950, *People's China*, May 16, 1950.

66. Mao Tse-tung, Address to the State Council, April 13, 1950.

67. *Soviet News*, February 11, 1950.

68. *Ibid.*, February 16, 1950.

69. *Ibid.*

70. Quoted by the CCP delegate to the Czech Party Congress of June 1949, NCNA, June 7, 1949.

71. Liu Shao-ch'i, address to WFTU Conference, NCNA, November 23, 1949.

72. See further H. Arthur Steiner, *The International Position of Communist China*, New York, 1958, pp. 8–15.

73. Lu Ting-yi, quoted in *Christian Science Monitor*, December 7, 1948.

74. Speeches of Mao and Liu to the People's Political Consultative Conference, NCNA, September 29, 1949.

75. Quoted in *New York Herald Tribune*, May 13, 1950.

76. Mme Sun Yat-sen, 'Shanghai's new day has dawned', NCNA, May 26, 1950.

77. Mikhail Suslov, Report to Plenary Session of the CPSU CC, February 14, 1964, 'The struggle of the CPSU for the unity of the international communist movement', *Soviet Booklets*, London, Vol II, No. 3.

78. CPSU CC, letter of the CCP CC, March 7, 1964, *Peking Review*, May 1964.

79. Report by Sydney Gruson of alleged remarks by Khrushchev at gathering of party leaders for funeral of Boleslaw Bierut in Warsaw, March 1956, *New York Times*, June 4, 1956.

Revolution and Intervention in Vietnam

RICHARD MORROCK

I

THE seven decades of French colonial rule in Vietnam (1884–1954) were by no means lacking in acts of popular resistance to foreign domination. The French regime in Indo-China was marked by racism, brutality, hopelessly backward economic, social and educational policies, and the most fierce exploitation of the indigenous workers and peasants. (5, p. 424; 31, p. 70.) It was hardly surprising, therefore, that few consecutive years passed without some attempt by the Vietnamese to restore their national independence.

Modern revolutionary nationalism, however—as opposed to traditionalist nationalism, which sought independence under the existing dynasty—became a force in Vietnam only in the 1929–30 period, when it was given an impetus by the worldwide depression. A party known as the Quoc Dan Dang, or Vietnamese Nationalist Party, had been formed a few years earlier in Canton, China. In February 1930, the Quoc Dan Dang, together with mutinous Vietnamese troops in the French colonial army, staged an insurrection in Tonkin (northern Vietnam). The rebellion was crushed by the French, who destroyed or exiled the entire Quoc Dan Dang leadership. (23, pp. 78–9.)

The abortive nationalist rising had coincided with the foundation of the Vietnamese Communist Party (subsequently named the Indo-China Communist Party, and still later the Lao Dong, or Workers' Party) in Canton by Ho Chi Minh, an experienced revolutionary organiser who had spent many years in exile from his homeland. This new Communist Party was extremely effective in Vietnam, especially among the peasants and landless agricultural labourers. During the summer of 1930 the Communists organised a peasant uprising in the provinces of Ha Tinh and Nghe An, in what is now the southern portion of North Vietnam. Revolutionary soviets were formed, arms were distributed to the peasants, and the holdings of the large landlords were divided up. The French crushed this rising within a matter of weeks, but it proved to be the first battle in a long and bloody struggle.

For ten years the Vietnamese Communists were in relative eclipse, although the Trotskyists picked up much support, especially among the Saigon workers. Whether the Trotskyists had as much support elsewhere in Vietnam is difficult to ascertain, since the French permitted elections only in Cochin-China, the southernmost of the three regions of Vietnam—even in Cochin-China, most of the population did not qualify for the franchise. Nevertheless, the Trotskyists obtained the overwhelming majority of the vote in the 1939 elections. Their criticism of the 'Stalinist' Communists was based upon the assumption that the proletariat, rather than the peasantry, should lead the revolution in Vietnam; and some of their theoreticians even attacked Mao Tse-tung for setting up peasant soviets in China, on the grounds that this was an ultra-left strategy. (32.) The Trotskyists, however, beset by internal divisions and insisting that the revolution be led by a class which had not been fully developed in Vietnam, rapidly lost ground to the Communist Party once changing conditions made it possible to think about revolution again.

This happened in 1940, when the Japanese occupied French Indo-China. Unlike the situation in the other South-East Asian colonial territories, the Japanese met with little resistance from the established authorities in Indo-China. The collaboration between the Vichy regime and the Germans found its counterpart in Asia in the collaboration between the French colonialists and the Japanese. During the first year of the Japanese occupation, the French suppressed with great severity two uprisings by the Vietnamese—one (in Tonkin) led by right-wing nationalists, the other (in the Mekong delta) led by the Communists. (17, pp. 24–5.)

With the urban proletariat too weak and too close to its peasant origins to lead the resistance, and with the peasants themselves suffering under the triple yoke of the Vietnamese landowners, the French colonialists and the Japanese invaders, it was evident that the resistance would have to be led by some broad front, uniting all patriotic Vietnamese regardless of class, but capable nevertheless of appealing to the most down-trodden members of society who had the most to gain from revolution. The Communist Party saw this need, and created, in May 1941, the Viet Nam Doc Lap Dong Minh, or Vietnamese Independence League. Besides the Communist Party, the Democratic Party and the Radical Socialist Party were represented in a united front, which was known for short as the Viet Minh. The Democratic Party was representative of the petty bourgeoisie, and the Radical Socialists represented the intellectuals. What was created was a 'bloc of three classes,' similar to Mao Tse-tung's 'bloc of four classes' (workers, peasants, petty bourgeoisie and national bourgeoisie) but without the national bourgeoisie, which did not exist in Vietnam. Within the Viet Minh, the Communist Party maintained its identity and its distinct Marxist-Leninist programme.

Late in 1944, the Viet Minh began organising armed guerrilla resistance bands in Tonkin. These guerrillas had the support of the American office of Strategic Services, which had a base in southern China. The rapid growth of the guerrilla movement was aided by the break-up of the alliance between the Japanese and the French. In March 1945, fearing that the French would switch sides, the Japanese put them in concentration camps, while declaring Vietnam 'independent.' The Viet Minh took advantage of this coup to extend its activities into central and southern Vietnam—where revolutionary bases were created which were never liquidated even at the zenith of Ngo Dinh Diem's power. (36, pp. 29–30.)

When Japan surrendered, five months later, its troops were still in occupation of ex-French Indo-China. Returning to their barracks, the Japanese troops handed power over to the Viet Minh, which was the only other force in the country at the time, and which still enjoyed the support of the western allies. The Democratic Republic of Vietnam was established in August 1945 in Hanoi, amidst great popular enthusiasm.

On September 14, 1945, the London *Times,* commenting on the political situation in Vietnam, explained to its readers: 'There seem to be only two parties of any significance at the moment, the Viet-min and the Communists. The Viet-min, which is the stronger, is especially active in the north.' (23, p. 130.)

After 1945 American far eastern policy underwent a change. Whereas during the war, the United States had been willing to cooperate with communist-led resistance movements in Asia, postwar American policy was directed entirely against communism, and was not loath to unite with colonialists and even former Japanese collaborators in the struggle against communist-led or supported movements for national liberation. The British, for their part, were consistent in their support of colonialism. Immediately after the Japanese surrender, a British division landed in Saigon on the pretext of disarming the Japanese; they were welcomed as allies and liberators by the Vietnamese and the Viet-Minh. Instead of disarming the Japanese, however, the British permitted them to keep their weapons, and used the Japanese troops for security duty. At the same time, they freed numerous French and Foreign Legion soldiers, who were given back their arms. Late in September 1945, these French and Foreign Legion troops attacked the Vietnamese in Saigon, carrying out a massacre and driving the Viet Minh authorities out of Saigon. (27, p. 226; 23, p. 130.)

In January 1946, the Viet Minh held nation-wide elections (in the occupied areas of southern Vietnam these elections were held underground). The northern two-thirds of the country had already been occupied by Chinese Nationalist troops, who brought with them cadres of the Quoc Dan Dang and other nationalist organisations. Although the Chinese did not use military force against the Viet Minh authorities, they did encourage these rival nationalist factions, and helped them seize control of several northern Vietnamese districts. When the Viet Minh held elections, it promised a certain number of seats in the National Assembly to these nationalist factions; thus the election took on the character of a plebiscite. Nevertheless, even an American source admits: '... the National Assembly that emerged as a result of the voting was a fairly representative body.' (32, p. 159.) Even the French realised that the pro-independence forces in Vietnam had widespread popular backing. In March 1946, France recognised the Democratic Republic of Vietnam as the legitimate government of all Vietnam. In the agreement signed by Ho Chi Minh and the Deputy High Commissioner for Indo-China, Jean Sainteny, France stated that she 'recognises the Republic of Vietnam as a free state having its government and its parliament, its army and its finances....' (20, pp. 52–3.) Vietnam agreed to be a member state of the ephemeral French Union, and French troops were permitted to relieve the Chinese Nationalists in Hanoi and Haiphong.

Some critics of the Viet Minh (21, p. 9) maintain that Ho Chi Minh could have obtained an even greater degree of independence from France in 1946 than he actually settled for. This argument overlooks the fact that had the Viet Minh not accepted the French offer (whose primary drawback was that French troops were to be permitted to remain), the French could have negotiated the same agreement with one of the other nationalist groups. The Viet Minh's People's Army had not yet been in existence for two years, and was in no position to carry on a simultaneous fight against both the French and the anti-Viet Minh nationalists. It is nevertheless true that the Viet Minh placed all too much hope on the influence that the French Communist Party could or would be willing to exert on the French government to take reasonable line in Indo-China. This was an understandable, if regrettable, mistake.

The Viet Minh took advantage of the respite obtained by means of the March agreement to eliminate several political groups which would certainly have given them trouble later on. In the north, these were the Quoc Dan Dang and some other nationalist parties. In the south, they were mainly the Trotskyists and the Hoa Hao. Of these, only the last-named offered any serious resistance.

Cochin-China has long been distinguished from the rest of Vietnam by the existence of the Hoa Hao and Cao Dai religious cults—the former a reform Buddhist sect, and the latter an eclectic combination of Confucianism, Buddhism and Roman Catholicism. Fervent adherents of these religions probably number not quite a million at the present time, but for historical reasons these two cults have had influence out of proportion to the number of their followers. The Cao Dais are concentrated in Tay Ninh province, due north of Saigon, while the Hoa Haos have their base in An Giang and Kien Phong provinces, along the upper Bassac river. Both base areas border Cambodia; both lie along important trade routes. Much of the trade between the Cochin-Chinese seaports and Cambodia was in the hands of these religious groups; and the Hoa Haos still monopolise the trade between the government-controlled and NLF-controlled zones of South Vietnam. (22, p. 101.)

The Hoa Haos in particular were strongly opposed to the Viet Minh, since their movement, originally based on craftsmen and traders, had subsequently come under the control of the large landowners. During the Japanese occupation, both religious groups organised their own armed forces, whose members were placed on the Japanese payroll. After World War II, the French took over the task of sponsoring these military organisations.

While the Viet Minh was fighting the Hoa Hao, the French were conspiring to overthrow the Ho Chi Minh government and to restore the colonial regime. They cut off the flow of rice from Cochin-China to northern Vietnam, causing a famine. The Viet Minh abolished taxes in Tonkin as a relief measure, leaving the Vietnamese government dependent upon customs for its finances. The French then demanded the right to control customs at the seaport of Haiphong; the Vietnamese resisted this demand, and the French retaliated by bombarding the Vietnamese quarter of Haiphong, killing thousands of civilians.

This bloodshed marked the beginning of the French-Indo-China War. By 1954, about half a million soldiers were involved on each side in the conflict: fighting for the Viet Minh were Vietnamese peasants, workers and intellectuals, plus smaller numbers of Laotians and Cambodians who carried the struggle into their own homelands; on the French side were troops from metropolitan France, from North Africa and from West Africa. There were also Indo-Chinese troops, who generally fought with singular lack of enthusiasm, at least according to French General Navarre. (23, p. 312.) There were, in addition, the soldiers of the Foreign Legion fighting on France's side, many of them former German Nazis and Italian Fascists. Their conduct was hardly calculated to endear the French cause to the Indo-Chinese peoples.

In 1947 the French—possibly on American advice—approached ex-Emperor Bao Dai, who was living in Hong Kong on a Viet Minh pension. Bao Dai had served as puppet ruler under the French during the 1930s—his first Minister of the Interior being Ngo Dinh Diem. Later he had served the Japanese, and had eventually abdicated voluntarily when the Viet Minh came to power. After cooperating with the Viet Minh briefly, he retired from public life. The French brought him back to Vietnam to head a puppet government, giving a fig leaf of legitimacy to the French colonialist endeavour.

The only significant group to defect from the independence struggle during the French-Indo-China War was the Catholic minority in Tonkin. French missionaries, over the years, had converted about ten per cent of the Vietnamese to Catholicism; in Tonkin, these converts lived in their own villages, under the political control of their priests (large landlords being very few outside the Mekong delta). The priests, in turn, followed the advice of their bishops and archbishops, many of whom were Frenchmen, Spaniards and Irishmen. Fanatically opposed to communism, the Catholic hierarchy in Vietnam succeeded in getting the Catholic peasants to accept Bao Dai rather than Ho Chi Minh. (22, p. 103.)

The majority of the Vietnamese population, however, gave enthusiastic support to the Viet Minh. Part of this support was due to the progressive social policies carried out in the liberated areas which were under Viet Minh control. For example, the Viet Minh campaigned against illiteracy, which had actually increased under French colonial rule. The Viet Minh also supported autonomy for the tribal minorities, who numbered $2\frac{1}{2}$ to 3 million, largely in the Tonkin mountains. The Viet Minh had their headquarters in one of the areas populated by the tribesmen, and many tribesmen rose to high positions in the Viet Minh and the Vietnamese People's Army.

Finally, the Viet Minh initiated a program of land reform, which had far-reaching effect in the Mekong delta; in this fertile region, most of the land belonged to a relative handful of extremely wealthy landowners. At first, the Viet Minh reduced rents and interest rates; when this caused most of the landowners to side with the French, the Viet Minh began confiscating the holdings of collaborators. This included most of the arable land in the Mekong delta; the large majority of the landowners spent the years of the anti-French struggle in Saigon. Finally, in 1953, the Viet Minh announced its intention of distributing the holdings of all large landowners, regardless of the latter's political views.

Once the Communists had emerged victorious in the Chinese Civil War, it was possible for the Viet Minh to receive assistance from the outside. However, one should not overestimate the importance of this aid. No Chinese or Soviet soldiers ever fought for the Viet Minh, and most of the weapons used by the Viet Minh had been captured from the other side. This is generally the case in guerrilla movements.

The French debacle at Dien Bien Phu was the occasion, rather than the cause, of the decision by Paris to terminate the war. The United States, apparently ready to fight to the last Frenchman, proposed a joint US-British-French offensive against the Viet Minh, which would include the use of nuclear weapons. For several reasons, this idea never came to fruition. First, the French people had been fighting a losing war in Indo-China for more than seven years, and were not anxious to prolong it. Second, Great Britain was reluctant to enter the war, since its own interests had not been directly threatened. Third, there was much opposition to intervention in the United States, where Eisenhower had been elected less than two years previously on a platform of ending the Korean War. (10, pp. 225–8.) Finally, it was not certain, nor even probable, that atomic weapons could have been effectively used against a guerrilla army.

Thus, in 1954, almost nine years after the creation of the Democratic Republic of Vietnam, the French-Indo-China War was ended at the conference table at Geneva. As could be seen by the refusal of American Secretary of State John Foster Dulles to shake hands with his Chinese opposite number, Chou En-lai, it was a bitter pill for the United States to swallow. Grumbled *US News and World Report:* 'The non-Communist white man, in a word, seems to be through in Asia. It's up to the non-Communist Asians now.' (42.)

II

According to the Geneva agreement, Vietnam was to be temporarily divided along the Ben Hai river, which ran through Annam (central Vietnam) near the 17th parallel. French Union forces, including the Vietnamese who had fought for France, were to be regrouped south of the armistice line, where Bao Dai still retained nominal authority. Viet Minh troops were to be withdrawn north of the line, where the Viet Minh was in control. Civilian sympathisers of one side or the other were given until 1956 to change zones. Elections were to be held throughout all of Vietnam no later than the summer of 1956, in order to set up a national government with genuine popular support. In the North, nearly all the Catholics in two bishoprics (Bui Chu and Phat Diem) left for the South, rather than live under the Viet Minh. (22, p. 105.) They were accompanied by former French Union soldiers of Vietnamese origin and their families. Altogether, these evacuees numbered about 875,000, mainly Catholics.

From the South, about 100,000 Viet Minh soldiers were evacuated. Civilian sympathisers of the Viet Minh, however, remained in the native villages, assuming that the anti-Communist interregnum in South Vietnam would be brief. Although the Viet Minh lost nearly all of its military strength south of the 17th parallel, it retained its political influence throughout the countryside, both in villages which had been in liberated zones during the war, and in villages from which the French withdrew after 1954. Joseph Alsop wrote that according to American informants in Saigon, '. . . outside the feudal domains of the military religious sects, anywhere from 50 to 70 per cent of the southern Indo-Chinese villages are subject to Viet Minh influence or control. French experts give still higher percentages, between 60 and 90.'* (18, p. 36.) In 1957, William Henderson stated in *Foreign Affairs*:

> The exact strength of the Communists in South Vietnam is a matter of speculation. After May 18, 1955, the date on which all Viet Minh forces were supposedly withdrawn from the South, the Communists continued to exercise effective political authority in many rural areas. They had extensively infiltrated the government apparatus, the police and the armed forces; and they enjoyed considerable support, or at least acquiescence, among large segments of the rural population. (19, pp. 288–9.)

And after the fall of Bao Dai in 1955, according to I. Milton Sacks, 'The Republic of Vietnam . . . had little real authority in the area that was nominally defined as its territory.' (32, p. 168.)

When the French withdrew, the official head of state in Saigon was Bao Dai, and his Prime Minister was Ngo Dinh Diem, who had taken office just before the start of the Geneva conference. After Geneva, Bao Dai followed his erstwhile sponsors back to France. Diem was left behind to manage the affairs of the tottering puppet regime.

The anti-Communist forces in South Vietnam made use of the two years of grace between the Geneva armistice and the mid-1956 deadline for the elections that never were to take place. Diem had no support, or even authority, in the countryside at that point, and even in Saigon he was being challenged by the Hoa Haos, the Cao Dais, the Binh Xuyen bandit group and dissident army elements; however, Diem knew that he could call on the United States for assistance . . . and this he did.

As soon as the armistice was in effect, the United States began the creation of 'Free Vietnam.' This project was carried out on two levels. In South Vietnam, about $250,000,000 per year in military and economic aid was poured in by the United States. Meanwhile, in the United States, a massive campaign was initiated to convince the American people that South Vietnam was a showcase of anti-Communism, inhabited by a 'brave little people' who had 'resisted

* *New York Herald Tribune*, March 1, 1955.

Communist aggression,' and who were heroically tackling the problems of poverty, illiteracy and underdevelopment under the leadership of the immensely popular, democratic, anti-Communist patriot, Ngo Dinh Diem.

A central factor in the establishment of 'Free Vietnam,' both in terms of its legitimacy at home and its image in the United States, was the election of October 1955. Between 1954 and 1955, Diem had succeeded in winning the loyalty of the generals in Bao Dai's army—this was accomplished when the United States made it clear that it would not give aid to any military clique which toppled Diem. Subsequently, Diem used the South Vietnamese army to crush the Binh Xuyen, the Cao Dai and the Hoa Hao. Without foreign subsidies, the armies of the cults lost most of their effectiveness.

Diem then chose to hold a plebiscite on the question of the continuation of the monarchy. The voters had a choice between a republic under Diem or the old monarchy under Bao Dai. Wrote David Hotham of the London *Times*: '. . . It would be well to destroy the myth that Diem's regime was ever a popular one. No one who was in Saigon in October 1955 [the month of the plebiscite], unless blind to realities, would dispute this.' (25, p. 347.) The results of the plebiscite were: Diem, 5,721,735; Bao Dai, 63,017. (5, p. 468.)

There are several remarkable things about this result. The total population of South Vietnam at the time was perhaps 13 million—of whom nearly a million were Chinese or French citizens, not eligible to vote. About half of the population was below the voting age, due to the low life expectancy common in colonial countries, and to the effects of the long war. Of the eligible voters, therefore, close to 95 per cent must have turned out for this election—which was held little more than one year after independence—and of these, almost 99 per cent voted for Diem. (One might compare this to India, where less than half of the eligible voters participate in national elections, of whom only about 50 per cent vote for the Congress Party.) Diem's overwhelming victory could only have been caused by two things: fraud on a gigantic scale; or a highly disciplined, loyal, efficient and mass-based political movement. There can be little argument as to which was responsible; Diem's mass organisation, the National Revolutionary Movement, was only formed *after* the 1955 election.

This political organisation, which was not a political party in the accepted sense of the term, was to play an important role in the newly-created Republic of Vietnam. It was a broad front, intended to mobilise popular support for the regime, especially among the youth. The NRM sponsored many meetings in the countryside, where, according to the Saigon press, innumerable Viet Minh cadres would 'recant their error' and 'rally to the government.' (40, p. 5.) Civil servants were obliged to belong to the NRM's auxiliary.

Real power lay with another political organisation, the Can Lao, or 'Labour and Personalism Party,' which was similar in structure and purpose to the Japanese Black Dragon Society or the South African Broederbond. It had five-man cells, and its members hid their affiliation. The members of the Can Lao joined other political groups in order to dominate them. They informed the government of the behaviour of civil servants and army officers. The Can Lao was the typical apparatus of a totalitarian fascist state. (14, pp. 48–9.)

The NRM and the Can Lao tried to make out of Diem a 'father-figure' who could compete with the Communists' 'Uncle Ho'. Wrote William Henderson:

> Public adulation of the President ... has reached startling proportions; and although Diem professes to be embarrassed by all the fuss, he has done little to stop it. A constant barrage of propaganda is laid down through the controlled press and radio. 'Spontaneous' demonstrations are staged with distressing frequency. There is even a strength-through-joy youth movement that stirs unhappy memories of the Nazi past. (19, p. 293.)

Numerous high posts in the South Vietnamese government went to members of Diem's family. His brother, Ngo Dinh Nhu, was the President's chief political adviser, and head of the NRM and the Can Lao. Nhu's wife was head of the women's organisation and chief government whip in the shadow parliament. Another brother, Ngo Dinh Can, was Viceroy of Central Vietnam; he ruled southern Annam from his headquarters at Hue, and had his own secret police force. Archbishop Ngo Dinh Thuc, another brother, had widespread economic interests in Cochin-China, as did a sister in Annam, who died in 1957. A fifth brother, Ngo Dinh Luyen, was ambassador to England, and Madame Nhu's father was ambassador to the United States. Much of the vast amount of American aid to South Vietnam was channelled through the ruling family's sticky fingers, and was used, in part, to finance the Can Lao. (14, p. 28.) Thus did the American taxpayers assist 'democratic growth' in 'Free Vietnam.' This was not even an improvement over the days of Bao Dai, when American aid was used to finance the construction of the world's largest house of ill repute. (23, p. 379.)

An official philosophy, known as 'personalism,' was espoused by the regime. This doctrine was a potpourri of right-wing Catholic spiritualism and Dulles-style anti-communism. One foremost characteristic of the Diem regime was the extent to which the Catholic minority—especially those Catholics from the North—was favoured. Until Diem's fall, for example, only Catholic chaplains were permitted in the predominantly Buddhist South Vietnamese army. This favouritism, together with the official propagation of the 'personalist' ideology, served to alienate the regime from even many anti-Communist groups in the country.

Before long, it appeared as if His Majesty the Emperor had been replaced by His Majesty the President. There was the same corruption, the same lack of contact with the masses, and the same subservience to a foreign power that had prevailed under Bao Dai. European writers, generally, were not taken in by the pretence of democracy. Bernard Fall wrote that the Diem government 'is, in terms of the actual relations between government and governed, an absolute monarchy, such as ... Franco's Spain has been since 1939.' (10, p. 237.) David Hotham wrote, under the heading *General Consideration of American Programs:*

> The chief hope of defending the south from the communism which threatened it at the time of Dien Bien Phu, and which still threatens it today [1959]—for the battle is not won, but hardly begun—was that somebody should succeed in uniting all the genuinely anti-Communist nationalist elements into a regime which would have the confidence of the southern people. Had that been done, the bastion would have been strong. But this is precisely what has not been done. Instead of uniting it, Diem has divided the south. Instead of merely crushing his legitimate enemies, the Communists, he has crushed all opposition of every kind, however anti-Communist it might be. In so doing, he has destroyed the very basis on which his regime should be founded. He has been able to do this, simply and solely because of the massive dollar aid he has had from across the Pacific, which kept in power a man who, by all the laws of human and political affairs, would long ago have fallen. Diem's main supporters are to be found in North America, not in Free Vietnam. This is an unnatural situation, and unnatural situations do not last long. (25, p. 348.)

On the other hand, Diem received much favourable publicity in the United States. There were some sceptics, at first, such as Joseph Alsop, who described Diem as 'narrow, obstinate and petty,'* (23, p. 348.) but most other writers—experts and journalists alike—showed almost unlimited enthusiasm for South Vietnam's dictator. He was hailed as 'The Miracle Man of Vietnam' (possibly for the skill with which he made his political opponents disappear), 'the Churchill of Asia,' 'the greatest little man in Asia,' and so forth. In 1956 the historian Alan Nevins said in a letter to the American Friends of Vietnam that 'Vietnam is a country of which the West may feel proud.' (38.) In 1959, Ellen Hammer stated, '... the service rendered by Diem to free Asia may well extend beyond the frontiers of the Republic of Vietnam,' (25, p. 41.) while Joseph Buttinger

* *New York Herald Tribune,* March 31, 1955.

concluded simultaneously: 'In Vietnam the Communists are now being deprived of total victory because the West is applying policies consonant with the principles of a democratic world.' (25, p. 31.)

American public and governmental opinion was thus poorly prepared for the rapid deterioration of Saigon's authority in the countryside which took place during the late 1950s. Regularly, Diem would hold 'free elections,' in which he, or parliamentary candidates running with his backing, would emerge with overwhelming majorities. Few bothered to check on certain anomalies in these elections. Why was the abstention rate 25 per cent in Saigon, but only five per cent in the countryside, where the percentage of illiteracy was higher? Why was Diem receiving two-thirds of the votes in Saigon, but 98 to 99 per cent in the provinces? And why were the highest percentages of votes for Diem or his protégés invariably recorded in those provinces which were under Viet Minh control, even during the apogee of Diemist power? (31, pp. 93–7.) The only way such results could have been achieved was through massive stuffing of ballot boxes.

Pro-'Free Vietnam' publicity in the United States made much of the 875,000 refugees who left North Vietnam to settle in the South between 1954 and 1956. Robert Scheer effectively debunks the argument that the flight of these people was proof that the Communists were hated by the majority of the Vietnamese. (30, esp. pp. 26–31.) Most of the refugees, of course, were Catholics, and nearly all had fought for the French. Many went to South Vietnam in the belief that they would be given land—a commodity in short supply in the Tonkin delta region. Several tens of thousands of these refugees were settled in the Cai San colony, a block of model villages in the Trans-Bassac area of South Vietnam. But hundreds of thousands more were concentrated in a ring around Saigon (22, p. 105); this area was already overpopulated, and it is certain that for so many newcomers to have been settled there, many of the original inhabitants would have to have been displaced.

The refugees, furthermore, were the only section of the South Vietnamese population which the Diem regime felt it could rely upon. With the assistance of the International Rescue Committee, educated Catholic refugees were brought into the Diem government to replace indigenous South Vietnamese, whom Diem distrusted as too pro-French. (30, p. 29.)

There was only one other social group in South Vietnam which placed itself entirely in Diem's camp—the large landowners from the Mekong delta. This small but important group had identified with the French cause for reasons of class interest, and supported Diem for the same reason.

When the French-Indo-China War ended, the Viet Minh had already distributed the extensive holdings of these gentlemen, without compensation. Once a certain amount of stability had been achieved in Saigon, however, the landlords decided that they wanted to get their property back, and some even hoped for the back rents for the years they had spent hiding in Saigon. Diem came to their assistance, drawing upon the services of the American expert, Wolf Ladejinsky. Ladejinsky produced a 'land reform' ordinance which served the interests of the landlords, rather than the peasants. This ordinance 'was in fact proclaimed at a time when large landowners seemed to be regaining influence in places of political power, and was in many respects an inadequate compromise measure.' (35, p. 81.) It was to be expected, of course, that the failure of the Viet Minh to gain control of South Vietnam would mean that its policies—for better or worse—would not be implemented south of the Ben Hai river. What was most ironic is that Ladejinsky, the man in charge of giving back the Mekong delta to the landlords, had himself once been labelled a communist by Senator Joseph McCarthy.

The program seemed progressive enough on the surface, if one did not know the realities of property relations in the South Vietnamese countryside after 1954. It called for the reduction of rents from the prewar 40–50 per cent to 15–25 per cent of the principal crop, depending upon the value of the land for the exact percentage. Interest charges on loans, and rent on tools and draft animals, was not to exceed 12 per cent. (25, p. 201.) As for land ownership, the landlords were 'limited' to 245 acres (although more land could be allotted them for 'religious purposes'), and the land that was confiscated was paid for. Ten per cent of its value was paid immediately in cash, and the remainder in government bonds. (9.) Regulations regarding abandoned land were favourable to the owners; landlords had only to 'declare their intention either to lease abandoned land or to cultivate it themselves; otherwise they were to be considered absent.' (25, p. 201.)

The reforms were made primarily for the purpose of impressing American public opinion with the 'democratic national revolution' that was supposedly taking place in South Vietnam. The provisions which restricted the landlords were, in fact, not always enforced. Furthermore, and most important, Diem's 'reforms' constituted actual retrogression. The government was 'reducing' rents which the Viet Minh had abolished, selling land which the Viet Minh had given away, and reestablishing estates which the Viet Minh had broken up!

Peasant resistance to these measures was widespread, foreshadowing the civil war which was to come. Already in the spring of 1955, Ladejinsky reported finding what the *New York Times* described as 'a strange land reform problem'. The *Times* elaborated: 'Usually it is the tenants who are most eager for land reform and the landlords who are reluctant. In the southern half of Vietnam, however, the landlords are accepting the Government's land reform plan more readily than the tenants.' (8.)

The government's ordinance provided for Agrarian Reform Committees, consisting of the district or provincial chief, plus equal numbers of representatives of tenants and landlords. The tenants, however, obstructed the election of their own representatives. They refused 'to have anything to do with the machinery of the new rent control law. In some areas many potential electors stayed away during balloting for tenant representatives, and there were even instances of tenants going to polling places in groups, then ostentatiously refusing to vote.' (35, pp. 84–5.) It often became necessary for the provincial chiefs to appoint the tenant 'representatives.'

The peasants, led by Viet Minh cadres, began to organise violent resistance to Diem's effort to undo the Viet Minh's land reform. 'Indeed,' wrote Wesley Fishel in 1959, 'the main target of the Communist effort in recent months has been the Government's land reform program. . . . Terrorist attacks on agents sent out from Saigon to explain the land reform idea or to carry out land surveys or division have caused delays. Nevertheless, some 750,000 of a total of about one million acres of eligible rice land in South Vietnam have been redistributed.' (12, p. 18.) Fishel does not specify in what manner the land was redistributed.

Ladejinsky and Diem viewed the growing resistance in the countryside not as a danger signal, but as a sign of success. 'The Viet Minh's opposition to South Vietnam's reforms,' wrote Ladejinsky in 1961, 'is violent precisely because they are successful.' (14, p. 175.) If violent resistance was the mark of a successful agrarian policy, one can only speculuate as to what might have caused Ladejinsky to consider the program a failure.

A similar discrepancy between theory and practice arose in other programs of 'social reform' initiated under Diem. Wrote Sidney Lens in 1964:

> The government, for instance, set up a national agricultural credit organisation to provide credit for the poor. But the local overlords administer it in such a way that only the wealthy can borrow money. The rules and requirements exclude the vast majority. After securing low-interest loans, the village rich then lend the money to the poor at usurious rates. (24, p. 23.)

The Saigon government's reactionary policies in the countryside were bad enough by themselves, and when the Diem regime also turned its back on industrialisation (14, p. 69) the situation became intolerable for the masses of South Vietnamese.

Yet another source of the revolt against the Diem regime was its policies towards the minorities. Whereas in Tonkin, the Northern government created two autonomous zones for the two million tribesmen who inhabit the area, in the South, where the mountains are populated by 500,000 to 1,000,000 tribesmen (or *montagnards*), no such autonomous area was formed. Even the individual provinces inhabited by the tribesmen were not given autonomy; their boundaries were shuffled around at will by the Saigon government. Thousands of Vietnamese from the lowlands, many of them Northern refugees, were colonised in *montagnard* territory in a government program which pleased neither the *montagnards* nor the Vietnamese settlers.

Almost half a million Cambodians, living in the Mekong delta, were also subjected to discriminatory treatment. They were forced to change their names to Vietnamese equivalents, prohibited from using their own language in their schools, denied the right to practise certain religious and cultural customs, and so forth. (29, p. 6.) Such policies of the Diem regime drove the majority of the Cambodians and *montagnards* into the Communist camp.

The realities of South Vietnam were, in a word, very different from the 'Miracle' that was presented to the American people—who were prevented by the anti-Communist hysteria in the United States from ever hearing the other side of the story. The regime which was ballyhooed as a 'democratic' and 'nationalist' alternative to Viet Minh rule was neither democratic nor nationalist. Its social base consisted entirely of the country's propertied élite plus the refugees from the North, both of these groups having sympathised with the French during the struggle for independence. Not only did the socio-economic policies of the South Vietnamese government harm the workers and peasants, but they even failed to win support from intermediate strata such as the intellectuals (many of whom emigrated to Paris) and the petty bourgeoisie (who were largely Chinese or members of the religious cults). South Vietnam was, of course, too small and backward to produce a national bourgeoisie. As a result, when South Vietnam began to slide back into civil war, there was no one to come to Diem's aid—except the Americans.

III

The first months of the Diem regime were marked by the repression of the non-Communist opposition, but it was not long before the government began to crack down on its most dangerous enemy, the former Viet Minh cadres who wielded great influence in the countryside. Wrote Philippe Devillers: 'The *de facto* integration of South

Vietnam with the American military defense structure implied that the region ought to be secure, and hence, ought to be purged of anything which might, however remotely, serve the Red cause.' (7, p. 12.)

The slaughter of Communists, Communist sympathisers and alleged Communists in South Vietnam brings to mind the excesses of the Spanish Fascists after their victory in 1939, or of the Indonesian rightists after October 1965. The American press, which seldom tired of reporting new 'miracles' in South Vietnam, was strangely silent on the question of this frightful purge which took the lives of perhaps as many as 75,000 people—most of them activists in the struggle for independence against the French. One exception was *Foreign Affairs* magazine, where William Henderson, after pointing out that 'the Communists in South Vietnam played a fairly passive role after Geneva,' went on to say:

> As the Diem régime waxed in strength and confidence, it gave increasing attention to rooting out the Communist danger. All the techniques of political and psychological warfare, as well as pacification campaigns involving extensive military operations, have been brought to bear against the underground. Some of the methods employed, such as anti-Communist denunciation rallies and self-criticism meetings, smack of practices which the Communists themselves perfected long ago; and it is clear that the usual democratic safeguards have not always been upheld. (19, pp. 288–9.)

The Diem regime itself made no secret of its desire to liquidate the 'Viet Minh remnants'. Diem personally headed the 'Campaign to Denounce Communists.' A semi-official Saigon publication states:

> President Ngo Dinh Diem's government had first to dedicate itself to the reestablishment of order and unity upon the privileges enjoyed by the great barons who defied governmental authority [i.e. the leaders of the religious sects]. Once this indispensable task was carried out it remained to free the country from a no less deadly plague—the subversive action of innumerable communist agents left on the spot by the Viet Minh to stalemate all efforts towards recovery. *It meant the waging of a new civil war* ... (40, pp. 2–3. Italics—R.M.)

Informers were used to help classify the population as 'loyal' or 'disloyal,' according to criteria which would have placed the majority of the South Vietnamese in the latter category. (4, p. 39.) Those denounced as Communists were labelled 'Viet Cong,' literally 'Vietnamese Communist.' This term was used instead of 'Viet Minh,' which was the name of a coalition organisation.

The repression grew in intensity between 1955 and 1959, by which time the victims had begun to fight back with increasing success. We return to Philippe Devillers, who described the slaughter of 'Communist agents'.

The Diem government ... launched out in 1957 into what amounted to a series of man-hunts. The population were called upon to redouble their vigilance and to denounce all Communist activity.... Guided by informers, 'mopping-up operations' became only too frequent, especially in the Centre, where the President's brother, Ngo Dinh Can, had recourse to the toughest of methods.

The pattern of these man-hunts was as follows:

... denunciation, searches and raids, arrest of suspects, plundering, interrogations enlivened sometimes by torture (even of innocent people), deportation and regrouping of population suspected of intelligence with the rebels, etc....
The Communists, finding themselves hunted down, began to fight back. Informers were sought out and shot in increasing numbers, and village chiefs who had presided over the denunciations, village notables, and members of the militia who took part, were frequently treated in the same way. (7, pp. 12–13.)

Conditions in Diem's prison camps staggered the imagination; cases of political prisoners (non-Communist in this case) being blinded, starved and deliberately maimed only came to light after Diem was overthrown. But even in December 1958, the North Vietnamese government reported that as many as a thousand prisoners in the Phu Loi 'reeducation centre' (Dr Wesley Fishel's phrase) had been killed by their guards. This atrocity, more than any other single event, signalled the beginning of the armed resistance to Diem's fascist regime.

The first targets of the resistance were the informers, sycophants and petty tyrants whom Diem and his brothers were relying on throughout the countryside. Once the informers had been assassinated or driven out, the government forces found it impossible to distinguish 'subversives' from the population at large. Next came the landlords, who fled to the safety of the cities, as they had done in the 1950s. Next, the government officials, who either joined the Communists, stayed at their posts with the tacit approval of the Communists, or lost their lives. By 1960, according to Bernard Fall, about 10,000 of Diem's civil servants, soldiers, police and informers in the villages had been killed. Because of this, wrote Fall, 'the Diem regime had lost a large part of the battle for South Vietnam before it had even begun in earnest....' (11.)

Frustrated by the inability of the government to deal with the spreading insurrection, the South Vietnamese army launched a coup d'état against Diem in November 1960. The purpose of the coup was to force Diem either to change his ways or to step down. Trapped in the presidential palace, Diem began to negotiate with the rebel troops, stalling them until loyal troops could arrive in Saigon and rescue him. The coup was crushed.

Because of this abortive coup, several things came to pass. First, Diem began to distrust his top generals, and from then on promoted officers on grounds of loyalty rather than competence. Second, the United States became aware of the Communist threat to 'Free Vietnam,' and of the inability of Diem to cope with it without direct foreign intervention. Third, the Communists and their allies, taking advantage of the upsurge of anti-government sentiment sparked by the coup, organised the National Liberation Front of South Vietnam in December 1960.

Like the Viet Minh, the National Liberation Front is a broad coalition—but due to the religious, cultural and political diversity in South Vietnam, the NLF is even broader than the Viet Minh. It includes the People's Revolutionary Party—the equivalent of the Lao Dong of North Vietnam; the Democratic Party and the Radical Socialist Party are also represented. Also included with in the NLF's leadership are the South Vietnamese peace movement, organised in 1954 to ensure the observance of the Geneva accords; the Binh Xuyen; organisations of the Cao Dai and Hoa Hao religions; and movements of tribesmen and Cambodians. The South Vietnamese Catholic community is represented among the leadership, and the 'Association of Militants for Peace,' an organisation of ex-members of the South Vietnamese army, also plays an important role.

Special branches of the NLF apparatus propagandise the various sections of the population. The Dan-Van performs such work among the peasants, the effectiveness of which has been noted by the Americans. The Tri-Van operates among the Saigon intellectuals. The Binh-Van works within the South Vietnamese army, in order to bring about defections. (10, p. 364.) No particular effort seems to have been made to win the urban workers by special appeals.

The NLF is organised in nearly every village in South Vietnam— as a permanent governing body in the liberated areas, as a governing body during the night in those areas which the Saigon troops hold by daylight, and as an underground organisation in those areas— including Saigon—which the government forces occupy on a permanent basis. The NLF controls the Liberation Armed Forces, within which there are three 'services.' The local militia are the most numerous; these are poorly armed, and are used to guard villages in the liberated areas. Regional troops are better armed, but not nearly as numerous, and generally operate within their native provinces. Finally, there are the regular troops, known as the 'hard-helmets' to the Americans. These are educated and politically conscious crack soldiers, who bear the brunt of the fighting. Together, these NLF fighters numbered about 225,000 at the beginning of 1966.

Jean Lacouture interviewed Pham Ngoc Thuan, a South Vietnamese veteran of the Viet Minh, and now North Vietnamese ambassador to East Germany, who compared the Viet Minh to the National Liberation Front:

> We [i.e. the Viet Minh] were very clumsy primitives. We tried to oppose the colonial system and its Vietnamese allies with a 'counter-state' with its own administration, currency, and educational system. ... But our successors, wherever they could, have made a great deal of progress and utilised our experiences and our failures by choosing another way: they make every attempt to infiltrate the state and utilise it. Rather than systematically oppose the existing legal framework, they prefer to use it, in order to substitute another one for it. In simple terms, I would say that in the old days, we were cutting roads to intercept vehicles. They prefer to step into existing automobiles. (22, p. 174.)

In one case, illustrative of the revolutionary creativity of the Liberation Armed Forces, the idea of stepping into existing automobiles was not merely a figure of speech. Faced with the problem of capturing a heavily-fortified 'strategic hamlet,' the NLF troops halted a bus which was en route to the hamlet, removed the passengers and put their own men on board. They then drove the bus right into the hamlet, bypassing its elaborate defences. (10, p. 364.)

As the Diem government came to rely more and more upon American assistance, US officials such as Ambassador Lodge and Secretary of State Rusk began making periodic statements dismissing the NLF as a foreign-supported terrorist outfit which had virtually no strength within South Vietnam. In fact, between 1960 and 1964, the area under the control of the NLF increased by about four times. When it was founded, the NLF exercised virtual control over three provinces (An Xuyen in the extreme south, Kien Tuong to the northwest of Saigon, and Quang Ngai along the central coast). By mid-1964, a *New York Herald-Tribune* reporter described 14 provinces as being 'virtually governed by the Communists.' They included Long An and Binh Duong, which are about as close to Saigon as New Jersey and Connecticut are to New York City. (6.)

Two years later, the NLF had liberated about three-quarters of South Vietnam. Only the large towns and provincial capitals remained under the Saigon regime—plus some of the main roads and a diminishing handful of fortified villages. Even in Saigon, the Liberation Armed Forces were able to carry out armed attacks against American-occupied installations and South Vietnamese police posts. The cities, furthermore, were the location of periodic strikes, riots and demonstrations which often tied the hands of whatever government was in power at the time.

How was this poorly-armed guerrilla movement able to drive a numerically superior military force—three times as large, better-equipped and better paid—from most of South Vietnam's territory? The essential factor was the support given to the NLF by the overwhelming majority of the population. Not only did this provide the NLF with an inexhaustible source of recruits—many of whom came over from the South Vietnamese army, together with their weapons and training—but it provided the guerrillas with a constant supply of accurate information about the movements and weaknesses of the enemy. At the same time the US and Saigon forces—while collecting food and taxes, and drafting soldiers, by force—found themselves unable to obtain the same sort of information about the 'Viet Cong'. Wrote the London *Economist*:

> The most serious military shortage is of information—accurate information—about the Vietcong. Normally where the conflicting sides are the same people speaking the same language there is a good two-way intelligence system. But this does not operate in Vietnam, although it is obvious that the Vietcong rebels have excellent information about South Vietnamese and American activities and plans. (37, p. 285.)

The *New York Times* correspondent Homer Bigart described one battle in the Mekong delta which highlighted the problem faced by the South Vietnamese government troops. This was an NLF ambush which resulted in a serious military defeat for the government forces.

> The ambush occurred on the outskirts of Bentre, a garrison town and on a heavily travelled highway. Yet the guerrillas moved into position in daylight, prepared the ambuscade in full view of the road and waited for three hours for the convoy to appear. They must have been observed by scores of peasants. Yet no one informed the garrison in Bentre. Could this have happened if the peasants felt any real identification with the regime? (3.)

What were the reasons for the support given by the people to the National Liberation Front? They were many and diverse. Perhaps most important of all was the fact that the NLF defended the land reform carried out by the Viet Minh during the war with the French. A captured NLF document was translated and published by the US State Department as a mimeographed pamphlet entitled *When the Communists Come . . .;* the text dealt with the efforts made by the NLF to win over the people of one village whose inhabitants were, at first, almost all hostile to communism. Within a few years, so many villagers had been won over that the Diem regime was no longer able to maintain any administrative apparatus there. The crucial factor in the loss of this originally loyal village to the NLF was the land question; government corruption played a secondary role.

Another important cause of the NLF's popularity is the realisation that the price of preserving an anti-communist state in South Vietnam is the continued partition of the Vietnamese nation. Most South Vietnamese are conscious of the fact that so-called 'Free Vietnam' is the heir to the French colonial regime, while North Vietnam is the creation of the struggle against the French. All of the North Vietnamese leaders, and many of the leaders of the National Liberation Front, were active in the fight for independence. Diem, on the other hand, spent the war years in exile in Belgium and the United States; General Nguyen Cao Ky, for his part, was a pilot in the French Air Force during the French-Indo-China War. The NLF stands for the reunification of the two zones of Vietnam on the basis of self-determination. Thus, the factor of nationalism, instead of being one of the subjective conditions impeding the growth of revolutionary consciousness, actually encourages it.

A third vital cause of the National Liberation Front's popular appeal is its constant struggle on behalf of democracy. In fact, the NLF's program of December 1960 speaks as much about democracy as about either national reunification or social reform.* Trade union rights, ethnic minority group rights and freedom from religious discrimination are particularly important planks in the platform.

It would be wrong, however, to assume that the outcome of an NLF victory would mean the establishment of a bourgeois democracy. Under the French colonial regime, and under the Diem regime which opposed any policy of industrialisation, no South Vietnamese bourgeoisie came into existence—with the exception of the comprador class, which included a large percentage of Chinese aliens. Bourgeois democracy is simply not a form of government which can exist for any length of time in a country without a bourgeoisie; under such circumstances, bourgeois democracy will either degenerate into a new form of reactionary dictatorship (as in Indonesia or Bolivia), develop into socialism (as in Cuba), or be overthrown (as in Brazil or Nigeria).

What determines the course that bourgeois democratic revolutions take in semi-colonial countries is which class controls the armed forces. When professional armies are left intact, they generally tend to side with the most conservative forces in the revolutionary movement, and at some point turn away from revolution and suppress the left. When professional armies, however, are replaced with revolutionary armies or militias, the probability is that the revolution will soon pass from its bourgeois democratic first stage into a socialist second stage.

---

* The program is reprinted in Herbert Aptheker, *Mission to Hanoi*, (See Reference 1), pp. 99–106.

In South Vietnam, the political organisation representing the workers, peasants, petty bourgeoisie and revolutionary intellectuals has retained control over the military arm of the revolutionary movement. Furthermore, the majority of members of the Liberation Armed Forces are militiamen, who farm by day and fight by night. This is in contrast with Algeria, where the FLN created a professional army in exile; this army eventually took over the country in order to halt the march towards socialism.

One should therefore not be misled by the disclaimers of some of the NLF leaders to the effect that the goal of the Front is nothing more than the elimination of American imperialism and the overthrow of the puppet regime. At the same time, one should not overlook the distinction between the first and second stages of the South Vietnamese revolution.* From a peasant-based movement with non-socialist goals, the National Liberation Front is most likely to develop into the instrument for the socialist transformation of South Vietnam.

IV

Following the 'loss' of Cuba by the 'free world,' there was a reappraisal of American foreign policy vis-à-vis revolutionary movements in the semi-colonial countries. It was evident that reliance on military and economic aid to 'anti-communist' regimes would, by itself, not suffice to halt the erosion of the capitalist zone of the world. The American ruling circles devised a strategy for the 'containment' of 'communist expansion' which assumed that Soviet and Chinese intervention on behalf of revolutionary movements would be kept to a minimum by means of nuclear blackmail. This new strategy was implemented at the outset of the Kennedy administration.

The strategy envisaged three stages, as it were, in the containment of revolution. In the first stage, United States commitment would be limited to the military aid programmes which already existed under Eisenhower. The second stage was 'counter-insurgency,' to be used in case the first stage failed; in this stage, American troops as well as American money were to be used to suppress revolutionary movements. Given the failure of the second stage, the third stage, known as 'limited war,' would be entered upon; here, the American strategists evisaged a Korean-type situation in which there would be open conflict between American troops and the armed forces of one or more nations of the socialist camp.

In South Vietnam, the United States entered the first stage even during the French-Indo-China War (although the US aid to the

* As does Adolfo Gilly (see Reference 15).

French was, of course, not then conceived of as the 'first stage' in a perpetually expanding American commitment). US assistance to the anti-Communist forces in Vietnam grew during the years of the Diem regime, so that in May 1961 the *New York Times* could report: 'United States authorities estimate that American military aid already covers 80 per cent of South Vietnam's defense budget. In addition, economic assistance has totalled more than $1,300,000,000 since 1955.' (33.)

In that month, the first of a long series of high-level official visits to Saigon took place. On the 12th, Vice-President Johnson met with Diem, pledging the latter increased military aid. Wrote the *New York Times* on May 12, 1961: 'Among measures which Mr Johnson did not announce, but which were reported by informed sources, is an expansion of the United States Military Advisory Group to about 1,650 men.' The Geneva accords had prohibited the use of more than 650 foreign advisers by either half of Vietnam.

The year 1961 marked the beginning of the 'counter-insurgency' effort in South Vietnam. The American scheme to crush the 'Viet Cong' was based on the experiences of the British in Malaya where they fought against 'communist terrorists.' What the American strategists ignored about the British experiences in Malaya proved to be more important than what they learned.

The Malayan guerrilla movement, first of all, was largely limited to the Chinese population, and never made any serious inroads among the Moslem and traditionalist Malays. Of the Chinese, only those who lived in the countryside were—for reasons of physical limitation—able to participate in the armed struggle. Most Chinese in Malaya lived in the cities; the ones who lived in the countryside were 'squatters,' who had moved there during the Japanese occupation. The British concentrated these people in 'New Villages,' managing to separate the guerrillas from their supporters. Thus, using a total of 300,000 troops (Malayan, British, Australian, New Zealand, Gurkha and African), the British suppressed about 8,000–12,000 communists in roughly fourteen years.

Obtaining the same numerical superiority over the 'Viet Cong' did not look difficult for the United States in 1961, since there were only about 10,000 guerrillas. What proved to be the big stumbling block was the fact that, unlike the situation in Malaya, the large majority of the peasants in South Vietnam were supporters of the guerrillas.

Nevertheless, the American and South Vietnamese governments went ahead with a resettlement program, in the hope of concentrating the peasants in 'strategic hamlets.' This program was, to put it mildly, less than successful. David Arnold, a former officer in the US Information Agency in South Vietnam, reported:

> Both Americans and Vietnamese were taking the strategic hamlet
> program seriously and were hailing it as the turning point in the
> struggle against the Viet Cong. I visited strategic hamlets in the
> Mekong Delta every day and saw differently. Fortified villages in
> Malaya probably did win the war. The British, through means never
> revealed to Parliament, managed to separate the Communist from
> the non-Communist before enclosing the village with a wall. The
> Vietnamese did not. Anyone could live in the strategic hamlet if he
> said he wanted to or could be forced to. In Malaya the walls were
> twelve feet high, the gates were closed at sundown, and anyone
> found outside the walls was shot on the spot, no questions asked.
> In the Delta, some walls managed to rise to three feet, and for the
> peasants who couldn't be bothered with stepping over them, the
> gates were always kept open. In Malaya, the inhabitants were kept
> armed, to ward off guerrilla attacks. In South Vietnam, weapons
> were kept locked in the hamlet chief's office and distributed in
> emergencies. Emergencies managed to come too fast for effective
> distribution. In Malaya, the Communists were effectively cut off
> from the peasants. In Vietnam, the flow of propaganda, terror,
> food and information continued unhindered. (2.)

Acting as adviser to the South Vietnamese government on the
question of the strategic hamlets was Robert Thompson, an English-
man who had served in a key capacity in Malaya during the war
against the 'communist terrorists.' Thompson's advice was to build
the hamlets in those areas which were relatively secure from the
NLF. Ngo Dinh Nhu, on the other hand, was more inclined to concentrate on those areas which were least secure. Nhu had his way.
Wrote Denis Warner:

> Instead of going slowly, South Vietnam went into mass production.
> Instead of concentrating on white (or Viet Cong free) areas, the
> government went for the red (or Viet Cong dominated). Operation
> Sunrise, which was intended to separate the Maquis D, the Viet
> Cong's main base in the rubber, jungle and swamps immediately
> north of Saigon from the capital, and the Maquis D itself from the
> Cambodian border, by the resettlement of the peasants, was almost
> Operation Sunset for the strategic hamlet concept. Without warn-
> ing, preparation or consent, peasants saw their homes, and often
> their belongings, burned behind them. They were uprooted at
> bayonet point and planted down in new areas which had not been
> prepared to receive them.... To add to their misfortunes, the
> villagers were not settled in their own localities, but were often
> moved considerable distances. This meant that they lost not only
> their homes but also their land. (34, pp. 34–5.)

The effect of the strategic hamlet program was the opposite of what the strategists of 'counter-insurgency' had expected it to be. Fearing the sort of 'resettlement' described by Warner, the peasants would flee whenever government troops approached. The hamlets themselves could not be defended effectively against the Liberation Armed Forces, inhabited, as they were, by people who sympathised with the NLF. One by one, the 'strategic hamlets' fell to the guerrillas; some were transformed into NLF fortresses, some were destroyed by their inhabitants. The arms with which the hamlets were to have been defended became the property of the Liberation Armed Forces. After the fall of Diem, the 'strategic hamlet' program was abandoned.

Side by side with the attempted resettlement of the peasants went the collective punishment of all those who escaped or resisted. In the 'red' areas, which were under NLF control, everything that moved was considered an enemy. Government troops were permitted, as a matter of policy, to loot all villages which they temporarily occupied in 'red' areas. Later, the Americans adopted the tactic of burning these villages to the ground, destroying everything in them, from cooking utensils to fruit trees. Where ground troops could not reach, aeroplanes bombed the defenceless villages with napalm. Rice fields were sprayed with special chemicals—a variety of weed-killer—which poisoned the crops. Whenever American troops captured NLF guerrillas, they turned them over to South Vietnamese government forces, who either killed the prisoners outright or tortured them for information. In the name of 'protecting freedom,' of 'halting aggression,' and of 'opposing tyranny,' the United States was conducting a campaign of genocidal nature against the political movement which had the support of the majority of the South Vietnamese people.

As the war progressed, a rift began to appear between the Diem regime and its American protectors. At long last it dawned on some Americans that the policies of the government in Saigon were a factor contributing to the growth of the guerrilla movement. They also began to realise that the hundreds of millions of dollars in American aid were reaching a relative handful of South Vietnamese. Far from making South Vietnam an anti-communist bastion, US aid to Diem was only furthering the growth of communism. Finally, the Diem government disagreed with the Americans on the conduct of the war; the Americans, in effect, wanted the South Vietnamese soldiers to take a more active part in the war against the National Liberation Front, while Diem preferred to avoid military engagements in which his troops might suffer high casualties.

In January 1963 two thousand government troops suffered a major defeat at the hands of two hundred NLF soldiers. Reverses such as this weakened the case of those American policy-makers who said, 'sink or swim with Diem.'

In May of that year, the 'Buddhist crisis' broke out. The Buddhists are the largest single religious denomination in South Vietnam, although they were, at that time, not as united or well-organised as the Roman Catholics. The crisis began when the police in Hue tore down religious flags on a pagoda. A government decree prohibited the flying of any flags except those of South Vietnam, but this had been overlooked only a few days earlier when the Catholics had flown Vatican flags in honour of the silver jubilee of Archbishop Ngo Dinh Thuc, the President's brother. On May 8, the Buddhists assembled a large demonstration in Hue to protest against the government's action. Government tanks opened fire on the crowd, killing eight or nine persons. 'All available evidence . . .', writes Wesley Fishel, 'supports the charge that the deaths resulted from the impact of cannon projectiles.' (13, p. 24.) The government refused to accept responsibility for the deaths, insisting that they had been caused by a 'Viet Cong' hand grenade.

This touched off massive demonstrations in Saigon, which spread to other cities. University and high school students joined the demonstrations with vigour. The demonstrations continued through the summer, and were put down with increasing brutality. Finally, in the fall, the government closed down the large Xa Loi pagoda in Saigon, arresting hundreds of monks. By that time, the erstwhile 'Miracle Man of South Vietnam' had become a millstone around Washington's neck. Any of the Diem regime's crimes could be defended in the United States on the grounds of 'anti-communism', except one—suppression of religion. Thus, the United States policy-makers belatedly came to the conclusion that Diem, the man who had supposedly 'saved' South Vietnam from communism, would have to be eliminated if South Vietnam were to be saved from communism!

Discontent with the anti-Buddhist policies of the regime (and with the absurd propaganda tales used to justify them) was rife among the South Vietnamese generals, who were themselves largely Buddhists. The regime could rely only upon its shock troops, the so-called Special Forces, who had been trained in guerrilla warfare as part of the American 'counter-insurgency' effort. In October 1963 these Vietnamese units were in Saigon fighting Buddhist monks instead of the 'Viet Cong'.

Jean Lacouture writes: '. . . The American Embassy told Diem that any financial aid still forthcoming would be stopped unless the "special forces" departed for the rice paddies to fight against the Viet Cong. The Ngos gave in; on October 30 their "SS" left the capital.' (22, p. 84.) This cleared the way for the army to strike, which it did only two days later. Diem and Nhu were killed. Ngo Dinh Can took refuge in the American consulate in Hue, to be turned over to his enemies for execution six months later. Crowds danced in the streets. The Diem dictatorship was no more.

Diem was replaced by a military junta; the fall of this junta less than three months later, when General Nguyen Khanh seized power in a bloodless coup, indicated that the otherthrow of Diem had been more than just a palace revolution—that the Diem regime had been so centralised, with so much power located within a single family, that the removal of this family could undermine the entire repressive apparatus, particularly the hated Can Lao organisation.

With the Diem regime gone, it soon became evident that no Saigon government could achieve even the relative stability which had existed between 1954 and 1963. First the junta of General Duong Van Minh, then the dictatorship of General Nguyen Khanh, then the short-lived civilian regime of Tran Van Huong, then Khanh again, and finally (as of July 1966) the military regime of General Nguyen Cao Ky, were faced with the same problem: balancing between those anti-Communist forces who had been 'in' during the Diem regime—mainly the Catholic refugees from the North—and those who had been 'out' —including the Buddhist leaders, the FULRO organisation among the *montagnards*, the students and a few coffee-house politicians. The first group had been totally discredited because of its association with Diem; the second group was distrusted by the Americans and their puppets, who feared that they entertained covert sympathies for the National Liberation Front.

By early 1965, the United States realised that it had reached a complete *impasse* in its 'counter-insurgency' program. The NLF had liberated most of South Vietnam's territory; no government seemed to be able to survive for any length of time in Saigon; and the South Vietnamese troops were deserting at an increasingly rapid rate—many of them going right over to the NLF. Rather than face defeat at the hands of the NLF, President Johnson decided to 'escalate' the war to North Vietnam.

The official pretext for the expansion of the war to North Vietnam was that the North Vietnamese were 'infiltrating' men and equipment into South Vietnam. In the eighteen months preceding the February 1965 escalation (claimed the State Department—43, Appendix D), no less than 173 weapons of Soviet, Chinese and Czechoslovak manufacture had been captured from the enemy by American and South Vietnamese troops. At that time, Washington was claiming 10,000 'Viet Cong' dead per year, or about 15,000 in an 18-month period; 173 weapons out of 15,000 enemy dead was hardly proof that the 'Viet Cong' owed its existence to outside support. As Hans Morgenthau commented: 'Let it be said right away that the [State Department] white paper is a dismal failure. The discrepancy between its assertions and the factual evidence adduced to support them borders on the grotesque.' (26, p. 87.)

In reality, one of the original reasons for the creation of an American client state in South Vietnam was the undermining and eventual destruction of the socialist government in North Vietnam. The northern part of the country contained most of the industry and natural resources, and was by far the more attractive half by the standards of any foreign imperialist power. If there was one fact about Vietnam that the United States was not blind to, it was this! Even while the United States was consolidating its grip on the southern half of the country, it was preparing to 'liberate' North Vietnam from its 'communist masters.'

The often-quoted French journalist, Georges Chaffard, wrote in *Le Monde* on August, 1964:

...American 'Special Services' for several years have encouraged and supported guerrilla operations against North Vietnamese territory.

Thus as early as 1957 there was created at Saigon a 'service of liason in the presidency,' headed by several American specialists and charged with the organisation, training and command of parachutist commandos specializing in intelligence and counter-espionage. Within this service, 'Section 45,' assisted by four American advisers, was trained for operations in the North...

Until 1960, however, the pace of these operations was very slow. The United States had not yet intervened directly in the second Indo-Chinese war and the southern commandoes lacked zeal. Things changed from 1961 on when Washington decided to step up its efforts in Vietnam. ... the government of Hanoi, from 1961 on, more and more often announced the capture of 'American-Diemist saboteurs, caught in the act.' ... Most of the agents intercepted had been recruited among Catholic refugees from Tonkin or former soldiers in the French army. (39.)

These operations soon became an open secret. In mid-1964, the following front-page story appeared in the *New York Times*:

Saigon, South Vietnam, July 22—The Commander of South Vietnam's Air Force confirmed today that 'combat teams' had been sent on sabotage missions inside Communist North Vietnam and that Vietnamese pilots were being trained for possible larger-scale attacks.

Teams have entered North Vietnam by 'air, sea and land,' Air Commodore Nguyen Cao Ky said at a news conference.

He indicated that clandestine missions had been dispatched at intervals for at least three years. This confirmed, in effect, charges of such penetration broadcast by the Hanoi radio.

From the evidence so far made known unofficially, these raids have had virtually no success. More than 80 per cent of under-cover teams were reported to have been apprehended before they had made any progress in their sabotage missions. (16.)

The United States was apparently learning the hard way that successful guerrilla movements could not be launched by means of 'infiltration' from outside.

Desirous none the less of bringing the war to the North, the United States encouraged the Saigon navy to attack radar installations on the North Vietnamese coast.* Hard upon these raids came the incident between the US destroyer *Maddox* and several North Vietnamese PT boats. This was followed by the first US air attacks upon North Vietnam, early in August 1964.

The real purpose of these attacks, in all probability, was the testing of American public opinion. When President Johnson found that he could escalate the war while still posing as a 'man of peace'—this thanks to Senator Goldwater—the decision was made for the partial entry into the 'third stage' of the campaign to crush the Vietnamese revolution.

The bombings of North Vietnam constituted one more in a long series of costly miscalculations on the part of American foreign policy-makers. The United States had miscalculated in the first place when it decided that a stable anti-Communist regime could be created in the southern half of Vietnam. It miscalculated further when it decided to base this regime entirely on the Northern refugees and the rich landlords. The 'counter-insurgency' campaign that took place after 1961 was a third grave miscalculation. In bombing North Vietnam, the American government was acting on the assumption that the source of the insurrection in South Vietnam could be found to the north of the 17th parallel. Was it just one more unfortunate case of official Washington falling victim to its own propaganda?

Among the many reflections provoked by the experiences of the Vietnamese people are those which concern the relationship between nationalist and socialist movements and the violent and peaceful attainment of their respective goals. Normally, there is a tendency to see the ideologies of nationalism and socialism as being in permanent opposition to one another. In fact, in many of the dependent and semi-colonial nations today, nationalist and socialist movements not only march along the same route, but are sometimes almost indistinguishable from one another. In some countries this works to the detriment of the socialists, but elsewhere—as in Vietnam —it works to their advantage.

* *New York Times* (editorial), August 4, 1964.

During the 1930s, some Vietnamese Marxists tended to overlook the strictly nationalist aspects of the struggle against the French. They behaved as if all that mattered was the class struggle between the Vietnamese proletariat—what there was of it—and the French ruling class. They ignored the fact that many Vietnamese who were not part of the proletariat had about as much to gain from the victory of the proletarian revolution as did the organised working class itself —and in the case of the peasants, they had even more to gain, being the most exploited segment of the population.

On the other hand, there were those 'nationalists,' Diem included, who sought a peaceful, rather than a revolutionary, surrender of power by the French to the Vietnamese. Most of these people were Catholics. Under French rule, Catholic education had been fostered while Buddhist and secular education had been relatively neglected, and as a result, a great many of the high posts in the French colonial administration that were held by Vietnamese were held by members of this religious minority. The sort of independence that they sought would have been similar to that obtained by India or Malaya—where those colonial subjects who had risen within the administration were not considered quislings, but leaders of the struggle for independence, men who had helped their compatriots gain freedom 'without violence.'

In Vietnam, however, a peaceful transition to independence would have changed little except the flags flying over Hanoi and Saigon. The French discouraged the growth of a Vietnamese bourgeoisie which would compete with French interests. Thus, without revolution, economic power (and thus real political power) would have remained in the hands of the French capitalists. Vietnam, under such conditions, would have enjoyed only a specious independence, with the same abysmal standard of living.

Vietnam is also proof of the fact that whenever a nation tries to put an end to the capitalist system, or even whenever a dependent nation seeks the abolition of its inferior status relative to some industrialised power, these efforts will be resisted by force and violence. South Vietnam was the first case where agreement was reached among the great powers that elections would be held (in 1956) to determine whether a country would take the capitalist or socialist path; if peaceful transition to socialism proved to be impossible in a country where the United States, England and France had already 'committed' themselves not to prevent it, then it is hardly likely that it will be possible anywhere else.

*   *   *

REFERENCES

1. Herbert Aptheker, *Mission to Hanoi*, New York, 1966.
2. David Arnold, 'Vietnam, Symptom of a World Malaise,' Fellowship of Reconciliation, May 1964.
3. Homer Bigart, 'Vietnam Victory Remote Despite US Aid to Diem,' *New York Times*, July 25, 1962.
4. Wilfred Burchett, *The Furtive War: The United States in Vietnam and Laos*, New York, 1963.
5. Joseph Buttinger, *The Smaller Dragon*, New York, 1958.
6. Beverly Deepe, ' "McNamara's Headache"—14 Viet Provinces,' *New York Herald Tribune*, May 24, 1964.
7. Philippe Devillers, 'The Struggle for the Unification of Vietnam,' *The China Quarterly*, London, January-March, 1962.
8. Tillman Durdin, 'Ladejinsky Finds Vietnam Paradox,' *New York Times*, April 5, 1955.
9. Tillman Durdin, 'Vietnam Extends Agrarian Reform,' *New York Times*, April 2, 1959.
10. Bernard Fall, *The Two Vietnams; A Political and Military Analysis*, New York, 1963.
11. — 'Vietnam, New Faces, More Chaos,' *The Nation*, New York, December 7, 1963.
12. Wesley Fishel, 'Vietnam's War of Attrition,' *The New Leader*, New York, December 7, 1959.
13. — *Vietnam: Is Victory Possible?* (Headline Series No. 163), New York, 1964.
14. Wesley Fishel (ed.), *Problems of Freedom: South Vietnam Since Independence*, East Lansing, Michigan, 1961.
15. Adolfo Gilly, *'Vietnam: A War of the Masses and a Socialist Revolution,' Monthly Review*, New York, December 1965.
16. Peter Grose, 'Sabotage Raids on North Confirmed by Saigon Aide,' *New York Times*, July 23, 1964.
17. Ellen J. Hammer, *The Struggle for Indo-China*, Stanford, Calif., 1954.
18. — *The Struggle for Indo-China Continues*, Stanford, Calif., 1955.
19. William Henderson, 'South Vietnam Finds Herself,' *Foreign Affairs*, New York, January 1957.
20. Leo Huberman and Paul Sweezy,, 'What Every American Should Know About Indo-China,' *Monthly Review*, June 1954.
21. Doug Jenness, *War and Revolution in Vietnam* (Young Socialist Pamphlet), New York, 1965.
22. Jean Lacouture, *Vietnam: Between Two Truces*, New York, 1966.
23. Donald Lancaster, *The Emancipation of French Indo-China*, London, 1961.
24. Sidney Lens, 'Vietnam: The Only Hope,' *The Progressive*, Wisconsin, November 1964.
25. Richard Lindholm (ed.), *Vietnam: The First Five Years*, Ann Arbor, Michigan, 1959.
26. Hans Morgenthau, 'We Are Deluding Ourselves in Vietnam,' *New York Times Magazine*, April 18, 1965.
27. Robert Payne, *The Revolt of Asia*, New York, 1947.
28. James Reston, 'Johnson and the Larger Crisis,' *New York Times*, July 1, 1966.
29. Huot Sambath, Declaration Before the General Assembly, Cambodian

Mission to the United Nations, September 25, 1963.

30. Robert Scheer, *How the United States Got Involved In Vietnam*, Santa Barbara, Calif., 1966.

31. Robert Scigliano, *South Vietnam, Nation Under Stress*, Boston, 1963.

32. Frank N. Trager (ed.), *Marxism in Southeast Asia*, Stanford, Calif., 1959; esp. chapter on Vietnam by I. Milton Sacks.

33. Robert Trumbull, *New York Times*, May 12, 1961.

34. Denis Warner, *The Last Confucian*, New York, 1963.

35. David Wurfel, 'Agrarian Reform in the Republic of Vietnam,' *Far Eastern Survey*, Yale, June 1957.

36. *Breaking Our Chains* (North Vietnamese documents of the August 1945 Revolution), Hanoi, 1960.

37. 'Faulty Line Between Americans and Vietnamese,' *Economist*, London, April 17, 1965.

38. *I. F. Stone's Bi-Weekly*, Washington, October 28, 1963.

39. *I. F. Stone's Bi-Weekly*, Washington, August 24, 1964.

40. *The Fight Against the Subversive Communist Activities in Vietnam* (*Review Horizons* reprint), Saigon, 1957.

41. *The Polemic on the General Line of the International Communist Movement*, Foreign Languages Press, Peking, 1965.

42. 'What Comes After Indo-China Truce?' *US News and World Report*, July 30, 1954.

43. *White Paper. Aggression From the North*, State Department, Washington, 1965.

Notes on Contributors

ISAAC DEUTSCHER. Among the many publications of this distinguished historian and biographer are *Stalin: A Political Biography* (1949), *Russia After Stalin* (1953), a three-volume biography of Trotsky (1954–63), *Ironies of History* (1966) and *The Unfinished Revolution* (1967). He is co-author of *The Era of Violence* (Vol. XII of *New Cambridge Modern History*, 1960).

WILLIAM APPLEMAN WILLIAMS is Professor of History at the University of Wisconsin and the author of several books including *The Tragedy of American Diplomacy* (Delta, New York) and *The Contours of American History* (Quadrangle, Chicago).

JOHN BAGGULEY was assistant editor of *Vietnam* (Eyre and Spottiswoode, London, 1965) and co-editor of *Authors Take Sides on Vietnam* (Owen, London and Simon and Schuster, New York, 1967); he has written a study of the British army which is to be published by MacGibbon and Kee, London.

HENRY H. BERGER is Assistant Professor of History at the University of Vermont. He is the author of 'American Labor Overseas', *The Nation*, January 16, 1967 and other articles.

TODD GITLIN was one of the leaders of Students for a Democratic Society (SDS) in the United States and the author of several articles published in *Studies on the Left* and other journals. He is currently an organiser with JOIN Community Union in Chicago.

JOHN GITTINGS, formerly a member of the Royal Institute of International Affairs, London, is now on the staff of the Institute of International Studies, University of Chile, Santiago. He is the author of a forthcoming study *The Role of the Chinese Army* (Oxford University Press, 1967).

DAVID HOROWITZ was educated at Columbia College (New York) and the University of California (Berkeley). He is the author of *Student* (Ballantine, 1962), *Shakespeare: An Existential View* (New York and London, 1965), *The Free World Colossus* (New York and London, 1965; translated into Swedish and Norwegian, and printed in a revised edition by Penguin under the title *From Yalta to Vietnam,* 1967). His most recent book is *The Russian Revolution and the Cold War* (1967; also translated into Norwegian). He is the editor of *Marx and Modern Economics* (MacGibbon and Kee, London, 1967). He is currently Director of the Bertrand Russell Centre for Social Research, London.

RICHARD MORROCK is a graduate student in international relations at Columbia University. He wrote his MA thesis on Vietnam and has published several articles.